W9-BYU-325

Brooks - Cork Library
Shelton State
Community College

DISCARDED

DATE DUE

FEB 1 8 2004

DEMCO, INC. 38-2931

)

T

Bedford/St. Martin's   Boston ◆ New York

For Bedford/St. Martin's

Developmental Editors: Karen Henry, Jennifer Rush
Production Editor: Ara Salibian
Senior Production Supervisor: Catherine Hetmansky
Marketing Manager: Brian Wheel
Editorial Assistant: Caroline Thompson
Production Assistant: Thomas P. Crehan
Copyeditor: Mary Lou Wilshaw-Watts
Text Design: Sandra Rigney
Composition: Karla Goethe, Orchard Wind Graphics
Printing and Binding: Haddon Craftsmen, Inc., an R. R. Donnelley & Sons Company

President: Charles H. Christensen
Editorial Director: Joan E. Feinberg
Managing Editor: Elizabeth M. Schaaf
Editor in Chief: Karen S. Henry
Director of Marketing: Karen Melton
Director of Editing, Design, and Production: Marcia Cohen

Library of Congress Catalog Card Number: 2001095037

Copyright © 2002 by Bedford/St. Martin's

All rights reserved. No part of this book may be reproduced, stored in a retrieval system, or transmitted by any form or by any means, electronic, mechanical, photocopying, recording, or otherwise, except as may be expressly permitted by the applicable copyright statutes or in writing by the Publisher.

Manufactured in the United States of America.

7 6 5 4 3 2
f e d c b a

For information write: Bedford/St. Martin's, 75 Arlington Street, Boston, MA 02116 (617-399-4000)

ISBN: 0–312–39653–8

Acknowledgments

Sissela Bok, from *Lying: Moral Choice in Public and Private Life* by Sissela Bok, copyright © 1978 by Sissela Bok. Used by permission of Pantheon Books, a division of Random House, Inc.

René Descartes, from *Discourse on the Method, The Philosophical Works of Descartes,* vol. 1, trans. E. S. Haldane and G. R. T. Ross. Reprinted with the permission of Cambridge University Press.

Harry G. Frankfurt, from "On Bullshit," *The Importance of What We Care About,* by Harry G. Frankfurt. Cambridge University Press, 1988. Reprinted with the permission of Cambridge University Press.

Galileo, from *Sidereus Nuncius,* or *The Starry Messenger,* trans. Albert van Helden. University of Chicago Press, 1990. Reprinted by permission of the University of Chicago Press.

Acknowledgments and copyrights are continued at the back of the book on page 199, which constitutes an extension of the copyright page. It is a violation of the law to reproduce these selections by any means whatsoever without the written permission of the copyright holder.

Brooks - Cork Library
Shelton State
Community College

To the Instructor: Helping Your Students Improve Their Writing

Philosophy instructors, like other academics, are largely preoccupied with presenting the subject matter of their courses; this is what absorbs our attention as we work at developing our own ideas while teaching the writings of others. We have too little time (or inclination) to spend on helping our students improve their writing skills; instead, we tend to accept whatever level of writing they offer us so that we can press ahead to explain and explore philosophical ideas, arguments, and themes.

In doing so, we risk overlooking some obvious facts:

Probably no more than one student in ten who takes an introductory philosophy course will take another, more advanced course. Of those who do, no more than one in ten will go on to major in philosophy; and out of any ten students who do that, at most one will go on to graduate study in the field. In other words, introductory philosophy courses in our colleges and universities today are largely service ventures in a liberal arts curriculum; they are preprofessional training grounds for only a handful of students.

We all know this. As a consequence, many teachers of introductory philosophy courses are all the more eager to make as great a philosophical impact as possible on their students, convinced that they will have only one opportunity to do so. This reinforces the preoccupation they have with the unique content of their courses — the philosophical issues themselves — and demotes to a secondary concern those aspects of their courses shared with other courses in the humanities and social sciences: the teaching of coherent thinking, analytical reading, evaluative criticism, and thoughtful writing *whatever the subject.*

But these general skills are not always taught with lasting effect elsewhere in the liberal arts curriculum, or in the way a philosophically trained instructor would teach them. Further, because critical thinking, reading, and writing are so central to philosophy, philosophy courses are ideal places for students to improve and apply such skills — skills that will stand them in good stead in whatever courses and careers they choose.

iii

Of course, if one thinks of writing as verbal filigree, decorative wrapping around the solid core of thought, and thus of no essential relevance to the grasp of ideas and the facility in stating and evaluating a theory or an argument, then one can complacently ignore the quality of student writing. But most teachers recognize that it is folly to cultivate too sharp a distinction between form and content in writing. To be sure, making a fetish out of footnote style, for example, or of other niceties in work headed for publication in a book or scholarly journal is just too trivial to inflict on beginning students in philosophy and certainly a waste of valuable classroom time. Yet the other extreme — studied indifference to how students use quotations in their papers and where they get them — is hardly defensible either. We must strike a balance, preferably one that will serve students well in other courses too. This book aims to help you strike such a balance; it guides students in thinking, reading, and writing about philosophy in a way that leaves you, the instructor, substantially freer to concentrate on the purely philosophical material of your courses.

This book also tries to help students learn some elementary lessons of philosophical analysis along the way, but only as needed to understand a reading assignment or to carry out a writing exercise. *Thinking and Writing about Philosophy* is not intended as a substitute for classroom guidance in informal logic, argumentative strategies, and the like. The emphasis throughout this book is on *writing* — specifically, the kinds of writing assigned in introductory philosophy courses.

The strategy of the book is quite simple. Students first learn to master fundamental assignments — like summarizing, abstracting, and outlining — in which they write to understand what they have read. They then learn how to evaluate argumentative prose and draft their own philosophical essays. The heart of *Thinking and Writing about Philosophy* is chapter 5, devoted to all of the stages of drafting and revising a philosophical essay, including revising a paper in response to comments from instructors and peers. Chapter 6 covers conventions for integrating quotations, avoiding plagiarism, and citing and documenting sources; chapter 7 provides an overview of library and internet resources that are most useful to students in introductory philosophy courses.

The abundant models of student writing in this book should inspire and encourage students. And because the writings are based on readings about classic philosophical issues — by eminent philosophers like David Hume, Friedrich Nietzsche, and Bertrand Russell and well-known contemporary philosophers like Edmund Gettier, Sisella Bok, and Judith Jarvis Thomson — students see how they and their peers can enter the discussion of perennial issues and questions. All the readings are of the sort found in current anthologies designed for and typically used in introductory courses.

Thinking and Writing about Philosophy should be an asset to any introductory philosophy course, regardless of focus (classic problems, current controversies), subject (ethics, epistemology), and other philosophical readings (an essay anthology, classic texts). The exercises and strategies presented on these pages are based on many years of experience and the conscious effort to help students help themselves.

ACKNOWLEDGMENTS

Modest though this book is, it exists only because of the valuable contributions by many during the course of its development. Without the inspiration and encouragement of my colleague and collaborator on other projects, Sylvan Barnet, I would not have had the temerity to undertake a book of this sort in the first place. Charles Christensen at Bedford/St. Martin's offered a contract for the book before the first words were written; an author cannot hope for a better endorsement. Constance Putnam, on whom I have learned to rely for many kinds of advice, provided indispensable assistance every step of the way. My editor for the first edition, Beth Castrodale, has put her stamp on the final product, improving the text I placed into her hands in countless ways. Jennifer Rush and Karen Henry have provided excellent editorial advice for the second edition. I have leaned on these associates; without them this book would not even have been countenanced, much less completed.

I would also like to thank others at Bedford/St. Martin's who helped make this book a reality. Jennifer Rush and Karen Henry have provided excellent editorial advice for the second edition.

Professional colleagues have also been of much help in persuading me to introduce various features in the book and to drop others. The following gave the kind of advice that only experienced teachers deeply concerned with improving their students' writing can give: Richard W. Burgh (Rider College), James B. Hart (Bridgewater State College), Erin Kelly (Tufts University), Kathleen Dean Moore (Oregon State University), Lisa Newton (Fairfield University), Gayle L. Ormiston (Kent State University), William Pohle (Lehmann College), Nelson Potter (University of Nebraska, Lincoln), Sue Stafford (Simmons College), Burke Townsend (University of Montana), Martha K. Woodruff (Middlebury College), and an anonymous reviewer whose brisk style and pointed criticisms aroused my respect and chagrin in about equal amounts. The book is much improved thanks to their comments and suggestions. At an early stage in the book's production, I wrote to several other colleagues across the country, soliciting their advice on the sort of writing projects they had found successful with their beginning philosophy students. Unfortunately, it seems I have misplaced beyond retrieval the list of their names. The best I can do to cover my embarrassment is to thank them collectively and anonymously.

This second edition has several new features. Three of the exercises for reading and writing are new, and so are three of the excerpts from classic philosophical texts. The result is a total of twelve different writing exercises and sixteen extracts from philosophical texts. Other new features include a list of internet resources of interest to philosophers, a glossary of philosophical terms, and a catalogue of fallacies to avoid. In addition, the book has been redesigned to open up the page and to highlight the different elements — excerpts, student writing, discussions of such writing — that make up the book. Finally, in order to put some flesh on the bare bones of the extracts, a brief biographical sketch of each of the philosophers whose work is excerpted is also included.

Finally, one of the delights in writing this book was the opportunity it afforded me to enlist the help of several Tufts undergraduates and to work with them in a fashion not possible in the usual student-teacher relationship. They contributed one of this book's central features, a series of written materials of varying difficulty appropriate for beginning students. It is a great pleasure to acknowledge this debt to Steven Calcote, Ashley de Marchena, David Hoberman, Noah Kriegel, Peter Miller III, Daniel Rosenberg, Stacey Schmidt, and Ellen Wheeler.

To the Student: Why Improving Your Writing Matters — to You

If you are enrolled in your first college course in philosophy, you are about to embark on an exciting and rigorous intellectual adventure. The readings and discussions that lie ahead in this course will introduce you to some of the great thinkers, classic and contemporary, and some of the great problems of philosophy. The diversity of views, the variety of arguments, and the perplexity and reflection they engender should prove stimulating.

In philosophy courses (as opposed to courses in formal logic) most of your work will consist of reading assigned material and then writing papers of various sorts — either in-class or take-home examinations or explanatory, evaluative, or argumentative essays written outside of class. This book is intended to make it easier for you to meet the challenges of such assignments by helping you improve your reading and writing skills. Don't misunderstand, however. This book is not addressed to those who need a course in remedial writing. Rather, it is intended for every beginner in philosophy regardless of prior preparation. No doubt you have already taken (or are currently enrolled in) freshman English or some equivalent course, and much you learned or will learn there can be transferred with profit to your written work in philosophy. But there is always more to learn, and philosophy places some special demands on its students. This book is intended to supplement your previous training by introducing you to a variety of writing tasks specifically, though not only, of interest and importance in the study of philosophy. The most powerful intellectual tool at your disposal — now and throughout your life — is your mastery of written English, and sharpening that tool cannot be left solely to introductory composition courses. Training in philosophy and philosophical writing is an ideal way to improve your expository, critical, analytic, and evaluative writing skills.

Unlike many other college courses, philosophy is peculiarly abstract in its subject matter. In philosophy, you will rarely find any call for narrative as you will in the study of history and religion, for example. Nor can you achieve precision in a philosophical essay by recourse to computations, statistics, graphs, or other mathematical tools. In your introductory course, you will learn how to read and analyze abstract materials and to write about them intelligently, even originally. Accordingly, the aim of *this* little book is to help you become a more accomplished writer during the course of your study of standard philosophical problems, puzzles, and controversies.

But there's more to gain than just learning to read and write philosophy. The strategies of critical reading and writing discussed in this book have unparalleled transfer value. For example, just as the ability to punctuate sentences and to use metaphor and simile — taught in English composition courses — transfers to whatever writing you do in history, fine arts, and philosophy, the ability to *evaluate and construct arguments* in epistemology or ethics similarly transfers to analyzing and constructing arguments about any subject. As you will see, the very vocabulary philosophers use to state and evaluate arguments originated in the logic and rhetoric that we owe to Aristotle. No wonder the study of philosophy is traditionally one of the principal fields of undergraduate concentration for students planning a career in law, where analytic and argumentative precision about a wide range of topics is so essential.

From ancient Greece to the present, philosophy has been at the center of the study of the humanities in Western culture and the liberal arts college curriculum in particular. The principal tool of inquiry, communication, and development of thought and knowledge in these fields is *written prose*. In fact, the more precise, clear, and coherent the thinking, the more precise, persuasive, and original the writing. Consequently, developing skill in thinking, reading, and writing is essential to success in any field of the liberal arts.

In approaching their own written work, many students yield to the temptation to contrast "content" — the philosophical substance of their writing, the insights expressed, the nuances revealed — with the "form" or style, in order to dismiss or subordinate the latter as mere drapery or decoration. On the contrary, your writing is like the skin on the surface of your body, an organ vital to — and reflective of — overall health even though it is wholly on the surface.

Why do instructors require students to write essays in philosophy courses, and what do they look for in those essays? Essentially they want to know how well you have understood an assigned reading. In evaluating your work, they will confront what you have written with the following types of questions:

- Have you *restated in your own words* the content (argument, theme, assumptions, consequences) of the reading?
- Have you *critically evaluated* the reading — assessed the cogency of the author's reasoning, the aptness of the examples and analogies used, the adequacy of the evidence offered to support claims made in the text?
- Have you *expressed* your views, interpretations, and arguments with clarity and cogency?

- Have you *quoted* your sources accurately?
- Have you *double-checked* for spelling and diction errors, typos, and revised other mechanical flaws that can serve as distractions?
- Have you said anything *original* about the topic under discussion?

These same criteria can apply to classroom quizzes or examinations, but because those writing tasks are done under time pressure, the characteristic feature of good writing — *rewriting* (critical rereading, revising, and polishing) — rarely comes into play. A take-home writing assignment, however, permits all these and more, and the conscientious student will appreciate the opportunity to take advantage of the additional time such assignments afford.

So much by way of introduction and motivation. The rest is largely up to you. Bon voyage and good luck!

Brief Contents

Contents

Exercises

1. First You Write

The unexamined life is not worth living.
— Socrates

And the examined life is not so hot, either.
— Kurt Baier

A SOCRATIC EXERCISE

You have enrolled in a philosophy course — perhaps your first — and the class is about to begin. The instructor walks in and, after a word or two of introduction, announces: "This is a course in philosophy, and right from the start I want us to *do* philosophy and not just *talk* about it. So here is your first assignment." The instructor then passes out a sheet of paper to each student. When you get your copy, this is what you see:

> In this course, we begin by reading Plato's famous dialogue, *The Apology,* in which Socrates asserts what is surely the most famous seven words of wisdom in the whole of Western philosophy: "The unexamined life is not worth living." Use the rest of this sheet to answer two questions: (1) What does this Socratic epigram mean to you, and (2) do you think it is true? After the class has spent ten minutes on this assignment, we'll discuss what you have written. (P.S. Don't worry, you won't have to turn in what you write for a grade.)

After the initial shock of being told to plunge right in has worn off, you reread the assignment and begin to think about it. What sorts of things occur to you that shed light on the two questions? (You might interrupt your reading now and try to answer these two questions.) Of course, no two students will write the same responses. Here, as an illustration, is what one student jotted down on this assignment:

What does Socrates mean? What is an "examined" life? The opposite of an unexamined life? And who is supposed to do the examining? I guess the idea is that each of us is supposed to examine our own life. But how do I do that? And what am I supposed to be looking for when I examine my life? I guess the idea is not to be too self-satisfied with the way things are going, unless I've examined what I'm doing. Examining my life would mean thinking about whether I find things to criticize. I suppose I could find myself saying "Get a life!" — what an awful thought. But it's true, examining my life might lead to changing — or trying to change — my life.

Is what Socrates said true? I don't know. You can't just take his word for it. Anyway, if I'm honest, I'd have to say I haven't really "examined" my life, whatever that means, in any thorough way. Yet I wouldn't go so far as to say that I think my life is worthless. Does that show Socrates is wrong? On the other hand, I agree that the more I look at what I am doing and compare it with what my friends are doing with their lives, the better I feel about my own life. Maybe Socrates is right.

TIME'S UP — *stop writing!* You've just finished what may be your first effort at writing philosophy. Of course, what you wrote in a few minutes isn't polished; you haven't really constructed an essay on the topic. All you have are some sentences loosely grouped together around each of the two main issues — What does Socrates *mean?* and Is he *right?* — two perennial and inescapable philosophical questions. Nevertheless, in these sentences you have before you the materials out of which you could (with more time and thought) construct a short essay in which you explain these famous words of wisdom, stating reflectively what they mean to *you,* based on *your* own thoughts, ideas, and examples. And that is exactly what philosophical thinking — investigation, criticism, reflection — is all about. The rest of this book is devoted to making such tasks more manageable, more productive, and more fun.

SOME IMPORTANT FEATURES OF WRITING PHILOSOPHY

Before going on, let's note five important features of writing philosophy that emerge in this initial exercise. We will look at each of them more closely in the pages ahead.

Definition   Explaining the idea of "examining a life" amounts to giving a definition of the phrase. Suppose you wanted to write out an explicit definition of the phrase "examining a life": What would you write? How would you go about it? And what would make one definition better than another?

Contrast   You can get a better idea of what an "examined life" is by explicitly thinking about the opposite or contrasting idea, in this case the idea of an *unexamined* life. Similarly, if you are writing a paper about justice, you'd be well advised to think about injustice; a paper on knowledge might well profit from reflections on ignorance, belief, and lucky guesses — all states of mind that contrast with knowledge.

Examples and analogy   Perhaps you have an aunt who seems to you to have examined her own life and found such introspection satisfying. Or perhaps you can think of other things that are unexamined but worth examining — say, a friendship or a college course in which you are enrolled. These might shed light by analogy on examining one's life.

Counterexamples   Testing the adequacy of any generalization involves considering whether there are counterexamples. (It just cannot be true that all swans are white if — as it turns out — some swans are black.) If you could honestly say that you know someone who has never examined his life and yet it's obvious to you that his life is worth living, then you have begun to cast doubt on the truth of Socrates's remark.

Questions   Philosophers, beginning with Socrates, have always been better at *asking* questions than at *answering* them. As you grope for responses to a writing assignment in philosophy, you can often jump-start your reflections by posing a few questions. Never mind how dumb or obvious they seem; just write them down as they occur to you. Then try to jot down some answers. One question, or its answer, will often lead to another, and to another, as in the student's response earlier. Before you know it you will have strung together a line of thinking that really does lay out something worth saying.

So much by way of extracting some general lessons from this first writing exercise. We will have occasion to look at these tactics again and in more detail, because all are useful in thinking about and writing a philosophical essay.

Before you attempt a full-length essay, however, you can profit from several preliminary kinds of writing exercises that pose modest challenges to your critical and creative faculties even as they help develop your ability to *understand what you have read*. The next chapter describes four such exercises. Some practice at these elementary tasks will help smooth the way toward the greater challenges presented later when you try to compose your own philosophical essays.

THE FIELDS OF PHILOSOPHY

The student-writing projects in this book, like those you will be expected to do in a philosophy course, will fall into one or another area of philosophy, depending on the subject matter of the course in which you are enrolled. As introductory courses vary widely in their subject matter, it might be useful to have a brief look at the scope and major subdivisions of the entire field of philosophy.

First and foremost, philosophy can be (and traditionally has been) organized into four major substantive areas: ethics, metaphysics, epistemology, and logic.

Ethics (or, more precisely, ethical theory or moral philosophy) can be divided into normative ethics, metaethics, and applied ethics. **Normative** ethics is the study and evaluation of the norms, standards, and principles governing our conduct. ("Are the biblical Ten Commandments the best set of ethical norms? Or is the commandment 'Do unto others as you would have them do unto you' a better norm?") **Metaethics** is the study of the nature and meaning of ethical concepts used in formulating ethical principles and standards. ("Can we explain the concept of 'justice' by reference to something more fundamental, such as the equality or respect for individual rights, or is 'justice' a fundamental moral concept that cannot be further defined?") **Applied** ethics deals directly with practical problems ("Under what conditions, if any, is one justified in breaking the law? Was Martin Luther King Jr. doing the right thing when he broke the law to protest racial segregation?")

In this book, there are more writing exercises involving ethical issues than any other topic. This is because introductory courses often focus on ethics; it is usually interest in ethical issues that brings students to study philosophy in the first place.

Metaphysics (in Greek, *meta ta physica,* "after the physics") is said to get its name from Aristotle's treatise on physics; his so-called metaphysical writings were assembled to follow his physical texts because they dealt with the abstract concepts used in those initial texts. Thus, metaphysics is the study of the most general concepts that we use to understand the world. The concept of cause, for example, underlies all scientific efforts to study the causes and effects of whatever events belong to a given natural or social science. But only metaphysics studies causation, an abstract concept not tied to any particular science. Metaphysics was traditionally subdivided into cosmology (the study of space and time), ontology (the basic kinds of things that exist), rational theology (the existence and nature of God, insofar as reason and experience can settle the issue), and rational psychology (the nature of the mind and its relation to the body).

Epistemology, or the theory of knowledge, is concerned with the criteria for knowledge and related concepts (belief, ignorance, truth, certainty, error). In other words, this area of philosophy studies how and whether we know what we think we know.

Logic, broadly speaking, is concerned with how to connect assertions, assumptions, and hypotheses with each other in order to reason with them correctly. Accordingly, logic concerns the criteria for valid inference in its most rigorous and economical forms, as well as certain special concepts (such as paradox, dilemma, syllogism, proof), and the nature and sources of fallacious reasoning. Logic is traditionally divided into formal deductive logic (nowadays taught as symbolic logic), inductive logic (generalization from a sample), and informal logic (criteria for good reasoning without reliance on formal systems or symbolization). Critical thinking and applied, or informal, logic are close neighbors. Courses in logic usually do not involve paper writing, unlike all other areas of philosophy, which typically do.

The rest of the substantive fields in philosophy are classified by discipline. A sketch of ten such fields follows:

Philosophy of art, or aesthetics, is the study of art in general, aesthetic value, and aesthetic experience. This field is traditionally preoccupied with the nature and criteria of the 'beautiful'.

Philosophy of education is the study of the principles and goals of education in whatever field of study, and of the differences between education and indoctrination, and teaching.

Philosophy of history is the use and study of the principles that distinguish historical understanding, interpretation, and explanation.

Philosophy of language is the field in which the nature of symbolic (verbal) meaning and reference, grammar and syntax, and natural versus artificial languages are studied.

Philosophy of law is the study of the nature of law, of legal standards and principles (especially in relation to and in contrast with moral principles), and of such basic concepts as crime, punishment, harm, offense, and legal obligation.

Philosophy of mathematics aims to provide a coherent account of the nature and methodology of mathematics, the concept of number, and the sources of necessity in mathematical truths.

Philosophy of mind is at the leading edge of psychological and neurobiological research into the nature of mental processes (reasoning) and mental entities (imagery); human, infrahuman, and artificial intelligence; consciousness and self-consciousness; and the mind-body problem. The new field of cognitive science overlaps (but does not coincide) with philosophy of mind.

Philosophy of politics (more usually called political philosophy) seeks to identify the concepts and principles by which societies can be organized and governments empowered.

Philosophy of religion is the study of the meaning and justification of religious claims about human nature and the world and the nature of faith and its role in religious belief.

Philosophy of science involves the study of the concepts and principles governing scientific knowledge and the roles of conjecture, experiment, and testability and falsifiability of hypotheses in scientific theory and practice.

Philosophical inquiry into any of these fourteen fields of philosophy may be undertaken in either (or both) of two ways: systematically or historically. **Systematic philosophy** endeavors to confront directly the problems that arise in a given field, often without any special attention to or reliance upon the work of earlier thinkers. **Historical inquiry** focuses on the philosophical problems, views, and theories of earlier thinkers and endeavors to determine exactly what those thinkers meant, whether they were correct, and how one might improve on their views.

There is, of course, much more to be said about the nature of philosophy and the many areas into which its problems can be sorted. But the foregoing should suffice for a purely introductory account of the entire field and should help you understand where your own reading and writing assignments fit into the broader picture of philosophy.

2. Writing to Understand Reading

> When I imagine the perfect reader, he always turns
> into a monster of courage and curiosity; moreover,
> supple, cunning, cautious; a born adventurer and
> discoverer.
> — Friedrich Nietzsche

Most writing assignments in philosophy courses, and certainly the typical writing assignment in an introductory course, require you to write an essay using assigned readings — usually readings discussed in class before the writing assignment is due. If you want such an essay to hit the mark, you must do the assigned reading carefully.

READING VERSUS SKIMMING

Philosophical books and articles — unlike texts that narrate, explain, or report information — cannot be skimmed for key facts and details. Rather, philosophical writing tends to be complex, advancing an argument, exploring a hypothesis, explaining a doctrine or theory, or evaluating a line of reasoning. Because of its complexity, philosophical writing demands close — and perhaps repeated — reading if justice is to be done to the author's intention. In that respect, it is like poetry. And, like poetry, philosophical texts require a creative and individual response from readers — such as an imaginary dialogue with the absent author. So be prepared to read carefully whatever philosophical materials are assigned to you, especially if you have been given a writing assignment based on them.

NOTE TAKING

Whether you read or skim a text, you may want to take some notes along the way — in the margins or on separate sheets or in a journal (in which you might also have notes from lectures and class discussions).

To be sure, if you have no special reading or writing assignment before you as you read, it is difficult to take appropriate notes on the reading, since it is unclear what is relevant and what isn't. Nevertheless, you will read more profitably if you keep your pen and highlighter handy to mark passages that look important; it will help even more if you jot down some notes for future reference, mentioning key words or phrases in the reading that seem of paramount interest and importance compared with other passages. At this stage you might also include some questions for further thought. Notes taken on your reading before class discussion are especially valuable; they will help you decide whether you are getting the essence of the reading on your own or are being distracted by ideas of lesser importance. Testing the adequacy of your note taking in this way is a valuable part of understanding the required reading and thus a useful preparatory tool to any future writing assignment.

REWRITING WHAT YOU HAVE READ:
FOUR ASSIGNMENTS

Writing assignments in a philosophy course can be quite varied, and some of the most useful do not require writing anything that could be called an essay. Instead, these assignments involve demonstrating that you have accomplished the fundamental goal of understanding the assigned reading and grasping its essential features. In these assignments, you reproduce in condensed form what you have read — in essence, rewriting what you have read.

In this chapter, we will examine four such writing assignments, any or all of which you might face in your first philosophy course and which you ought to be able to undertake whether or not they are assigned by your instructor. They are writing a *summary,* writing an *abstract,* extracting an author's *thesis,* and writing an *outline.* Each sample assignment requires you to read carefully a philosophical text (usually a brief one); it will not require you to evaluate what you have read, although it will help prepare you to do that later. Once you have mastered these assignments, you not only will be prepared to get the most from any reading assignment but will also be ready for the more challenging task of writing a philosophical essay of your own.

EXERCISE 1: Writing a Summary

Annually for many years, Clarence Irving Lewis (1883–1962), one of Harvard's most distinguished professors of philosophy, taught a course in the philosophy of Immanuel Kant (1724–1804). He concentrated on Kant's great treatise in epistemology and metaphysics, *The Critique of Pure Reason* (1781). Lewis required several kinds of writing assignments from students; the principal one was a weekly *summary* of a dozen or so pages of Kant's book. By the end of the term, each student had summarized all seven hundred pages of this forbiddingly difficult text — an exercise few of those students will ever forget.

The experience of teaching Kant had evidently convinced Lewis that there was no better way for beginners to come to grips with Kant's complex arguments. Besides, one cannot sensibly criticize Kant — or any other philosopher — without first making the effort to understand the philosopher's work. A helpful step toward understanding a philosophical text is to restate, *in one's own words*, the argument of the text, the concepts and principles used, the definitions proposed — page by page, chapter by chapter, from beginning to end.

Many readers *underline* or *highlight important passages* in a text to help them remember key points. The simple physical act of using a pen or highlighter to mark a passage actually helps etch that passage into their memory. (Please do not make marks in library books.) As effective as highlighting an assigned text can be, even more effective is *summarizing a text* by writing notes about it, either in the margins or — better still — in a notebook kept for this purpose. Writing creates a *tactile memory,* engraving in your mind what you have read. It also forces you to face the question of whether you really understand what you have read. It is far easier to deceive yourself that you have understood what you have read if all you do is pass your eyes over the page, line by line, highlighting or underlining here and there. If, instead, you write down in your own words, paragraph by paragraph, an author's thesis, key ideas, and basic arguments, you will have made some progress toward both understanding and remembering those central points.

Some Guidelines for Writing an Effective Summary

Following are some points to keep in mind as you summarize a text:

- Remember that the summary must be considerably briefer than the text itself, typically one-third or less the length of the original. If your summary runs longer, this could be a sign that you have not understood the text well enough to condense it in your own words.
- It can be useful to *number the paragraphs in the original and use those same numbers to mark the sentences in your summary.* This step correlates the text and your summary of it and also helps ensure that you don't forget to summarize a key point.
- To achieve brevity, *try to write no more than one or two sentences for each paragraph of the original.*
- *Quote infrequently and not at length. Instead, rely on paraphrasing* lest you preserve too much of the original. Extensive quotation may seduce you into thinking you understand the original better than you really do.

At least two purposes are achieved by summarizing an assigned reading. *First,* summarizing helps you understand the content and sequence of ideas in a reading; it focuses your attention so that as you read the text closely, you can extract its main points. *Second,* because summarizing is an exercise in writing — though not in critical thinking — it is a useful step in making the transition from reading to writing, from absorbing and evaluating what others have said to expressing your own thoughts on paper.

With these thoughts in mind, let's turn to our first text to be summarized.

Summarizing an Extract

Introduction   The following text is from *Dialogues Concerning Natural Religion*, written in the 1770s by the Scottish philosopher David Hume (1711–1776) but not published until several years after his death. The whole book runs to about a hundred pages and is divided into twelve parts. The extract reprinted here constitutes the most important section of the text, seven paragraphs of varying length and interest from part 2. In these paragraphs, three fictional characters debate what is probably the most popular traditional argument in theology, variously called the "argument from design," the "argument by analogy," and "the argument *a posteriori*" (that is, from something known based on experience). (Why this argument has these several names should become clear as you read the extract itself.)

Part 2 of Hume's *Dialogues* opens with remarks from Demea, a character whom Hume has fashioned into a stalwart if rather unresourceful defender of conventional religious belief and practice as well as of traditional metaphysics. Demea's brief remarks are followed by those of Philo, a self-styled "skeptic." Philo shares with Demea a belief in the weakness of human reason and the limitations of human experience when confronted with the supernatural. Unlike Demea, however, Philo is very resourceful in argument and confident of the powers of reason and experience in natural science. The third figure, Cleanthes, is at odds with both Demea and Philo; it is his role to carry the burden of the argument in the *Dialogues* by stating and defending as well as he can what is called (in the language of the eighteenth century) "natural religion."

Natural religion, as described in part 1 of the *Dialogues* (not reprinted here), is the attempt to explain the *nature* of God by appeal only to reason and experience (thus excluding revelation, miracles, and holy writ). Taken for granted in the *Dialogues* is that God exists; the three-way conversation among Demea, Philo, and Cleanthes proceeds on this unargued assumption. Hume depicts Cleanthes as a "modern" thinker who believes that the ways of scientific inference (used with such success by Copernicus, Galileo, and Newton to extend and organize knowledge about the physical universe) can be put to good effect in philosophy and metaphysics as well. Cleanthes's "argument *a posteriori*," as he calls it, illustrates such an outlook. Demea opposes Cleanthes's argument because he thinks it threatens traditional belief and practice, which rest in part on faith. Philo opposes Cleanthes's argument for a very different reason; he thinks Cleanthes's style of argument employs principles and assumptions that exceed the powers of the human mind and that the evidence for Cleanthes's analogy between God and the human mind is far weaker than Cleanthes believes.

You might want to try your hand at summarizing Hume's text before turning to the sample student summary on pages 13–14.

DAVID HUME
from *Dialogues Concerning Natural Religion*

Not to lose any time in circumlocutions, said Cleanthes, addressing   1
himself to Demea, much less in replying to the pious declamations of Philo, I shall briefly explain how I conceive this matter. Look round the world: Contemplate the whole and every part of it: You will find it to be nothing but one great machine, subdivided into an infinite number of lesser machines, which again admit of subdivisions to a degree beyond what human senses and faculties can trace and explain. All these various machines, and even their most minute parts, are adjusted to each other with an accuracy which ravishes into admiration all men who have ever contemplated them. The curious adapting of means to ends, throughout all nature, resembles exactly, though it much exceeds, the productions of human contrivance — of human design, thought, wisdom, and intelligence. Since therefore the effects resemble each other, we are led to infer, by all the rules of analogy, that the causes also resemble, and that the Author of Nature is somewhat similar to the mind of man, though possessed of much larger faculties, proportioned to the grandeur of the work which he has executed. By this argument *a posteriori*, and by this argument alone, do we prove at once the existence of a Deity and his similarity to human mind and intelligence.

I shall be so free, Cleanthes, said Demea, as to tell you that from   2
the beginning I could not approve of your conclusion concerning the similarity of the Deity to men, still less can I approve of the mediums by which you endeavor to establish it. What! No demonstration of the Being of God! No abstract arguments! No proofs

---

David Hume, Scotland's most eminent philosopher, had the bitter experience of watching his brilliant first book, *A Treatise of Human Nature* (1739–1740) — as he memorably put it — "fall dead-born from the press." Despite this discouragement, he persisted as a writer and shifted his efforts to history and essays. His multivolume *History of England* (1754–1762) was a great success and established his literary reputation. In his philosophical essays on a wide variety of topics in metaphysics, epistemology, and moral theory, he restated his views in the *Treatise* in a more palatable form and earned himself immediate acclaim. In France he was a celebrity; there he met Jean-Jacques Rousseau (1712–1778). Their friendship soon deteriorated under Rousseau's paranoid conviction that Hume was out to ruin him.

His posthumous *Dialogues Concerning Natural Religion* has often been praised as second in quality and style only to Plato's dialogues; an excerpt is reprinted here.

a priori![1] Are these which have hitherto been so much insisted on by philosophers all fallacy, all sophism? Can we reach no farther in this subject than experience and probability? I will say not that this is betraying the cause of a Deity; but surely, by this affected candor, you give advantages to atheists which they never could obtain by the mere dint of argument and reasoning.

What I chiefly scruple in this subject, said Philo, is not so much 3 that all religious arguments are by Cleanthes reduced to experience, as that they appear not to be even the most certain and irrefragable of that inferior kind. That a stone will fall, that fire will burn, that the earth has solidity, we have observed a thousand and thousand times; and when any new instance of this nature is presented, we draw without hesitation the accustomed inference. The exact similarity of the cases gives us a perfect assurance of a similar event, and a stronger evidence is never desired or sought after. But wherever you depart, in the least, from the similarity of the cases, you diminish proportionably the evidence; and may at last bring it to a very weak *analogy,* which is confessedly liable to error and uncertainty. After having experienced the circulation of the blood in human creatures, we make no doubt that it takes place in Titius and Maevius; but from its circulation in frogs and fishes it is only a presumption, though a strong one, from analogy that it takes place in men and other animals. The analogical reasoning is much weaker when we infer the circulation of the sap in vegetables from our experience that the blood circulates in animals; and those who hastily followed that imperfect analogy are found, by more accurate experiments, to have been mistaken.

If we see a house, Cleanthes, we conclude, with the greatest 4 certainty, that it had an architect or builder because this is precisely that species of effect which we have experienced to proceed from that species of cause. But surely you will not affirm that the universe bears such a resemblance to a house that we can with the same certainty infer a similar cause, or that the analogy is here entire and perfect. The dissimilitude is so striking that the utmost you can here pretend to is a guess, a conjecture, a presumption concerning a similar cause; and how that pretension will be received in the world, I leave you to consider.

I would surely be very ill received, replied Cleanthes; and I 5 should be deservedly blamed and detested did I allow that the proofs of a Deity amounted to no more than a guess or conjecture. But is the whole adjustment of means to ends in a house and in the universe so slight a resemblance? the economy of final causes? the order, proportion, and arrangement of every part? Steps of a stair are plainly contrived that human legs may use them in mounting; and this inference is certain and infallible. Human legs are also contrived for walking and mounting; and this inference, I allow, is not altogether so certain because of the dissimilarity which you remark; but does it, therefore, deserve the name only of presumption or conjecture?

---

1. Obtained through reason as opposed to experience. [Ed.]

Good God! cried Demea, interrupting him, where are we? Zeal- 6
ous defenders of religion allow that the proofs of a Deity fall short
of perfect evidence! And you, Philo, on whose assistance I depended
in proving the adorable mysteriousness of the Divine Nature, do
you assent to all these extravagant opinions of Cleanthes? For what
other name can I give them? or, why spare my censure when such
principles are advanced, supported by such an authority, before so
young a man as Pamphilus?

You seem not to apprehend, replied Philo, that I argue with 7
Cleanthes in his own way, and, by showing him the dangerous consequences of his tenets, hope at last to reduce him to our opinion.
But what sticks most with you, I observe, is the representation which
Cleanthes has made of the argument *a posteriori;* and, finding that
that argument is likely to escape your hold and vanish into air, you
think it so disguised that you can scarcely believe it to be set in its
true light. Now, however much I may dissent, in other respects,
from the dangerous principle of Cleanthes, I must allow that he has
fairly represented that argument. . . .

Sample Student Summary

A Summary of Hume's

Dialogues Concerning Natural Religion,

the Beginning of Part 2

by

Noah Kriegel

Cleanthes says that he views the universe as one
giant machine, whose workings parallel, though they
much surpass, machines of human design. By analogy
we may infer that since these "effects" resemble each
other, their "causes" must also resemble, and so "the
Author of Nature" must be akin to, though much
greater than, the mind of a human. He insists that
by this "argument a posteriori" we prove both the
"existence" of God and God's "similarity to human
mind and intelligence" (para. 1).

Demea objects to Cleanthes's argument primarily
because it implies a "similarity of the Deity to
men," and secondly because it relies upon experience
and not upon "proofs a priori" (para. 2). Philo is

not so concerned with the fact that Cleanthes's argument relies on experience as he is with the weakness of the analogy. Experience clearly tells us, he argues, that whenever we see a house we know that it has a builder, but any analogy between the universe and a house is so disproportionate that we cannot possibly infer that their causes must be similar (paras. 3-4).

Cleanthes replies by arguing that the analogy is not as weak as Philo claims. He holds that the "order, proportion, and arrangement" of both the house and the universe, while not being totally analogous, are still deserving of serious consideration (para. 5).

Demea interrupts to express his horror at the idea of theologians conceding that "the proofs of a Deity" are not perfect, and he calls the reasoning of Cleanthes nothing more than "extravagant opinions" (para. 6).

Philo states that, while he may have some worries about the argument a posteriori, he believes that Cleanthes has stated the argument well (para. 7).

Discussion   Let's notice a few basic features of Noah Kriegel's summary. First, it runs to less than three hundred words, roughly one-fifth the length of the original. This is well within the suggested length of a summary (see p. 9). Second, Kriegel tightened the argument by collapsing the seven paragraphs into five. He frequently departed, however, from the suggestion to confine the summary to one or two sentences for each paragraph of the original. Because Hume's paragraphs tend to be lengthy, the suggested two-sentence limit was perhaps too restrictive to follow consistently. Third, Kriegel incorporated some pithy quotations that capture the flavor of the original, focusing attention on key ideas and phrases. Judged by these rather mechanical considerations, then, his summary is a good one.

The real test of a summary is whether it effectively conveys the gist of the original, so that a reader unfamiliar with what the author actually wrote could nevertheless get all the main ideas by reading only the summary. Kriegel's summary passes this test. Cleanthes's argument —

the main issue presented by Hume — is adequately captured in the summary, even if some of the details that add color and texture are necessarily omitted.

In sum, whether evaluated for its probable help to Kriegel in grasping Hume's basic points or for use as evidence that Kriegel understood the reading, the summary is a success.

Could the summary be shortened even more? Or could it be revised so that some paragraphs in the original are handled in more detail according to their relative importance? Has anything in the original been blurred or unintentionally misrepresented? Look over each paragraph of the summary, measure it against the original, and judge for yourself. You might even try your hand at editing Kriegel's summary by adding or subtracting whatever you think might improve it.

EXERCISE 2: Writing an Abstract

In 1610, Galileo Galilei (1564–1642) published a short treatise in astronomy, *The Starry Messenger*, in which he announced to the world the remarkable discoveries he had recently made by using a telescope (indeed, he claimed to be the first to use this new instrument). The title page of his treatise, in the original Latin, looked like this:

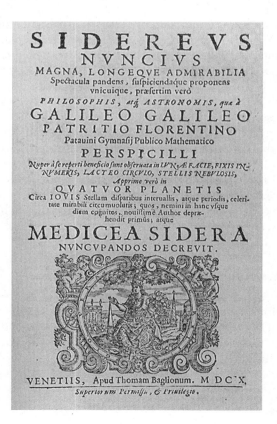

Translated from Latin into English, the title page reads as follows:

SIDEREAL MESSENGER
unfolding great and very wonderful sights
and displaying to the gaze of everyone,
but especially philosophers and astronomers,
the things that were observed by
GALILEO GALILEI,
Florentine patrician
and public mathematician of the University of Padua,
with the help of a spyglass lately devised by him,
about the face of the Moon, countless fixed stars,
the Milky Way, nebulous stars,
but especially about
four planets
flying around the star of Jupiter at unequal intervals
and periods with wonderful swiftness;
which, unknown by anyone until this day,
the first author detected recently
and decided to name
MEDICEAN STARS

As this page shows, Galileo was not above a little self-dramatization and self-promotion; his tantalizing promises — especially his phrase "displaying to the gaze of everyone" — are shrewdly calculated to arouse the reader's interest. Yet, looked at in another way, Galileo's title page can be seen as a primitive version of what we would call a *scientific abstract*. Today, every article published in a scientific journal is prefaced by an abstract, usually written by the article's author, that runs a paragraph or so (rarely more than 250 words) and appears immediately after the title and the author's name on the first page.

Much as did Galileo's title page of four centuries ago, modern abstracts inform busy readers of an article's essence. Abstracts usually include the *main results* being reported. (Galileo lists four different discoveries, in order of ascending importance to heighten interest in his announcement of the last one.) They also describe the *method* by which these results were obtained. (Galileo gives credit to his new instrument, the telescope.)

Some Guidelines for Writing an Effective Abstract

What contemporary scientific readers look for in the abstracts of professional journals — some version of Galileo's results-plus-methodology approach — won't do for philosophers. For one thing, there is usually no brief way to state the "methodology" guiding the philosophical writer to his or her conclusions; certainly there is nothing comparable to the telescope or other experimental apparatus in a philosopher's methods of analysis and argument. For another, not all philosophical essays are designed to yield "results," as reports of scientific research are. However, the features of philosophical abstracts are somewhat parallel to those of scientific abstracts. In their abstracts philosophers do a minimum of three things:

- State in a few words the main idea, theme, or thesis of their article
- Indicate or sketch the line of argument being used to establish this idea
- Restate any definition, distinction, principle, and so on necessary to understand the article

How, then, does an *abstract* differ from a *summary*? To be sure, there is no hard and fast distinction between the two; a long abstract can amount to a short summary, and vice versa. Still, unlike a summary, an abstract is always *very* brief. The brevity is achieved by ignoring all side issues, details, examples, illustrations, and anything else not essential to fulfilling the three requirements just mentioned. Note also that abstracts, like summaries and paraphrases, lack the subordination characteristic of an outline.

Choosing between writing a summary or writing an abstract of a given text will turn on what you are trying to accomplish. If your purpose is to record the content and sequence of ideas in the author's argument and to create some tactile memory of the text, then only a summary will do. But if your purpose is to capture the very essence of the text, then an abstract is what you want.

Why might authors in philosophy (and other disciplines) prepare abstracts of their own work? In short, to help readers. Because an abstract provides just the essence of an essay or an article, it allows readers to browse through a vast amount of material. Without publications like *The Philosopher's Index*, which abstracts hundreds of articles published annually in the scholarly journals of philosophy, it would be all but impossible for interested readers to keep up with recent publications in the field.

With these ideas in mind, let's look at an example of a philosophical text and a student's abstract of it.

Writing an Abstract

Introduction   Hardin's essay is one of the most provocative arguments of the past century; he opposes aid to the poor in nations facing starvation. His metaphors — lifeboat ethics, Spaceship Earth — depict our nation's situation (fortunate) and that of others (unfortunate) in a manner most readers find sobering in the extreme.

You might try your hand at writing an abstract of Hardin's article before you turn to the sample student abstract on page 23. Try hard not to exceed 250–300 words.

GARRETT HARDIN
from *On Not Feeding the Starving*

No generation has viewed the problem of the survival of the 1
human species as seriously as we have. Inevitably, we have entered
this world of concern through the door of metaphor. Environmental-
ists have emphasized the image of the earth as a spaceship — Spaceship Earth. Kenneth Boulding is the principal architect of this metaphor. It is time, he says, that we replace the wasteful "cowboy
economy" of the past with the frugal "spaceship economy" required
for continued survival in the limited world we now see ours to be.
The metaphor is notably useful in justifying pollution control measures.

Unfortunately, the image of a spaceship is also used to promote 2
measures that are suicidal. One of these is a generous immigration
policy, which is only a particular instance of a class of policies that
are in error because they lead to the tragedy of the commons. These
suicidal policies are attractive because they mesh with what we un-
thinkingly take to be the ideals of "the best people." What is missing
in the idealistic view is an insistence that rights and responsibilities
must go together. The "generous" attitude of all too many people
results in asserting inalienable rights while ignoring or denying match-
ing responsibilities.

For the metaphor of a spaceship to be correct the aggregate of people 3
on board would have to be under unitary sovereign control. A true ship
always has a captain. It is conceivable that a ship could be run by a
committee. But it could not possibly survive if its course were determined by bickering tribes that claimed rights without responsibilities.

What about Spaceship Earth? It certainly has no captain, and no 4
executive committee. The United Nations is a toothless tiger, because the signatories of its charter wanted it that way. The spaceship metaphor is used only to justify spaceship demands on common resources without acknowledging corresponding spaceship
responsibilities.

An understandable fear of decisive action leads people to embrace 5
"incrementalism" — moving toward reform in tiny stages. As we shall
see, this strategy is counterproductive in the area discussed here if it
means accepting rights before responsibilities. Where human survival
is at stake, the acceptance of responsibilities is a precondition to the
acceptance of rights, if the two cannot be introduced simultaneously.

Garret Hardin (b. 1915) received his Ph.D. in biology from Stanford in 1941. After
a brief teaching stint at Stanford and then at the Carnegie Institute, he joined the
faculty of the University of California at Santa Barbara, where he taught for over
thirty years (1946–1978). His interests focused on problems of human ecology, overpopulation, and food production and distribution. His first book in this area, coed-
ited with John Boden, was *Managing the Commons* (1977). Since then he has published *The Limits of Altruism* (1977), *Filters against Folly* (1988), *Living within Limits*
(1993), *The Immigration Dilemma* (1995), and *The Ostrich Factor* (1999).
Reprinted here is an extract from a journal article originally published in 1974,
in which Hardin defended (and popularized) "lifeboat ethics."

LIFEBOAT ETHICS

Before taking up certain substantive issues let us look at an alterna- 6
tive metaphor, that of a lifeboat. In developing some relevant examples the following numerical values are assumed. Approximately
two-thirds of the world is desperately poor, and only one-third is
comparatively rich. The people in poor countries have an average
per capita GNP (Gross National Product) of about $200 per year; the
rich, of about $3,000. (For the United States it is nearly $5,000 per
year.) Metaphorically, each rich nation amounts to a lifeboat full of
comparative rich people. The poor of the world are in other, much
more crowded lifeboats. Continuously, so to speak, the poor fall out
of their lifeboats and swim for a while in the water outside, hoping
to be admitted to a rich lifeboat, or in some other way to benefit
from the "goodies" on board. What should the passengers on a rich
lifeboat do? This is the central problem of "the ethics of the lifeboat."

First we must acknowledge that each lifeboat is effectively lim- 7
ited in capacity. The land of every nation has a limited carrying
capacity. The exact limit is a matter for argument, but the energy
crunch is convincing more people every day that we have already
exceeded the carrying capacity of the land. We have been living on
"capital" — stored petroleum and coal — and soon we must live on
income alone.

Let us look at only one lifeboat — ours. The ethical problem is 8
the same for all, and is as follows. Here we sit, say 50 people in a
lifeboat. To be generous, let us assume our boat has a capacity of 10
more, making 60. (This, however, is to violate the engineering principle of the "safety factor." A new plant disease or a bad change in
the weather may decimate our population if we don't preserve some
excess capacity as a safety factor.)

The 50 of us in the lifeboat see 100 others swimming in the 9
water outside, asking for admission to the boat, or for handouts.
How shall we respond to their calls? There are several possibilities.

One. We may be tempted to try to live by the Christian ideal of 10
being "our brother's keeper," or by the Marxian ideal of "from each
according to his abilities, to each according to his needs." Since the
needs of all are the same, we take all the needy into our boat, making a total of 150 in a boat with a capacity of 60. The boat is swamped,
and everyone drowns. Complete justice, complete catastrophe.

Two. Since the boat has an unused excess capacity of 10, we 11
admit just 10 more to it. This has the disadvantage of getting rid of
the safety factor, for which action we will sooner or later pay dearly.
Moreover, *which* 10 do we let in? "First come, first served"? The best
10? The neediest 10? How do we *discriminate?* And what do we say
to the 90 who are excluded?

Three. Admit no more to the boat and preserve the small safety 12
factor. Survival of the people in the lifeboat is then possible (though
we shall have to be on our guard against boarding parties).

The last solution is abhorrent to many people. It is unjust, they 13
say. Let us grant that it is.

"I feel guilty about my good luck," say some. The reply to this is   14
simple: *Get out and yield your place to others.* Such a selfless
action might satisfy the conscience of those who are addicted to
guilt but it would not change the ethics of the lifeboat. The needy
person to whom a guilt-addict yields his place will not himself feel
guilty about his sudden good luck. (If he did he would not climb
aboard.) The net result of conscience-stricken people relinquishing
their unjustly held positions is the elimination of their kind of conscience from the lifeboat. The lifeboat, as it were, purifies itself of
guilt. The ethics of the lifeboat persist, unchanged by such momentary aberrations.

This then is the basic metaphor within which we must work out   15
our solutions. Let us enrich the image step by step with substantive
additions from the real world.

REPRODUCTION

The harsh characteristics of lifeboat ethics are heightened by repro-   16
duction, particularly by reproductive differences. The people inside
the lifeboats of the wealthy nations are doubling in numbers every
87 years; those outside are doubling every thirty-five years, on the
average. And the relative difference in prosperity is becoming greater.

Let us, for a while, think primarily of the U.S. lifeboat. As of   17
1973 the United States had a population of 210 million people, who
were increasing by 0.8% per year, that is, doubling in number every
87 years.

Although the citizens of rich nations are outnumbered two to   18
one by the poor, let us imagine an equal number of poor people
outside our lifeboat — a mere 210 million poor people reproducing
at a quite different rate. If we imagine these to be the combined
populations of Colombia, Venezuela, Ecuador, Morocco, Thailand,
Pakistan, and the Philippines, the average rate of increase of the
people "outside" is 3.3% per year. The doubling time of this population is 21 years.

Suppose that all these countries, and the United States, agreed   19
to live by the Marxian ideal, "to each according to his needs," the
ideal of most Christians as well. Needs, of course, are determined by
population size, which is affected by reproduction. Every nation
regards its rate of reproduction as a sovereign right. If our lifeboat
were big enough in the beginning it might be possible to live *for a
while* by Christian-Marxian ideals. *Might.*

Initially, in the model given, the ratio of non-Americans to Ameri-   20
cans would be one to one. But consider what the ratio would be 87
years later. By this time Americans would have doubled to a population of 420 million. The other group (doubling every 21 years)
would now have swollen to 3,540 million. Each American would
have more than eight people to share with. How could the lifeboat
possibly keep afloat?

All this involves extrapolation of current trends into the future,   21
and is consequently suspect. Trends may change. Granted: but the

change will not necessarily be favorable. If — as seems likely — the rate of population increase falls faster in the ethnic group presently inside the lifeboat than it does among those now outside, the future will turn out to be even worse than mathematics predicts, and sharing will be even more suicidal.

RUIN IN THE COMMONS

The fundamental error of the sharing ethics is that it leads to the [22] tragedy of the commons. Under a system of private property the man (or group of men) who own property recognize their responsibility to care for it, for if they don't they will eventually suffer. A farmer, for instance, if he is intelligent, will allow no more cattle in a pasture than its carrying capacity justifies. If he overloads the pasture, weeds take over, erosion sets in, and the owner loses in the long run.

But if a pasture is run as a commons open to all, the right of [23] each to use it is not matched by an operational responsibility to take care of it. It is no use asking independent herdsmen in a commons to act responsibly, for they dare not. The considerate herdsman who refrains from overloading the commons suffers more than a selfish one who says his needs are greater. (As Leo Durocher says, "Nice guys finish last.") Christian-Marxian idealism is counterproductive. That it *sounds* nice is no excuse. With distribution systems, as with individual morality, good intentions are no substitute for good performance.

A social system is stable only if it is insensitive to errors. To the [24] Christian-Marxian idealist a selfish person is a sort of "error." Prosperity in the system of the commons cannot survive errors. If *everyone* would only restrain himself, all would be well; but it takes *only one less than everyone* to ruin a system of voluntary restraint. In a crowded world of less than perfect human beings — and we will never know any other — mutual ruin is inevitable in the commons. This is the core of the tragedy of the commons. . . .

WORLD FOOD BANKS

In the international arena we have recently heard a proposal to cre- [25] ate a new commons, namely an international depository of food reserves to which nations will contribute according to their abilities, and from which nations may draw according to their needs. Nobel laureate Normal Borlaug has lent the prestige of his name to this proposal.

A world food bank appeals powerfully to our humanitarian im- [26] pulses. We remember John Donne's celebrated line, "Any man's death diminishes me." But before we rush out to see for whom the bell tolls let us recognize where the greatest political push for international granaries comes from, lest we be disillusioned later. Our experience with Public Law 480 clearly reveals the answer. This was the law that moved billions of dollars worth of U.S. grain to food-short, population-long countries during the past two decades. When P.L. 480 first came into being, a headline in the business magazine *Forbes* revealed the power behind it: "Feeding the World's Hungry Millions: How it will mean billions for U.S. business."

And indeed it did. In the years 1960 to 1970 a total of $7.9 billion was spent on the "Food for Peace" program, as P.L. 480 was called. During the years of 1948 to 1970 an additional $49.9 billion were extracted from American taxpayers to pay for other economic aid programs, some of which went for food and food-producing machinery. (This figure does *not* include military aid.) That P.L. 480 was a give-away program was concealed. Recipient countries went through the motions of paying for P.L. 480 food — with IOUs. In December 1973 the charade was brought to an end as far as India was concerned when the United States "forgave" India's $3.2 billion debt. Public announcement of the cancellation of the debt was delayed for two months: one wonders why. . . . 27

What happens if some organizations budget for emergencies and others do not? If each organization is solely responsible for its own well-being, poorly managed ones will suffer. But they should be able to learn from experience. They have a chance to mend their ways and learn to budget for infrequent but certain emergencies. The weather, for instance, always varies and periodic crop failures are certain. A wise and competent government saves out of the production of the good years in anticipation of bad years that are sure to come. This is not a new idea. The Bible tells us that Joseph taught his policy to Pharaoh in Egypt more than 2,000 years ago. Yet it is literally true that the vast majority of the governments of the world today have no such policy. They lack either the wisdom or the competence, or both. Far more difficult than the transfer of wealth from one country to another is the transfer of wisdom between sovereign powers or between generations. 28

"But it isn't their fault! How can we blame the poor people who are caught in an emergency? Why must be punish them?" The concepts of blame and punishment are irrelevant. The question is, what are the operational consequences of establishing a world food bank? If it is open to every country every time a need develops, slovenly rulers will not be motivated to take Joseph's advice. Why should they? Others will bail them out whenever they are in trouble. 29

Some countries will make deposits in the world food bank and others will withdraw from it: There will be almost no overlap. Calling such a depository-transfer unit a "bank" is stretching the metaphor of *bank* beyond its elastic limits. The proposers, of course, never call attention to the metaphorical nature of the word they use. 30

Sample Student Abstract

An Abstract of Hardin's

On Not Feeding the Starving

by

Ashley de Marchena

The purpose of this essay is to explain why giving handouts to poor countries will not work in the long run. The total population of poor countries currently outnumbers that of rich countries two to one. As a rich country, how is the United States to deal with its responsibilities to poorer countries? If we go by the Christian-Marxian ideal of being "our brother's keeper," or "from each according to his abilities, to each according to his needs," we will quickly exceed our resources. If we help only as many as we can, how should we choose? There is no fair system of distribution. The other option, which most people think is unjust, is simply not to help these foreigners at all. The rationale for this option is brought to light by the problem of population growth. Impoverished nations have a much higher birthrate than the affluent nations, so even if it is possible to help them now, the gap between the rich and the poor will widen, making it harder to help them as time goes by. Another problem with trying to help all in need is that the Christian-Marxian idealism is just that: idealism. It is not realistic and it doesn't work; all it takes is one less-than-perfect person to ruin the system for everyone. World food banks are also shortsighted. Certain countries always give and certain other countries always take. This does not teach the needy countries to prepare for emergencies, for they believe that they will always be bailed out whenever they are in trouble.

Discussion   De Marchena's abstract conforms to the length restriction; she uses 267 words to tell the reader what Hardin has to say in some 2,700 words — a 90% reduction of the original. Notice that she abandons the four section headings that Hardin provides. These headings help the reader organize and retain the main points of the essay, but they are not needed in the abstract because of its brevity.

How well does de Marchena's abstract convey to the reader the high points of Hardin's article? She does not preserve the flavor of Hardin's essay as well as she might because she retains almost none of his language. This is not a very severe criticism; still, she could have used at least two of his most distinctive phrases ("lifeboat ethics," "tragedy of the commons") to good advantage. In any case, Hardin's central claim — that charity to poor nations is ultimately a self-defeating practice — comes across loud and clear in her abstract.

Of course, few readers of the abstract are likely to be persuaded to agree with Hardin; at the very least, they would need the details his essay provides but for which there is no room in the abstract. This is not, however, a defect in the abstract. The purpose of the abstract is not to persuade; it is to inform. Any effective alternative to de Marchena's abstract is going to share this feature.

EXERCISE 3: Extracting an Author's Thesis

Argumentative essays typically have a **thesis,** which is the essay's central idea. Considered together, a summary, an abstract, and the author's thesis are a bit like a Chinese box: Inside the summary lies hidden an even briefer version of the text, the abstract; and inside the abstract there is the thesis. Writing each of these is a slightly different way to develop tactile memory (see p. 9) and the analytic skills needed for effective reading and note taking. Further, because summarizing, abstracting, and extracting a thesis all involve writing and analysis, they are very useful in helping you make the transition from critical reading to critical writing.

Philosophical writing, as we have already seen in the excerpts from Hume and Hardin, is usually argumentative writing. The heart of such prose is the author's *thesis,* the central point that he or she is trying to defend, explain, justify, or otherwise convince the reader to believe based on whatever rational considerations the author can muster. This means two things. First, when you *read* such an essay you ought to be looking for the author's thesis. Without a good grip on the author's thesis, you cannot understand and evaluate the author's argument. Second, when you *write* such an essay yourself, you want to make sure your readers know what your thesis is. On page 109 we will take up how to *write* a thesis. Here we want to look more closely at how to *extract* an author's thesis. Often, philosophers (and other authors of arguments) open with their thesis, but sometimes they don't present the thesis until much later. In other cases, their thesis is implicit but never clearly stated. Because authors vary so widely in how they present their theses, and because extracting a thesis is such a vital part of reading in preparation for writing, we will look at a series of progressively more difficult examples.

A good example of a philosophical text in which the author states his thesis quite clearly is the widely read short book *On Liberty* by John Stuart Mill (1806–1873), published in 1859. What, exactly, is it about "liberty" that Mill argues for or against in this essay? Eventually, in the ninth of the very long paragraphs that open his book, Mill answers this question:

> The object of this essay is to assert one very simple principle, as entitled to govern absolutely the dealings of society with the individual in the way of compulsion and control, whether the means used be physical force in the form of legal penalties, or the moral coercion of public opinion. That principle is, that the sole end for which mankind are warranted, individually or collectively, in interfering with the liberty of action of any of their number, is self-protection. That the only purpose for which power can be rightfully exercised over any member of a civilized community, against his will, is to prevent harm to others. His own good, either physical or moral, is not a sufficient warrant.

The paragraph goes on a few more lines, but the portion quoted is all that matters here; it contains the thesis of Mill's book. Can that thesis be stated even more concisely, perhaps in only *one sentence*? Yes, it can. In your reading notes, you might restate his thesis this way:

The sole legitimate reason for state interference with individual liberty is to prevent harm to others.

Not only does Mill say this is his thesis (he calls it "one very simple principle," which it is "the object of this essay . . . to assert"), but a careful reading of his whole treatise confirms that it really *is* his central point. All the rest of his book is devoted to applying, illustrating, and defending this claim. Readers of *On Liberty* have always been grateful to Mill for the explicitness with which he sets out his thesis — even if he doesn't present it at the very beginning of his book.

In another work Mill was even more helpful. A decade after he published *On Liberty*, another important book-length essay of his appeared: *On the Subjection of Women* (1869). Once again he clearly states

---

John Stuart Mill was the precocious son of James Mill (himself a philosopher of sorts) and the heir to Jeremy Bentham's radicalism. He is chiefly remembered today for authoring three slender volumes: *On Liberty* (1859), *Utilitarianism* (1861), and *The Subjection of Women* (1869). All three of these books are classics of their kind and continue to be widely read and discussed. Mill's interests covered the entire range of philosophy, from logic to jurisprudence, ethics to metaphysics. Even so, his energies and talents were not confined to philosophy; following in his father's footsteps, he was employed as the director of Britain's East India Company, was an active contributor to the liberal journal *The Westminster Review,* and served a term in Parliament. He worked entirely at home and never held any permanent academic appointment.

his thesis, only this time he does so in the very first paragraph of the book:

> The object of this Essay is to explain as clearly as I am able, the grounds of an opinion which I have held from the very earliest period when I had formed any opinions at all on social or political matters, and which, instead of being weakened or modified, has been constantly growing stronger by the progress of reflection and the experience of life: That the principle which regulates the existing social relations between the two sexes — the legal subordination of one sex to the other — is wrong in itself, and now one of the chief hindrances to human improvement; and that it ought to be replaced by a principle of perfect equality, admitting no power or privilege on the one side, nor disability on the other.

Extracting Mill's thesis from this paragraph is fairly easy. You could restate it in your reading notes in one sentence, like the following:

The legal subordination of women to men--wrong in itself and a hindrance to human improvement--ought to be replaced with perfect equality between the two sexes.

Why does it matter whether a reader can identify the writer's thesis? Why should writers try to express, in clear language, the central idea of their book or article? The answer lies in a point that has been made before and will be made again in this book in various forms and contexts: The central purpose of writing is *communication* between the author and the reader. (This applies even to the special case where you play both roles — writer and reader — as when you take notes for yourself.) Writers will communicate ideas more effectively if they make a conscious effort to inform readers of their thesis rather than leaving it concealed in a thicket of prose, forcing readers to guess what the central issue is.

Some Guidelines for Extracting an Author's Thesis

As the two examples from John Stuart Mill indicate, extracting an author's thesis can be easy if the author states the thesis as clearly as Mill does. But as the following exercises will show, identifying the thesis isn't always so simple. What should you look for to help you find it?

One tip is to be guided by *the author's own title* for the text. If you can find a sentence or two in the text that restates what the author has put into the title, you may very well have identified the thesis. For example, Mill establishes a clear connection between the title of each of his two works and what turns out to be the thesis in each. But be careful — don't confuse an author's *topic*, perhaps expressed in the title, with the author's *thesis*. Garret Hardin's topic (p. 18) is the problem of overpopulation, but his thesis is that affluent nations ought not to open their coffers to the needy nor open their doors to starving immigrants.

Another and more fundamental tip in thesis hunting is to try to discern the main point the author is trying to make, around which the examples, analogies, evidence, and illustrative details cluster. If you can find such a main point, you probably have put your finger on the author's thesis.

If the going gets difficult, and you can't confidently point to any sentence or two in a text that you think expresses the author's thesis, step back a bit and think: Is the text you are reading really a piece of argumentative prose? Not every writer, and not even every philosopher, always writes with the intention of conveying an argument. And without an argument there may be no thesis — no particular stand, however subtle, that the author takes and defends.

Finally, after you have identified what you believe to be the author's thesis, you should try to state that thesis as precisely and briefly as you can. Try to force yourself to restate the thesis in one declarative sentence, that is, a sentence that makes a statement (i.e., asserts a proposition). If you find yourself writing more than one sentence, you are on your way to giving an abstract of the author's text (see p. 15). Forcing yourself to be brief not only will further test your skill in thinking and writing but will confirm whether you really have grasped the author's thesis.

Extracting the thesis

Introduction   The eleven paragraphs reprinted here are from an essay by the eminent English philosopher Bertrand Russell (1872–1970), written in 1952, two years after he won the Nobel Prize. Read over this essay and see whether by the end you can state Russell's thesis.

BERTRAND RUSSELL
from *Three Essentials for a Stable World*

Thought about public affairs in recent years has been so com-   1
pletely absorbed by the problem of relations between Russia and the West that various other problems, which would remain even if that one were solved, have not received as much attention as they

Bertrand Russell, whom many would judge the most eminent philosopher of the twentieth century, was known for his pioneering work in mathematics, logic, epistemology, and metaphysics, as well as in social and political philosophy. During most of his life he earned his way as a writer, but many of his popular books and articles added little if any luster to his reputation. When asked in his later years to describe his career, he said (more or less in these words), "When I was young I did mathematics; when that became too difficult I turned to logic. When that became too hard, I turned to philosophy. Now I write detective stories." During World War I he was a pacifist, which led to his losing his fellowship at Cambridge University and being briefly imprisoned at His Majesty's pleasure in 1918. He was awarded the Nobel Prize for literature (there being none for philosophy) in 1950, and during the cold war of the 1960s, he was both an active leader and spokesperson for nuclear disarmament and a vigorous critic of America's war in Vietnam.

deserve. The world during the last 150 years has been undergoing transformation so rapid that ideas and institutions have been unable to keep pace with modern needs. And, what is proving in some ways even more serious, ideas which might be beneficent if they spread slowly have spread with the rapidity and destructiveness of a prairie fire.

When Rousseau[1] preached democracy, it appeared after some   2 two hundred pages of rhetoric that there was only one small corner of the world where democracy could be successfully practiced, namely, the city of Geneva. His disciples gave it a somewhat wider extension: It was permitted in America and for a few bloodstained years in France. Very slowly it was adopted in England. By this time Rousseau's moderation and caution had been forgotten. Democracy was to be a panacea for all the ills of all the countries in the world.

But somehow it looked a little different when it acquired new   3 habitats. In a certain Balkan country, where the elections had produced an almost even balance, one party came into the chamber with loaded revolvers and shot enough of the other party to secure a working majority. Neither Locke[2] nor Rousseau had thought of this method. In Latin America, where the original insurgents against the power of Spain were fervent disciples of Rousseau, there was a system of checks and balances quite different from that advocated by Montesquieu. The party in power falsified the register, and after a while the party out of power conducted a successful revolution.

In the period of United States imperialism after the Spanish-   4 American War, this system was upset by the intrusion of Jeffersonian legality. The falsification of the register was still tolerated; but revolution was frowned upon. In various ways, in various regions that lay outside the purview of eighteenth-century Liberals, the orderly process of parliamentary government, in accordance in general elections, broke down. The idea of democracy persisted, but the practice encountered unforeseen difficulties.

The same kind of thing happened with the idea of nationality.   5 When one reads the works of Mazzini,[3] one finds one's self in a tidy little world which he imagines to be the cosmos. There are about a dozen European nations, each with a soul which, once liberated, will be noble. The noblest, of course, is Italy, which will be the conductor of the wholly harmonious orchestra. It is only tyrants, so Mazzini thought, that cause nations to hate one another. In a world of freedom, they will be filled with brotherly love.

There was only one exception and that was Ireland, because the   6 Irish supported the Pope in his opposition to Italian unity. But except for this tiny chink, the light of reality was not permitted to penetrate the dim halls of his utopia. But in regard to nationality, as

1. Jean-Jacques Rousseau (1712–1778), political philosopher whose works were influential among leaders of the French Revolution (1789–1815). [Ed.]

2. John Locke (1632–1704), English political and educational philosopher. Like Rousseau and the French philosopher Montesquieu (1689–1755), Locke championed democratic ideas, especially that individuals must be protected from oppressive and arbitrary acts of rulers. [Ed.]

3. Giuseppe Mazzini (1805–1872), revolutionary who fought for a unified and independent Italy and ruled the country briefly in the mid-nineteenth century. [Ed.]

in regard to democracy, although the reality has offered unpleasant problems to traditional Liberalism, the ideal has remained unchallenged and none of us can resist the appeal of a nation rightly struggling to be free, whatever oppressions and barbarities may be the goals for which freedom is desired.

Scientific technique is another of these ideals that seem to have 7 gone astray. The world has not developed as Cobden[4] imagined that it would. He imagined two industrial nations, America and Britain, supplying by machine production a great wealth of goods to grateful agriculturists distributed throughout the less civilized parts of the world. Commerce and division of labor were to secure universal peace; and each nation would love every other, since each would be the customer of every other.

But, alas, this dream proved as utopian as Mazzini's. As soon as 8 the power of machine industry had been demonstrated, other countries than those in which it had originated decided to become competitors. Germany, Japan, and Russia, each in turn, have developed large-scale industry. And every nation which has the faintest chance of following their example attempts to do so. The consequence is that a very large part of the productive capacity of every advanced nation is devoted to the production of engines for the destruction of the inhabitants of other advanced nations. So long as this system persists, every improvement in technique is a misfortune, since it enables nations to set aside a larger proportion of the population for the purpose of mutual extermination.

Owing to the spread of education, Western ideals have come to 9 be accepted, though often in distorted forms, in parts of the world that have not had the previous history needed to make these ideals beneficent. Old-style imperialism has become very difficult, because those who are subjected to it know much better than they formerly did what it is that their imperialistic masters are keeping to themselves. And the formerly imperialistic nations themselves have so far accepted the watchwords for Liberalism that they cannot practice old-style imperialism without a bad conscience, even when it is obvious that its sudden cessation will bring chaos.

When the Romans taught military discipline to the barbarians 10 the result was the fall of Rome. We have taught industrial discipline to the barbarians of our time; but we do not wish to suffer the fate of Rome. Our world inevitably includes self-determining nations whom the eighteenth and nineteenth centuries never thought of as independent powers. We cannot return to the security and stability that was enjoyed by our grandfathers until a way has been found of satisfying the claim of hitherto subject peoples without, in the process, producing universal chaos. If this is to be achieved, the ideals of Liberalism, however valid they may remain, are insufficient, since they offer no obstacle to anarchical disaster.

There are three things that must be achieved before stability can 11 be recovered: the first of these is a world government with a monopoly of armed force; the second is an approximate equality as regards standards of life in different parts of the world; the third is a

4. Richard Cobden (1804–1865), English politician who defended free trade. [Ed.]

population either stationary or very slowly increasing. I do not say that these three things will be achieved. What I do say is that unless they are, the present intolerable insecurity will continue. There are those who imagine that, if once we had defeated the Russians, all would be well. In 1914–18,[5] they thought this about the Germans. Ten years ago[6] they thought it about the Germans and Japanese. But no sooner were they defeated than we had to set to work to restore their power. Defeat of enemies in war, however necessary, is not a constructive solution of social problems.

Discussion   Russell's title — "Three Essentials for a Stable World" — alerts you to his main point and tells you to look out for the "three essentials," which aren't discussed until his final paragraph, although they have been supported in all the preceding paragraphs. (Russell even enumerates the points — "first," "second," "third" —so that you can hardly miss them.) Here is one way you might express Russell's thesis in your notes:

> *Three things are necessary for a stable world: a world government with a monopoly of armed force, approximate equality around the world in standard of living, and a fixed or slowly increasing human population.*

True, this is a rather long and complex sentence (still well short of an abstract, however), but nothing shorter or simpler will do in this case. If you want to convey the essence of Russell's position, you must state all three things he mentions, and that cannot be done in much less than three dozen words.

Extracting the Thesis

Introduction   A considerably more subtle challenge to one's ability to state an author's thesis is found in the following extract, from *The Genealogy of Morals*, written by the German philosopher Friedrich Nietzsche (1844–1900) and published in 1887 (the translation used here is by Walter Kaufmann). Unlike Russell, Nietzsche gave no title to this portion of his book, so you will have to look for other clues to the thesis. This passage is one of many in Nietzsche's writings in which his distinctive insights emerge in memorable epigrammatic form.

FRIEDRICH NIETZSCHE
from *The Genealogy of Morals*

The concept "punishment" possesses in fact not *one* meaning but a whole synthesis of "meanings": the previous history of punishment in general, the history of its employment for the most various purposes, finally crystallizes into a kind of unity that is hard to dis- [1]

5. Time span of World War I. [Ed.]
6. During World War II. [Ed.]

entangle, hard to analyze, and, as must be emphasized especially, totally *indefinable*. (Today it is impossible to say for certain *why* people are really punished: All concepts in which an entire process is semiotically concentrated elude definition; only that which has no history is definable.) At an earlier stage, on the contrary, this synthesis of "meanings" can still be disentangled, as well as changed; one can still perceive how in each individual case the elements of the synthesis undergo a shift in value and rearrange themselves accordingly, so that now this, now that element comes to the fore and dominates at the expense of the others; and under certain circumstances one element (the purpose of deterrence perhaps) appears to overcome all the remaining elements.

To give at least an idea of how uncertain, how supplemental, how accidental "the meaning" of punishment is, and how one and the same procedure can be employed, interpreted, adapted to ends that differ fundamentally, I set down here the pattern that has emerged from consideration of relatively few chance instances I have noted. Punishment as a means of rendering harmless, of preventing further harm. Punishment as recompense to the injured party for the harm done, rendered in any form (even in that of a compensating affect). Punishment as the isolation of a disturbance of equilibrium, so as to guard against any further spread of the disturbance. Punishment as a means of inspiring fear of those who determine and execute the punishment. Punishment as a kind of repayment for the advantages the criminal has enjoyed hitherto (for example, when he is employed as a slave in the mines). Punishment as the expulsion of a degenerate element (in some cases, of an entire branch, as in Chinese law: thus as a means of preserving the purity of a race or maintaining a social type). Punishment as a festival, namely as the rape and mockery of a finally defeated enemy. Punishment as the making of a memory, whether for him who suffers the punishment — so-called "improvement" — or for those who witness its execution. Punishment as payment of a fee stipulated by the power that protects the wrongdoer from the excesses of revenge. Punishment as a compromise with revenge in its natural state when the latter is still maintained and claimed as a privilege by powerful clans. Punishment as a declaration of war and a war measure against an enemy of peace, of the law, of order, of the authorities, whom, as a danger to the community, as one who has broken the contract that defines the

Friedrich Nietzsche was trained as a classical scholar and at the tender age of twenty-four was appointed professor of philology at Basle University in Switzerland. Although he lacked any formal training in philosophy, his first book, *The Birth of Tragedy* (1872), showed the influence of Schopenhauer's anti-Kantian metaphysical treatise, *The World as Will and Representation* (1818). Nietzsche's career as a writer and thinker came to an end in 1889, when at the age of forty-four he suffered a physical and mental collapse. In less than two decades, he had produced a series of books that had enormous influence, especially among recent European thinkers. The style and substance of his works are highly personal and are perhaps most easily appreciated in *The Genealogy of Morals* (1887), a brief excerpt of which is reprinted here. One of the great cultural absurdities of the twentieth century was the use of some of his ideas ("the blonde beast," *"Übermenschen"*) by the Nazis in the 1930s. Had he lived to experience fascism he probably would have denounced it for its corruption of values, disgusting racism, and senseless brutality.

conditions under which it exists, as a rebel, a traitor, and breaker of
the peace, one opposes with the means of war. —

This list is certainly not complete; it is clear that punishment is 3
overdetermined by utilities of all kinds. . . .

Discussion   The excerpt opens with a sentence that looks as if it might
indeed be the thesis ("The concept 'punishment' possesses in fact not
one meaning but a whole synthesis of 'meanings'"). The belief that the
first sentence is the thesis is further supported by the second paragraph,
where Nietzsche develops the idea of punishment having different meanings by giving a dozen or so examples of punishment, each with its own
"meaning." But trouble arises when one gets to the last sentence of the
excerpt (". . . it is clear that punishment is overdetermined by utilities of
all kinds"). The problem is that this sentence, too, seems to state the
point of the excerpt, yet it and the sentence that begins the excerpt
seem to point the reader in different directions.

Let's look at this problem more closely. Nietzsche begins by saying
(1) punishment has not one but a whole synthesis of meanings. He ends
by saying (2) punishment is overdetermined by utilities of all kinds. But
are (1) and (2) merely two ways of saying exactly the same thing? It
seems not, because the "meanings" of punishment, so nicely illustrated
by his dozen examples, are quite distinct from whatever he means by
the many "utilities" of punishment. To put it precisely, someone who
wanted to agree with Nietzsche could assert sentence (1) but deny sentence (2), or just the reverse — deny sentence (1) but assert sentence
(2). If that is possible, surely the two sentences cannot be identical in
what they mean and so they must be somewhat independent of each
other.

Does this mean we must choose between these two sentences in
trying to state Nietzsche's thesis? Suppose we drop for the moment the
three troubling terms Nietzsche uses ("meanings," "overdetermined,"
"utilities") and, guided mainly by his instructive list of examples, restate
his main ideas in this way:

*Punishment has had many different purposes or functions, and society gets
many different kinds of benefits from punishing wrongdoers.*

This pretty well states the *theme* that holds together the extract. It
does so by suggesting a close connection between what Nietzsche calls
the "meanings" of punishment (the purposes it serves) and its "utilities"
(the benefits from its use). So far so good.

But this version of his thesis fails to take into account his idea,
stated in the final sentence, that punishment is "overdetermined." Roughly,
Nietzsche's thought here seems to be this: An event is "determined" if it
is the effect of some cause (see the meaning of "determinism" discussed
in connection with the essay by Jennifer Trusted, pp. 143–49). If so,

then an event is "overdetermined" if it is the effect of many different and independent causes. If, then, punishment is "overdetermined by its utilities," it must be because punishment is the effect of several causes, each of which constitutes some benefit to society, thereby explaining the persistence of punishment. With this in mind, one might improve the preceding version of Nietzsche's thesis by restating it as follows:

> *Punishment has had many meanings (or purposes), with benefits (or utilities) in each case, and more than enough of both to account for its use by all societies.*

In trying to restate the thesis of this excerpt from Nietzsche, you can see how even a very brief philosophical text can be challenging. You can also see how the reflection required to extract the thesis helps make sure you have understood the author's main point.

Extracting the Thesis

Introduction   In this essay, Edmund Gettier challenges what appears to be the main philosophical conclusion of Plato's dialogue *Meno* — namely, that knowledge is true belief justified. Since its publication in 1963, Gettier's essay has been widely reprinted in anthologies and other collections on epistemology. Few philosophical essays of recent decades can rival this one in having spawned a whole philosophical literature, in this instance a literature devoted to what has been called "Gettier examples." (When you have read the essay, you'll see what they are.) Brief though the essay is, it is pretty challenging to beginners, which is precisely why working through it carefully in search of Gettier's thesis is worth doing. If you can't find the thesis, it is going to be difficult to come to grips with his argument. Before you tackle Gettier's essay to extract its thesis, you may find the following tips helpful.

Like other analytic philosophers, Gettier uses various abbreviations to formulate his ideas. At the opening of his essay, he writes this definition:

> (a) S knows that P   *IFF*   (i) P is true,
> (ii) S believes that P, and
> (iii) S is justified in believing that P.

The complex statement (a) is a way of stating that there are three conditions, (i), (ii), and (iii), to be satisfied before it is true to say that someone (call that person "S") *knows* something (call what is known "P," and think of "P" as a proposition that can be stated in a declarative sentence, like "Grass is green"). Thus, statement (a) is one way of expressing the idea that knowledge is true belief justified, the very notion Gettier intends to put in question (as his title shows). Gettier designates this definition as (a) because he wants to be able to refer to it later without having to write it all out each time. Later he uses the abbreviations (b) and (c) to designate alternative ways of stating the doctrine that knowledge is justified true belief.

One further tip: Gettier uses the expression *"IFF,"* as many philosophers do, to abbreviate the phrase "if and only if." "If and only if" is the conjunction of ". . . if," expressing a sufficient condition, and ". . . only if," expressing a necessary condition. Together "if and only if" or *"IFF"* express necessary and sufficient conditions. This expression is an important logical connective, called the *biconditional.* Its role is to link two statements, one to the left of *"IFF"* and the other to the right, as in this example:

You're taller than I   *IFF*   I'm shorter than you.

This sentence in effect asserts that if it is true to say "You're taller than I" then it is also true to say "I'm shorter than you"; conversely, if either of these propositions is false, then so is the other. Thus a biconditional statement asserts that its two component statements are equivalent in truth value — either both are true or both are false, there being no third alternative.

Armed with these definitions of Gettier's abbreviations within statement (a), we can rewrite the statement as follows:

A person knows that something — some proposition — is the case if and only if three conditions are satisfied: First, the proposition is true; second, the person believes the proposition; and third, the person is justified in believing it.

The same kinds of substitutions will work for the abbreviations in the next two statements Gettier offers, (b) and (c).

Before turning to the discussion of Gettier's essay on pages 36–37, try to state Gettier's thesis yourself, in no more than one sentence.

EDMUND GETTIER
Is Justified True Belief Knowledge?

Various attempts have been made in recent years to state necessary and sufficient conditions for someone's knowing a given proposition. The attempts have often been such that they can be stated in a form similar to the following:[1]

    (a) S knows that P *IFF*   (i) P is true,
                                 (ii) S believes that P, and
                                 (iii) S is justified in believing that P.

1. Plato seems to be considering some such definition at *Theaetetus* 201, and perhaps accepting one at *Meno* 98.

Edmund Gettier (b. 1927) received his Ph.D. from Cornell in 1961 after joining the philosophy faculty at Wayne State University in Detroit, where he taught from 1957 until 1967. He left Detroit for the University of Massachusetts in Amherst where he has taught courses in metaphysics, modal logic, formal semantics, and the philosophy of language. His very short article, "Is Justified True Belief Knowledge?" (1963), reprinted here has provoked many times its volume in critical discussion.

For example, Chisholm has held that the following gives the necessary and sufficient conditions for knowledge:[2]

(b) S knows that P *IFF*   (i) S accepts P,
                            (ii) S has adequate evidence for P, and
                            (iii) P is true.

Ayer has stated the necessary and sufficient conditions for knowledge as follows:[3]

(c) S knows that P *IFF*   (i) P is true,
                            (ii) S is sure that P is true, and
                            (iii) S has the right to be sure that P is true.

I shall argue that (a) is false in that the conditions stated therein do 2 not constitute a *sufficient* condition for the truth of the proposition that S knows that P. The same argument will show that (b) and (c) fail if "has adequate evidence for" or "has the right to be sure that" is substituted for "is justified in believing that" throughout.

I shall begin by noting two points. First, in that sense of "justi- 3 fied" in which S's being justified in believing P is a necessary condition of S's knowing that P, it is possible for a person to be justified in believing a proposition that is in fact false. Secondly, for any proposition P, if S is justified in believing P, and P entails Q, and S deduces Q from P and accepts Q as a result of this deduction, then S is justified in believing Q. Keeping these two points in mind, I shall now present two cases in which the conditions stated in (a) are true for some proposition, though it is at the same time false that the person in question knows that proposition.

CASE I

Suppose that Smith and Jones have applied for a certain job. 3 And suppose that Smith has strong evidence for the following conjunctive proposition:

(d) Jones is the man who will get the job, and Jones has ten coins in his pocket.

Smith's evidence for (d) might be that the president of the company assured him that Jones would in the end be selected, and that he, Smith, had counted the coins in Jones's pocket ten minutes ago. Proposition (d) entails:

(e) The man who will get the job has ten coins in his pocket.

Let us suppose that Smith sees the entailment from (d) to (e), and accepts (e) on the grounds of (d), for which he has strong evidence. In this case, Smith is clearly justified in believing that (e) is true.

But imagine, further, that unknown to Smith, he himself, not 4 Jones, will get the job. And, also, unknown to Smith, he himself has

2. Roderick M. Chisholm, *Perceiving: A Philosophical Study,* Cornell University Press (Ithaca, New york, 1957), p. 16.
3. A. J. Ayer, *The Problem of Knowledge,* Macmillan (London, 1957), p. 34.

ten coins in his pocket. Proposition (e) is then true, though proposition (d), from which Smith inferred (e), is false. In our example, then, all of the following are true: (i) (e) is true, (ii) Smith believes that (e) is true. But it is equally clear that Smith does not *know* that (e) is true; for (e) is true in virtue of the number of coins in Smith's pocket, while Smith does not know how many coins are in Smith's pocket, and bases his belief in (e) on a count of the coins in Jones's pocket, whom he falsely believes to be the man who will get the job.

CASE II

Let us suppose that Smith has strong evidence for the following proposition:

(f) Jones owns a Ford.

Smith's evidence might be that Jones has at all times in the past within Smith's memory owned a car, and always a Ford, and that Jones has just offered Smith a ride while driving a Ford. Let us imagine, now, that Smith has another friend, Brown, of whose whereabouts he is totally ignorant. Smith selects three place names quite at random and constructs the following three propositions:

(g) Either Jones owns a Ford, or Brown is in Boston.
(h) Either Jones owns a Ford, or Brown is in Barcelona.
(i) Either Jones owns a Ford, or Brown is in Brest-Litovsk.

Each of these propositions is entailed by (f). Imagine that Smith realizes the entailment of each of these propositions he has constructed by (f), and proceeds to accept (g), (h), and (i) on the basis of (f). Smith has correctly inferred (g), (h), and (i) from a proposition for which he has strong evidence. Smith is therefore completely justified in believing each of these three propositions. Smith, of course, has no idea where Brown is.

But imagine now that two further conditions hold. First, Jones does *not* own a Ford, but is at present driving a rented car. And secondly, by the sheerest coincidence, and entirely unknown to Smith, the place mentioned in proposition (h) happens really to be the place where Brown is. If these two conditions hold, then Smith does *not* know that (h) is true, even though (i) (h) *is* true, (ii) Smith does believe that (h) is true, and (iii) Smith is justified in believing that (h) is true.

These two examples show that definition (a) does not state a *sufficient* condition for someone's knowing a given proposition. The same cases, with appropriate changes, will suffice to show that neither definition (b) nor definition (c) do so either.

Discussion   As noted earlier, Gettier does not explicitly state the thesis of his essay. But his title does give some guidance, even if not as much as we found in the title of Bertrand Russell's essay (p. 27). After reading through Gettier's essay, you might state his thesis as follows:

> *Justified true belief is not a correct definition of knowledge.*

Now it is true that Gettier believes this; the argument of his essay implies that this statement must be true. But this statement of his thesis does not reflect the particular form of his attack on the doctrine that knowledge can be defined as justified true belief.

One can see this if one asks: Does Gettier think that your having a justified true belief about something is completely irrelevant to any claim you might make to have knowledge about that something? A careful reader of his essay must answer "No." Instead, what Gettier does assert is that having a justified true belief in some proposition P is *not enough of a basis on which to claim* the knowledge of P. His whole argument turns on how a person can have a belief, and a true one, and even be justified in this belief — and yet *not* have knowledge. Since Gettier never argues that a person can know some proposition P without believing that proposition, or that one could know some proposition P even though P is false, or that one could know that P without any evidence whatever for P, it follows that he must think justified true belief is at least a *necessary* condition for knowledge (otherwise, he has been very careless in not eliminating this possibility); further, it looks as if his sole concern is to show that satisfying these three conditions — and especially the condition of justification — is *not sufficient* for knowledge.

So, as a second approximation of Gettier's thesis, you might note:

> *Justified true belief is not a sufficient condition of knowledge.*

Improved though this version is over its predecessor, it would be better still if it retained the idea of inadequate definition that appeared in the first version and connected that idea to the point about sufficient condition. With this in mind, you might revise in your reading notes for a third version of Gettier's thesis:

> *Justified true belief cannot be the definition of knowledge because it isn't a sufficient condition of knowledge.*

Is it a problem that this version of Gettier's thesis does not convey anything of the style of *argument* Gettier uses to establish his thesis? No. This is not a fair criticism of a *thesis*, though it would be a fair criticism of this statement as a *summary* or even an *abstract* of the essay. The statement of an author's *thesis* is not to be viewed as an attempt at a concise *abstract* or *summary* of the writer's whole essay.

EXERCISE 4: Outlining an Essay

Essay outlines can be useful in any of three ways: (1) to lay bare the structure of someone else's essay you are reading, (2) to assist you as an author in sketching the structure of the essay you want to write, and (3) to test the adequacy of the structure of the penultimate draft of an essay you have written. Let us look first at outlining someone else's essay.

Every philosophical essay, chapter, or book presents ideas in a certain sequence and in a certain *structure*, usually in which some dominant points are explained or illustrated by subordinate points. The concise presentation of that sequence and structure is the *outline* of the material. (The general form of such an outline is set out on p. 39.) With a little skill and practice, you can produce an outline to reduce a rather lengthy and complex philosophical essay to a few pages. Because outlining is a skill that you can use in developing your own writing, we will spend some time on it here.

Outlining someone else's essay may turn out to be a more creative task than you might initially think, especially if the author of the essay has not given much thought to structure. Because there is often more than one way to outline a given reading, a classroom exercise in which all students undertake to outline the same essay will often reveal not only differences in student abilities but also different ways to "read" the structure of an essay.

Writing an effective outline is a more challenging and time-consuming task than writing either an abstract or a summary, but it can be well worth the extra effort. An outline preserves the sequence of ideas in the original and conveys the content as well. It does so by laying bare the structure of the essay in a way that no abstract or summary can. And it does this by helping to reveal the arguments, one by one, and their interrelation.

In preparing an outline of a text, you will want to treat some paragraphs (or parts of paragraphs) as more important than others because they are more central or prominent in the original. The outline will reflect this hierarchy by introducing a *visible subordination* of some ideas to others, a subordination not always evident in the original. *Subordination* is the distinctive feature of an outline; it plays little or no role in either a summary or an abstract. A good outline shows the contrast between important and less important or supporting details in two ways: Sequential *enumeration* and successive *indentation*. The finished outline thus plainly displays both the sequential structure and the various levels of the essay's argument. That is, it models the very logic of the discourse in the essay itself.

Is there an optimum length or degree of detail for an outline? Probably not, but here are a couple of guidelines. First, try to state each entry in your outline briefly, in a sentence or sentence fragment. Second, write no more than a few entries for each page of the original; one entry per paragraph is a useful rule of thumb. As with a summary, you don't want the length and detail of your outline to rival those of the original. The point is to condense and especially to lay bare the structure.

The General Form of an Outline

All outlines have the same general form or structure, in which major ideas are contrasted with and followed by subordinate ideas. In theory, there is no limit to the levels or degree of subordination, but two usually suffice. The result is a pattern of the following sort:

```
I. First major idea
   A. First subordinate idea
      1. First sub-subordinate idea
      2. Second sub-subordinate idea
   B. Second subordinate idea

II. Second major idea (and so on)
```

A Sample Outline

Here is a sample outline of the first part of Gettier's essay (pp. 34–35).

```
          A Partial Outline of E. Gettier,
      "Is Justified True Belief Knowledge?"


 I. Attempts to state sufficient and necessary condi-
    tions of knowledge agree that someone, S, knows
    something, P, IFF P is true, S believes P, and S
    has adequate evidence for P.
    A. Plato's version
    B. Chisholm's version
    C. Ayer's version

II. All versions fail because they do not state a
    sufficient condition. The proof that they fail
    relies on two assumptions.
    A. It is possible for someone to be justified in be-
       lieving a proposition that is false.
    B. If S is justified in believing P, and P entails
       Q, and S accepts Q for this reason, then S is
       justified in believing Q.
```

As this fragment of an outline shows, it is possible to capture the main features of Gettier's reasoning (at least in the opening paragraphs of his essay) by using only two levels of discourse — the main level (indicated by large roman numerals) and the subordinate level (indicated by capital letters). Other essays, or the rest of Gettier's essay, may require three or even four levels of discourse.

How does one discover the structure of the essay so that its contents can be set out in such a sequence? Following is some advice.

Some Guidelines for Writing an Effective Outline

First, notice whatever structural markers the writer has used. For instance, many writers break their essays into parts (often marked with capital roman numerals), and those parts ought to be salient in your outline.

But suppose the author of the essay did not mark any of its parts in some manner. In that case, try first to find the major sections into which the essay naturally falls. For example, every essay has an opening and a closing paragraph. Try treating the former as the introduction, and set it off in your (provisional) outline like this:

```
I. Introduction
```

Next, mark off the closing paragraph and designate it in your outline as "Conclusion." (You can't number it with a roman numeral yet, however, because so far you have no idea how many numbers you will need for what comes after "Introduction" and before "Conclusion.") What remains between these two paragraphs is of course the bulk of the essay. So far, you have a three-part initial structural outline — not much, to be sure, but at least you've made a start.

Now you are ready to take two further steps (the order in which you do them doesn't much matter). One is to give some *content* in your outline for the paragraph you dubbed "Introduction." For instance, if the author explicitly states a thesis in the opening paragraph, you ought to summarize the thesis in a few phrases or a sentence.

The other is to break up the middle third of the essay into some appropriate parts, designating each with a roman numeral in sequence. To do this properly, you must read the essay carefully and see how the author's argument unfolds. The following are a few suggestions that should help no matter what essay you are trying to outline.

Start by treating each of the author's paragraphs as a unit to be designated with a separate numeral or letter in your outline. Try to detect any signs of subordination *between* the paragraphs, keeping your eye out for phrases like "For example" or "My second reason is" at the beginning of a paragraph. To show the subordination you have detected, label the more important ideas with large roman numerals and the less important or supporting ideas with capital letters or arabic numerals. Finally, look for subordination *within* each paragraph.

Unfortunately, it's impossible to provide one simple recipe for outlining because outlining someone else's essay is rarely a mechanical matter. Rather, it calls for careful attention and analysis of the original so that you can enter into the author's thinking as it is worked out in the essay. Nevertheless, the tips presented here will prove useful. If they don't, perhaps the problem lies not in you but in the original — it may not be a very well organized essay; in that case your outline will reflect this.

Writing an Outline

Introduction   The following excerpt is taken from an essay by Charles
Sanders Peirce (1839–1914); published in 1878, it was probably the most
significant philosophical essay written in the nineteenth century by any
American philosopher. In this essay, Peirce argues for a new criterion of
meaning and a new concept of truth, both of which are influential to
this day among philosophers who think of themselves as empiricists,
positivists, operationalists, behaviorists, and above all — of course —
pragmatists.

After reading the essay, try your hand at preparing an outline in
which you show the essay's major divisions, subdivisions, and overall
structure. Try to keep the outline to 3 or 4 pages (double-spaced, typed).
When you are done, check your work against the sample student outline on pages 51–53.

CHARLES SANDERS PEIRCE
from *How to Make Our Ideas Clear*

Whoever has looked into a modern treatise on logic of the com- 1
mon sort, will doubtless remember the two distinctions between
clear and *obscure* conceptions, and between *distinct* and *confused*
conceptions. They have lain in the books now for nigh two centuries, unimproved and unmodified, and are generally reckoned by
logicians as among the gems of their doctrine.

A clear idea is defined as one which is so apprehended that it 2
will be recognized wherever it is met with, and so that no other will
be mistaken for it. If it fails of this clearness, it is said to be obscure.

A distinct idea is defined as one which contains nothing which 3
is not clear. This is technical language; by the *contents* of an idea
logicians understand whatever is contained in its definition. So that
an idea is *distinctly* apprehended, according to them, when we can
give a precise definition of it, in abstract terms. Here the professional logicians leave the subject; and I would not have troubled the
reader with what they have to say, if it were not such a striking

Charles Sanders Peirce, pioneer of pragmatism — America's most distinctive philosophical outlook — graduated from Harvard in 1859. Trained as a mathematician,
chemist, and geophysicist, he nonetheless turned to philosophy. He taught for varying terms at Harvard and Johns Hopkins, but his eccentric life-style earned him few
friends. He took no advanced degrees and held no permanent academic post. His
entire career appears to have been a series of frustrations. Although he published no
books during his lifetime, his collected papers fill half a dozen large volumes. He is
best known for two essays, "The Fixation of Belief" (1877) and "How to Make Our
Ideas Clear" (1878), the second of which is reprinted in part here. Although he was
overshadowed during his lifetime by his two cofounders of pragmatism, William
James (1842–1819) and John Dewey (1859–1953), his reputation is secure among
philosophers.

example of how they have been slumbering through ages of intellectual activity, listlessly disregarding the enginery of modern thought, and never dreaming of applying its lessons to the improvement of logic. It is easy to show that the doctrine that familiar use and abstract distinctness make the perfection of apprehension has its only true place in philosophies which have long been extinct; and it is now time to formulate the method of attaining to a more perfect clearness of thought, such as we see and admire in the thinkers of our own time. . . .

The very first lesson that we have a right to demand that logic   4 shall teach us is, how to make our ideas clear; and a most important one it is, depreciated only by minds who stand in need of it. To know what we think, to be masters of our own meaning, will make a solid foundation for great and weighty thought. It is most easily learned by those whose ideas are meagre and restricted; and far happier they than such as wallow helplessly in a rich mud of conceptions. A nation, it is true, may, in the course of generations, overcome the disadvantage of an excessive wealth of language and its natural concomitant, a vast, unfathomable deep of ideas. We may see it in history, slowly perfecting its literary forms, sloughing at length its metaphysics, and, by virtue of the untirable patience which is often a compensation, attaining great excellence in every branch of mental acquirement. The page of history is not yet unrolled that is to tell us whether such a people will or will not in the long run prevail over one whose ideas (like the words of their language) are few, but which possesses a wonderful mastery over those which it has. For an individual, however, there can be no question that a few clear ideas are worth more than many confused ones. A young man would hardly be persuaded to sacrifice the greater part of his thoughts to save the rest; and the muddled head is the least apt to see the necessity of such a sacrifice. Him we can usually only commiserate, as a person with a congenital defect. Time will help him, but intellectual maturity with regard to clearness is apt to come rather late. This seems an unfortunate arrangement of Nature, inasmuch as clearness is of less use to a man settled in life, whose errors have in great measure had their effect, than it would be to one whose path lay before him. It is terrible to see how a single unclear idea, a single formula without meaning, lurking in a young man's head, will sometimes act like an obstruction of inert matter in an artery, hindering the nutrition of the brain, and condemning its victim to pine away in the fullness of his intellectual vigor and in the midst of intellectual plenty. Many a man has cherished for years as his hobby some vague shadow of an idea, too meaningless to be positively false; he has, nevertheless, passionately loved it, has made it his companion by day and by night, and has given to it his strength and his life, leaving all other occupations for its sake, and in short has lived with it and for it, until it has become, as it were, flesh of his flesh and bone of his bone; and then he has waked up some bright morning to find it gone, clean vanished away like the beautiful Melusina of the fable, and the essence of his life gone with it. I have myself known such a man; and who can tell how many histories of circle-squarers, metaphysicians, astrologers, and what not, may not be told in the old German [French!] story?

The principles set forth in the first part of this essay [not re- 5 printed here] lead, at once, to a method of reaching a clearness of thought of higher grade than the "distinctness" of the logicians. It was there noticed that the action of thought is excited by the irritation of doubt, and ceases when belief is attained; so that the production of belief is the sole function of thought. All these words, however, are too strong for my purpose. It is as if I had described the phenomena as they appear under a mental microscope. Doubt and Belief, as the words are commonly employed, relate to religious or other grave discussions. But here I use them to designate the starting any question, no matter how small or how great, and the resolution of it. If, for instance, in a horsecar, I pull out my purse and find a five-cent nickel and five coppers, I decide, while my hand is going to the purse, in which way I will pay my fare. To call such a question Doubt, and my decision Belief, is certainly to use words very disproportionate to the occasion. To speak of such a doubt as causing an irritation which needs to be appeased, suggests a temper which is uncomfortable to the verge of insanity. Yet, looking at the matter minutely, it must be admitted that, if there is the least hesitation as to whether I shall pay the five coppers or the nickel (as there will be sure to be, unless I act from some previously contracted habit in the matter), though irritation is too strong a word, yet I am excited to such small mental activity as may be necessary to deciding how I shall act. Most frequently doubts arise from some indecision, however momentary, in our action. Sometimes it is not so. I have, for example, to wait in a railway-station, and to pass the time I read the advertisements on the walls. I compare the advantages of different trains and different routes which I never expect to take, merely fancying myself to be in a state of hesitancy, because I am bored with having nothing to trouble me. Feigned hesitancy, whether feigned for mere amusement or with a lofty purpose, plays a great part in the production of scientific inquiry. However the doubt may originate, it stimulates the mind to an activity which may be slight or energetic, calm or turbulent. Images pass rapidly through consciousness, one incessantly melting into another, until at last, when all is over — it may be in a fraction of a second, in an hour, or after long years — we find ourselves decided as to how we should act under such circumstances as those which occasioned our hesitation. In other words, we have attained belief.

In this process we observe two sorts of elements of conscious- 6 ness, the distinction between which may best be made clear by means of an illustration. In a piece of music there are the separate notes, and there is the air. A single tone may be prolonged for an hour or a day, and it exists as perfectly in each second of that time as in the whole taken together; so that, as long as it is sounding, it might be present to a sense from which everything in the past was as completely absent as the future itself. But it is different with the air, the performance of which occupies a certain time, during the portions of which only portions of it are played. It consists in an orderliness in the succession of sounds which strike the ear at different times; and to perceive it there must be some continuity of consciousness which makes the events of a lapse of time present to us. We certainly only perceive the air by hearing the separate notes; yet we cannot be said to directly hear it, for we hear only what is present at the instant, and an orderliness of succession cannot exist in an instant. These two sorts of objects, what we are *immediately* conscious of and what we are *mediately* conscious of, are found in all consciousness. Some elements (the sensations) are completely present at every instant so long as they last, while others (like thought) are actions having beginning, middle, and end, and consist in a congruence in the succession of sensations which flow through the mind. They cannot be immediately present to us, but must cover some portion of the past or future. Thought is a thread of melody running through the succession of our sensations. . . .

And what, then, is belief? It is the demi-cadence which closes a 7 musical phrase in the symphony of our intellectual life. We have seen that it has just three properties: First, it is something that we are aware of; second, it appeases the irritation of doubt; and, third, it involves the establishment in our nature of a rule of action, or, say for short, a *habit*. As it appeases the irritation of doubt, which is the motive for thinking, thought relaxes, and comes to rest for a moment when belief is reached. But, since belief is a rule for action, the application of which involves further doubt and further thought, at the same time that it is a stopping-place, it is also a new starting-place for thought. That is why I have permitted myself to call it thought at rest, although thought is essentially an action. The *final* upshot of thinking is the exercise of volition, and of this thought no longer forms a part; but belief is only a stadium of mental action, an effect upon our nature due to thought, which will influence future thinking.

The essence of belief is the establishment of a habit; and differ- 8 ent beliefs are distinguished by the different modes of action to which they give rise. If beliefs do not differ in this respect, if they appease the same doubt by producing the same rule of action, then no mere differences in the manner of consciousness of them can make them different beliefs, any more than playing a tune in different keys is playing different tunes. Imaginary distinctions are often drawn between beliefs which differ only in their mode of expression; — the wrangling which ensues is real enough, however. To believe that any objects are arranged among themselves as in Fig. 1, and to believe that they are arranged [as] in Fig. 2, are one and the same belief; yet it is conceivable that a man should assert one proposition and deny the other. Such false distinctions do as much harm as the confusion of beliefs really different, and are among the pitfalls of which we ought constantly to beware, especially when we are upon metaphysical ground. One singular deception of this sort, which often occurs, is to mistake the sensation produced by our own unclearness of thought for a character of the object we are thinking. Instead of perceiving that the obscurity is purely subjective, we fancy that we contemplate a quality of the object which is

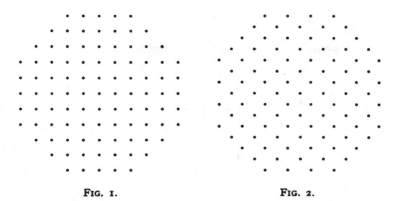

FIG. 1.   FIG. 2.

essentially mysterious; and if our conception be afterward presented to us in a clear form we do not recognize it as the same, owing to the absence of the feeling of unintelligibility. So long as this deception lasts, it obviously puts an impassable barrier in the way of perspicuous thinking; so that it equally interests the opponents of rational thought to perpetuate it, and its adherents to guard against it.

Another such deception is to mistake a mere difference in the 9 grammatical construction of two words for a distinction between the ideas they express. In this pedantic age, when the general mob of writers attend so much more to words than to things, this error is common enough. When I just said that thought is an *action,* and that it consists in a *relation,* although a person performs an action but not a relation, which can only be the result of an action, yet there was no inconsistency in what I said, but only a grammatical vagueness.

From all these sophisms we shall be perfectly safe so long as we 10 reflect that the whole function of thought is to produce habits of action; and that whatever there is connected with a thought, but irrelevant to its purpose, is an accretion to it, but no part of it. If there be a unity among our sensations which has no reference to how we shall act on a given occasion, as when we listen to a piece of music, why we do not call that thinking. To develop its meaning, we have, therefore, simply to determine what habits it produces, for what a thing means is simply what habits it involves. Now, the identity of a habit depends on how it might lead us to act, not merely under such circumstances as are likely to arise, but under such as might possibly occur, no matter how improbable they may be. What the habit is depends on *when* and *how* it causes us to act. As for the *when,* every stimulus to action is derived from perception; as for the *how,* every purpose of action is to produce some sensible result. Thus, we come down to what is tangible and conceivably practical, as the root of every real distinction of thought, no matter how subtle it may be; and there is no distinction of meaning so fine as to consist in anything but a possible difference of practice.

To see what this principle leads to, consider in the light of it 11 such a doctrine as that of transubstantiation. The Protestant churches generally hold that the elements of the sacrament are flesh and blood only in a tropical sense; they nourish our souls as meat and the juice of it would our bodies. But the Catholics maintain that they are literally just meat and blood; although they possess all the sensible qualities of wafer-cakes and diluted wine. But we can have no conception of wine except what may enter into a belief, either —

1. That this, that, or the other, is wine; or,
2. That wine possesses certain properties.

Such beliefs are nothing but self-notifications that we should, upon occasion, act in regard to such things as we believe to be wine according to the qualities which we believe wine to possess. The occasion of such action would be some sensible perception, the motive of it to produce some sensible result. Thus our action has exclusive reference to what affects the senses, our habit has the same bearing as our action, our belief the same as our habit, our conception the same as our belief; and we can consequently mean nothing by wine but what has certain effects, direct or indirect, upon our senses; and to talk of something as having all the sensible characters of wine, yet being in reality blood, is senseless jargon. Now, it is not my object to pursue the theological question; and having used it as a logical example I drop it, without caring to anticipate the theologian's reply. I only desire to point out how impossible it is that we should have an idea in our minds which relates to anything but conceived sensible effects of things. Our idea of anything *is* our idea of its sensible effects; and if we fancy that we have any other we deceive ourselves, and mistake a mere sensation accompanying the thought for a part of the thought itself. It is absurd to say that thought has any meaning unrelated to its only function. It is foolish for Catholics and Protestants to fancy themselves in disagreement about the elements of the sacrament, if they agree in regard to all their sensible effects, here and hereafter.

It appears, then, that the rule for attaining the third grade of clearness of apprehension is as follows: Consider what effects, that might conceivably have practical bearings, we conceive the object of our conception to have. Then, our conception of these effects is the whole of our conception of the object. 12

Let us illustrate this rule by some examples; and, to begin with the simplest one possible, let us ask what we mean by calling a thing *hard*. Evidently that it will not be scratched by many other substances. The whole conception of this quality, as of every other, lies in its conceived effects. There is absolutely no difference between a hard thing and a soft thing so long as they are not brought to the test. Suppose, then, that a diamond could be crystallized in the midst of a cushion of soft cotton, and should remain there until it was finally burned up. Would it be false to say that that diamond was soft? This seems a foolish question, and would be so, in fact, except in the realm of logic. There such questions are often of the greatest utility as serving to bring logical principles into sharper relief than real discussions ever could. In studying logic we must not put them aside with hasty answers, but must consider them with 13 attentive care, in order to make out the principles involved. We may, in the present case, modify our question, and ask what prevents us from saying that all hard bodies remain perfectly soft until they are touched, when their hardness increases with the pressure until they are scratched. Reflection will show that the reply is this: There would be no *falsity* in such modes of speech. They would involve a modification of our present usage of speech with regard to the words hard and soft, but not of their meanings. For they represent no fact to be different from what it is; only they involve arrangements of facts which would be exceedingly maladroit. This leads us to remark that the question of what would occur under circumstances which do not actually arise is not a question of fact, but only of the most perspicuous arrangement of them. For example, the question of free-will and fate in its simplest form, stripped of verbiage, is something like this: I have done something of which I am ashamed; could I, by an effort of the will, have resisted the temptation, and done otherwise? The philosophical reply is, that this is not a question of fact, but only of the arrangement of facts. Arranging them so as to exhibit what is particularly pertinent to my question — namely, that I ought to blame myself for having done wrong — it is perfectly true to say that, if I had willed to do otherwise than I did, I should have done otherwise. On the other hand, arranging the facts so as to exhibit another important consideration, it is equally true that, when a temptation has once been allowed to work, it will, if it has a certain force, produce its effect, let me struggle how I may. There is no objection to a contradiction in what would result from a false supposition. The *reductio ad absurdum* consists in showing that contradictory results would follow from a hypothesis which is consequently judged to be false. Many questions are involved in the free-will discussion, and I am far from desiring to say that both sides are equally right. On the contrary, I am of opinion that one side denies important facts, and that the other does not. But what I do say is, that the above single question was the origin of the whole doubt; that, had it not been for this question, the controversy would never have arisen; and that this question is perfectly solved in the manner which I have indicated. . . .

Let us now approach the subject of logic, and consider a con- 14
ception which particularly concerns it, that of *reality*. Taking clearness in the sense of familiarity, no idea could be clearer than this. Every child uses it with perfect confidence, never dreaming that he does not understand it. As for clearness in its second grade, however, it would probably puzzle most men, even among those of a reflective turn of mind, to give an abstract definition of the real. Yet such a definition may perhaps be reached by considering the points of difference between reality and its opposite, fiction. A figment is a product of somebody's imagination; it has such characters as his thought impresses upon it. That those characters are independent of how you or I think is an external reality. There are, however, phenomena within our own minds, dependent upon our thought, which are at the same time real in the sense that we really think them. But though their characters depend on how we think, they do not de-

pend on what we think those characters to be. Thus, a dream has a real existence as a mental phenomenon, if somebody has really dreamt it; that he dreamt so and so, does not depend on what anybody thinks was dreamt, but is completely independent of all opinion on the subject. On the other hand, considering, not the fact of dreaming, but the thing dreamt, it retains its peculiarities by virtue of no other fact than that it was dreamt to possess them. Thus we may define the real as that whose characters are independent of what anybody may think them to be.

But, however satisfactory such a definition may be found, it would   15 be a great mistake to suppose that it makes the idea of reality perfectly clear. Here, then, let us apply our rules. According to them, reality, like every other quality, consists in the peculiar sensible effects which things partaking of it produce. The only effect which real things have is to cause belief, for all the sensations which they excite emerge into consciousness in the form of beliefs. The question therefore is, how is true belief (or belief in the real) distinguished from false belief (or belief in fiction). Now, . . . the ideas of truth and falsehood, in their full development, appertain exclusively to the experiential method of settling opinion. A person who arbitrarily chooses the propositions which he will adopt can use the word truth only to emphasize the expression of his determination to hold on to his choice. . . . Since the time of Descartes, the defect in the conception of truth has been less apparent. Still, it will sometimes strike a scientific man that the philosophers have been less intent on finding out what the facts are, than on inquiring what belief is most in harmony with their system. It is hard to convince a follower of the *a priori* method by adducing facts; but show him that an opinion he is defending is inconsistent with what he has laid down elsewhere, and he will be very apt to retract it. These minds do not seem to believe that disputation is ever to cease; they seem to think that the opinion which is natural for one man is not so for another, and that belief will, consequently, never be settled. In contenting themselves with fixing their own opinions by a method which would lead another man to a different result, they betray their feeble hold of the conception of what truth is.

On the other hand, all the followers of science are animated by   16 a cheerful hope that the processes of investigation, if only pushed far enough, will give one certain solution to each question to which they apply it. One man may investigate the velocity of light by studying the transits of Venus and the aberration of the stars; another by the oppositions of Mars and the eclipses of Jupiter's satellites; a third by the method of Fizeau; a fourth by that of Foucault; a fifth by the motions of the curves of Lissajoux; a sixth, a seventh, an eighth, and a ninth, may follow the different methods of comparing the measures of statical and the dynamical electricity. They may at first obtain different results, but, as each perfects his method and his processes, the results are found to move steadily together toward a destined centre. So with all scientific research. Different minds may set out with the most antagonistic views, but the progress of investigation carries them by a force outside of themselves to one and the same conclusion. This activity of thought by which we are carried, not where we wish, but to a fore-ordained goal, is like the operation of destiny. No modification of the point of view taken, no selection of other facts for study, no natural bent of mind even, can enable a man to escape the predestinate opinion. This great hope is embodied in the conception of truth and reality. The opinion which is fated to be ultimately agreed to by all who investigate, is what we mean by the truth, and the object represented in this opinion is the real. That is the way I would explain reality.

But it may be said that this view is directly opposed to the ab- 17 stract definition which we have given of reality, inasmuch as it makes the characters of the real depend on what is ultimately thought about them. But the answer to this is that, on the one hand, reality is independent, not necessarily of thought in general, but only of what you or I or any finite number of men may think about it; and that, on the other hand, though the object of the final opinion depends on what that opinion is, yet what that opinion is does not depend on what you or I or any man thinks. Our perversity and that of others may indefinitely postpone the settlement of opinion; it might even conceivably cause an arbitrary proposition to be universally accepted as long as the human race should last. Yet even that would not change the nature of the belief, which alone could be the result of investigation carried sufficiently far; and if, after the extinction of our race, another should arise with faculties and disposition for investigation, that true opinion must be the one which they would ultimately come to. "Truth crushed to earth shall rise again," and the opinion which would finally result from investigation does not depend on how anybody may actually think. But the reality of that which is real does depend on the real fact that investigation is destined to lead, at last, if continued long enough, to a belief in it.

But I may be asked what I have to say to all the minute facts of 18 history, forgotten never to be recovered, to the lost books of the ancients, to the buried secrets.

> Full many a gem of purest ray serene
>   The dark, unfathomed caves of ocean bear;
> Full many a flower is born to blush unseen,
>   And waste its sweetness on the desert air.

Do these things not really exist because they are hopelessly beyond the reach of our knowledge? And then, after the universe is dead (according to the prediction of some scientists), and all life has ceased forever, will not the shock of atoms continue though there will be no mind to know it? To this I reply that, though in no possible state of knowledge can any number be great enough to express the relation between the amount of what rests unknown to the amount of the known, yet it is unphilosophical to suppose that, with regard to any given question (which has any clear meaning), investigation would not bring forth a solution of it, if it were carried far enough. Who would have said, a few years ago, that we could ever know of what substances stars are made whose light may have been longer in reaching us than the human race has existed? Who can be sure of what we shall not know in a few hundred years? Who can guess what would be the result of continuing the pursuit of science for ten thousand years, with the activity of the last hundred? And if it were to go on for a million, or a billion, or any number of years you please, how is it possible to say that there is any question which might not ultimately be solved?

But it may be objected, "Why make so much of these remote 19 considerations, especially when it is your principle that only practical distinctions have a meaning?" Well, I must confess that it makes very little difference whether we say that a stone on the bottom of the ocean, in complete darkness, is brilliant or not — that is to say, that it *probably* makes no difference, remembering always that that stone *may* be fished up tomorrow. But that there are gems at the bottom of the sea, flowers in the untraveled desert, etc., are propositions which, like that about a diamond being hard when it is not pressed, concern much more the arrangement of our language than they do the meaning of our ideas.

It seems to me, however, that we have, by the application of our 20 rule, reached so clear an apprehension of what we mean by reality, and of the fact which the idea rests on, that we should not, perhaps, be making a pretension so presumptuous as it would be singular, if we were to offer a metaphysical theory of existence for universal acceptance among those who employ the scientific method of fixing belief. However, as metaphysics is a subject much more curious than useful, the knowledge of which, like that of a sunken reef, serves chiefly to enable us to keep clear of it, I will not trouble the reader with any more Ontology at this moment. I have already been led much further into that path than I should have desired; and I have given the reader such a dose of mathematics, psychology, and all that is most abstruse, that I fear he may already have left me, and that what I am now writing is for the compositor and proofreader exclusively. I trusted to the importance of the subject. There is no royal road to logic, and really valuable ideas can only be had at the price of close attention. But I know that in the matter of ideas the public prefer the cheap and nasty; and in my next paper I am going to return to the easily intelligible, and not wander from it again. The reader who has been at the pains of wading through this paper, shall be rewarded in the next one by seeing how beautifully what has been developed in this tedious way can be applied to the ascertainment of the rules of scientific reasoning.

We have, hitherto, not crossed the threshold of scientific logic. It 21 is certainly important to know how to make our ideas clear, but they may be ever so clear without being true. How to make them so, we have next to study. How to give birth to those vital and procreative ideas which multiply into a thousand forms and diffuse themselves everywhere, advancing civilization and making the dignity of man, is an art not yet reduced to rules, but of the secret of which the history of science affords some hints.

Sample Student Outline

An Outline of an Excerpt from

Charles Sanders Peirce's Essay

"How to make our Ideas clear"

by

Daniel Rosenberg

I. Introduction: The logical distinctions between
   <u>clear</u> and <u>obscure</u> conceptions, and between distinct
   and <u>confused</u> conceptions, have been unimproved for
   centuries (para. 1).
   A. Clearness is familiarity with an idea so that it
      is always recognizable (para. 2).
   B. Distinctness is the absence of unclear ideas
      (para. 3).
   C. How to make our ideas clear is the first goal of
      logic (para. 4).

II. The principles set forth here will lead to a method
    of clarifying thought to a higher degree than
    distinctness (para. 5).
    A. The irritation of doubt is relieved by the
       process of thought if belief is obtained (para.
       5).
       1. Here, "doubt" and "belief" are used broadly
          (para. 8).
       2. Doubts, real or feigned, stimulate the mind
          to thought and belief.
    B. There are two kinds of things of which we are
       conscious (para. 6).
       1. We are immediately conscious of sensations.
       2. We are mediately conscious of other objects
          via our thoughts.
    C. What is a belief?
       1. It has three properties (para. 7).
          a. It is something of which we are aware.
          b. It appeases the irritation of doubt.
          c. It establishes a habit.
       2. The upshot of thinking is "the exercise of
          volition."
       3. Beliefs are individualized by the habits they
          establish (para. 8).
          a. example of a false attempt to divide one
             belief into two: believing that Fig. 1
             could be formed without also forming Fig.
             2.
          b. another example: believing our confusion is
             inherent in the object of our thought, and
             then failing to recognize our own thought
             when it is later presented clearly to us

        c. another example: mistaking a grammatical difference between two phrases for differences in the ideas they express (para. 9).

   D. The ultimate result of thought is the production of a habit (para. 10).

     1. "What a thing means is simply what habits it involves"

     2. The identity of a habit is determined by what it causes us to do.

     3. All distinctions of meaning boil down to differences in practice

        a. example: this principle applied to the doctrine of transubstantiation (para. 11)

        b. Since "our idea of anything is our idea of its sensible effects," and since Protestants and Catholics agree on these effects, they are foolish to disagree about what they cannot possibly experience.

   E. A new rule for attaining the third degree of clarity: "Consider what effects, that might conceivably have practical bearings, we conceive the object of our conception to have. Then, our conception of these effects is the whole of our conception of the object (para. 12). Examples applying this rule:

     1. What do we mean by "hard"? (para. 13)

     2. What do we mean by "free will" versus "fate"?

III. Let us return to logic and consider clarifying the idea of "reality" (para. 14).

   A. First degree of clarity: The real is what we are familiar with.

   B. Second degree of clarity: The real is what is independent of what anybody may think it to be.

   C. Third degree of clarity: The real is what causes our true beliefs (para. 15).

     1. Earlier philosophers acted as if a true belief is any belief adamantly held.

     2. Recent philosophers seem to think that we will never be able to settle whether our beliefs are true or false.

     3. Scientific thinkers believe agreement on what is true is possible (para. 16).

     4. Conclusion: "The opinion that is fated to be ultimately agreed to by all who investigate it, is what we mean by the truth, and the object represented in this opinion is the real."

   D. A revised conception of the "real" (para. 17)

     1. The real is independent of the thought of what a finite number of persons think; it is not independent of thought altogether.

     2. Objection: Where does this leave the reality of things about which at present we know nothing? (para. 18) Answer: In time all questions can in theory be answered.

> 3. Objection: Isn't that a repudiation of the
>   emphasis on the practical? (para. 19) Answer:
>   No; the hardness of an object, though never
>   scratched or pressed, remains an object of
>   possible experience, but that is all.
> IV. Conclusion. The new rule for obtaining clarity
>   invites us to construct an entire metaphysics of
>   existence (para. 20).
>   A. To do so here would strain the reader's pa-
>   tience.
>   B. Never forget: Ideas can be clear without being
>   true (para. 21).

Discussion   The first thing one will notice in constructing an outline of Peirce's essay is that Peirce gives no help in this task: He inserts no headings or subheadings anywhere in his essay. Worse than that, he rarely begins a paragraph with a sentence that connects with the prior paragraph or that forecasts what lies ahead. So, it is not surprising that Rosenberg found Peirce's paragraphing of uneven value in constructing his outline. Finding a structure in the twenty-one paragraphs of this essay is no easy matter, and many different versions of an outline can probably be developed with equal plausibility.

The key to an effective outline is *subordination,* within and between paragraphs. Subordination shows up in the levels of detail used in the outline. Rosenberg usually manages to get by with two levels of subordination, but occasionally he needs three. It is unlikely that a different outline of this essay would need more than three levels, or that it would be a better outline if it did.

What is the most important idea in Peirce's essay, and does it emerge with due prominence in Rosenberg's outline? Peirce's third rule of clarity is clearly stated in section II, subsection E: "Consider what effects, that might conceivably have practical bearings, we conceive the object of our conception to have. Then, our conception of these effects is the whole of our conception of the object." Rosenberg's outline gives this sentence the prominence it warrants.

How does Rosenberg's outline measure up in other respects? In a couple of places he maintains the flavor of Peirce's essay by using a quotation in his section headings; he might have done this in a few other cases as well. The careful reader will note that he made no use of Peirce's paragraph 3, a bold deletion but not unreasonable. In at least one case, the heading for section III.D.3, he uses language ("object of possible experience") that captures Peirce's meaning in paragraph 19 but goes well beyond what Peirce *actually* says. As to length, Rosenberg uses nearly 800 words (780 to be exact) to outline Peirce's essay of about 7,250 words. It would be difficult to do an outline of this essay in significantly fewer words.

In sum, the outline is a good one, neither so detailed as to virtually reproduce the essay nor so sketchy as to fail to give the reader the gist of each phase of Peirce's text. What more could one reasonably ask?

3. Evaluating Argumentative Prose

> All my ideas hold together, but I cannot elaborate
> them all at once.
> — Jean-Jacques Rousseau

Your most important writing assignments in a philosophy course are probably not going to be like any of those so far discussed — summarizing or abstracting an essay, extracting an author's thesis, or outlining someone else's chapter or article. Assignments of these sorts, designed mostly to help you make sure you have understood what you have read, are only preparation for more serious and challenging assignments in which you make a *critical examination of an argument*, probably a philosophical argument found in the readings assigned for your course. Evaluating another's argument is a good task to undertake before trying to construct an argument of your own; it is much easier to criticize someone else's line of thinking than it is to develop a position of your own and then argue for it. Indeed, most aspiring philosophers begin their studies by examining and evaluating the views and arguments other philosophers have developed. Each of the exercises later in this chapter will show some of the ways this can be done.

What intellectual tools do well-equipped philosophers use to think critically about philosophical issues and arguments? Unfortunately, it is not possible to set out in a neat and exhaustive list all such tactics and strategies — and certainly not in a book like this, devoted primarily to helping you write better and only secondarily to helping you reason better. Some of the more important basic tools are discussed in chapter 1 (e.g., definition, counterexample, analogy) and will be used in later writing exercises. Several others will be mentioned shortly. But philosophical thinking at its best is not achieved by learning and following certain set methods. One need not go so far as to agree with the Oxford philosopher Gilbert Ryle (1900–1976) when he observed, "The idea of a well-trained philosopher is a contradiction in terms." Were Ryle entirely correct, there would be little to gain in trying to teach beginners what has served others well in the past. Still, Ryle had an important point:

Philosophical thinking at its best crosses the frontiers of the known and the settled; it breaks new ground, bursts the confines of the prevailing categories, and so is untamed and unpredictable at its edges. In other words, it is creative. Even beginning students can witness some of this in classroom lectures and discussions in an introductory course, as well as in their reading assignments.

But most philosophical thinking — certainly the sort typically expected of beginners — calls less for creative or truly original thinking than it does for critical reflection. Not hostile or contentious criticism, of course, but thoughtful evaluation. For this purpose some standard and widely used strategies need to be learned — and learned so well that they become second nature.

ARGUMENT VERSUS DISPUTATION AND PERSUASION

Central to the work of philosophy is *argument*. Argument as used by philosophers is a *technique* or *method of inquiry,* not a bludgeon with which to beat others into submission. By pressing for reasons in favor of some belief or thesis, you probe the plausibility, the probability, the necessity of that belief or thesis. You shape and reshape your thinking about a belief or thesis as the reasons for it (and the reasons against it) emerge bit by bit as the product of your critical thinking. This process is evident in the excerpts in chapter 2 from Hume, Hardin, Russell, Nietzsche, and Gettier. These writers share nothing in subject matter or style; they do demonstrate a concern to *argue* for their views.

So argument is essential to philosophy — but not if it is confused with opinionated *disputation*. Contentiousness and disagreement just for the sake of disagreement (perhaps colored by ill-tempered and discourteous remarks) have no useful role in philosophy any more than they do in science. Of course, philosophers are only human; like others they often get overexcited, impatient, and stubborn during the sometimes heated exchanges that occur in philosophical discussion. But what alone matters in philosophy is the argument, as that term is used here, aimed at the *truth* of the matter under discussion, by using *rational* means that all can understand and evaluate.

By contrast with argument, *persuasion* aims at achieving agreement whether or not rational methods are used. Threats in particular can be very persuasive. (Not for nothing in the old gangster movies is a handgun known as a "persuader.") And we all know that we can be persuaded to believe and do things contrary to our better judgment, or despite lack of adequate evidence, and perhaps even in the face of a preponderance of facts that indicate that we should believe or act otherwise. Philosophers strive to persuade by the sheer weight — cogency, precision, detail, scope — of their *rational* argument.

To sum up, it may be useful (even if a bit unfair) to contrast the lawyer's interest in argument and persuasion with the philosopher's. It is often said that whereas a lawyer has many clients, a philosopher has only one: the Truth. Where lawyers seek to prevail on behalf of their clients, using whatever methods of persuasion the courts will allow — for example, threatening protracted litigation if the other side won't settle out of court — philosophers seek to establish the truth, using only the methods that unbiased reason allows. Like most generalizations, this one oversimplifies, but it does serve to remind us how central the rational search for truth is to philosophical thinking and writing.

ARGUMENT IN DETAIL

Let's look more closely at the nature of argument to develop the minimal working vocabulary needed to evaluate arguments. We can define an *argument* as a set of statements or propositions that perform two different but related functions. One function is to state a *conclusion*, the thesis or position being argued for. The other function is to provide the *reasons* for the conclusion. All arguments, whatever their content or subject matter and no matter how complex they may be, are built out of these two elements.

Reasons, which in an argument are called *premises*, can usually be expressed in declarative sentences. In a good argument, all the reasons will be made explicit, rather than left implicit; implicit premises are often treated as tacit *assumptions*. Thus, in reading an argument, learn to ask: "What are the reasons the author is proposing and relying on?"

The premises are in support of the *conclusion*, the point of the argument, what the argument is trying to establish, prove, or warrant. Like each premise, the conclusion can usually be stated in a single (sometimes very complex) declarative sentence. We have already seen the importance of confronting every argument with the question "What is the thesis or conclusion the author is trying to defend?"

In addition to the statements that constitute the premises and the statement that constitutes the conclusion of an argument, there is the invisible connective tissue that ties the premises to the conclusion. This connection is usually marked with *transitional expressions* like "therefore" (which may be indicated by the symbol "∴"), "thus," "accordingly," or "as a consequence." Such expressions indicate that the author of the argument believes that the conclusion is acceptable on the basis of the reasons given.

In light of the preceding definition of an argument, consider the following three statements about three republics in the former nation of Yugoslavia. Do the statements constitute an argument?

Bosnia was destroyed by Serbia in 1993.

Serbia has deep grievances against some of its neighbors.

Croatia is partly at fault for the destruction of Bosnia.

Obviously, all three statements have roughly a common topic, the collapse of Yugoslavia and the dismemberment of Bosnia by Serbia and Croatia. However, though all three statements may be true, they are isolated from one another and lack any logical interconnection. Certainly, the last sentence does not logically flow from the two previous ones. In other words, in this set of sentences we cannot point to premises or to a conclusion. This is not to deny that, with a little ingenuity, we could think up some further statements that, if added to these three, would enable us to cite one as the conclusion and the others as the premises. As things stand, however, given only these three statements, no argument is before us.

Now consider the following three statements:

Bosnia was destroyed by Serbia and Croatia in 1993.

Bosnia did not deserve to be destroyed.

The destruction inflicted on Bosnia in 1993 by Serbia and Croatia was undeserved.

These statements do constitute an argument. Why? Because the first two sentences pretty clearly constitute reasons — perhaps very good reasons — for believing the third one. In other words, they are premises that *imply* — establish or justify — the conclusion. To indicate the connection between the premises and conclusion, the third statement could properly be preceded by the word "therefore."

This brings us to an important lesson. Keep in mind that "therefore" and similar transitional expressions are crucial concepts in argumentation. Their true role is not to provide a pause between disconnected thoughts and utterances; rather, it is to express the connection that exists between reasons and a conclusion that follows from those reasons. If you can't rightly say "Statements A and B imply statement C," then you can't rightly say "Statements A and B, therefore statement C." Learn to keep a sharp eye on how you and others use "therefore," and be ready to question instances where it seems to have been misused.

Next we will discuss four different writing exercises, each of which is based on considering some kind of argument. The first involves formulating and evaluating a *definition;* the second involves explaining a definition by *exclusion* and *contrast;* the third requires evaluating an *analogy;* and the fourth involves evaluating a *formal argument.* For each assignment we'll examine a brief passage from a philosopher, consider what is involved in evaluating the passage, look at a student's written evaluation, and end with some comments on what the student wrote.

EXERCISE 5: Formulating and Evaluating a Definition

Philosophers are probably more likely than other academics to insist that you define your terms before getting very deeply into a discussion of your subject. Of course, a premature demand for definition can squelch discussion instead of focusing it, so teachers are often rightly cautious about insisting at the outset that students define their terms. Nevertheless, in examinations and sometimes even in short papers, particularly classroom exercises, you will almost certainly be asked to write a definition of some important term that appears in the reading or that has come up in classroom discussion. This ought to lead to useful reflections about the nature and purpose of definitions: What counts as a definition? What makes one definition better than another? How can inadequate definitions be improved?

Constructing a Definition

Introduction   Let us answer some of these questions by considering how we might construct a definition of "atheist" from "A Defense of Atheism," by Ernest Nagel. After reading the text, we'll examine some general approaches to formulating definitions. Then we'll evaluate a student's definition of "atheist" based on Nagel's text.

ERNEST NAGEL
from *A Defense of Atheism*

I must begin by stating what sense I am attaching to the word 1 "atheism," and how I am construing the theme of this paper. I shall understand by "atheism" a critique and a denial of the major claims of all varieties of theism. And by theism I shall mean the view which holds, as one writer has expressed it, "that the heavens and the earth and all that they contain owe their existence and continuance in existence to the wisdom and will of a supreme, self-consistent, omnipotent, omniscient, righteous, and benevolent being, who is distinct from, and independent of, what he has created."

Discussion   How could you use what Nagel says about atheism to define the term "atheist"? Don't say: "Well, an atheist is anyone who believes in atheism." That's true, of course, but trivially so, because it's *circular*. It uses one version of the term to define another version of the

Ernest Nagel (1901–1985) grew up in New York City, received his Ph.D. from Columbia, and taught there (apart from brief appointments elsewhere) for his entire career. His philosophical interests were concentrated on the philosophy of science and related topics. His commitments were to a pragmatism sharpened by the analytic methods championed by the logical positivists. Known (and admired) for his acute critical eye, he used it to good effect against many philosophers who enjoyed greater esteem and public recognition than he did. In *Sovereign Reason* (1954) and *Logic without Metaphysics* (1956) he reprinted many of these trenchant essays. His textbook, *Introduction to Logic and Scientific Method* (1934), coauthored with Morris R. Cohen, was widely regarded for many years as the best book of its kind. His long-awaited treatise, *The Structure of Science* (1961), unfortunately appeared just as the fancy of younger philosophers was taking the field in a different direction.

same term, thereby shedding no light on what the term itself means. What you want to do is transform, or reformulate, what Nagel says about atheis*m* so that you get a definition of what it is to be an athei*st*.

There are several ways of defining something and this writing exercise will help familiarize you with some of them. First, we can define a term by pointing to an *example* of what the term applies to. In this way you could define the term "planet" by pointing to Mars or Venus because they are often easily visible at night. This is called an **ostensive** definition (from the Latin *ostendo,* "I show"). However, this is not a very plausible way of defining abstract terms such as "atheist," and it can't be used effectively in written work.

Second, you can state *what something is*, in essence, completing a sentence like this:

`An atheist is . . .`

A definition framed this way promises to state the essential properties of the *thing* being defined. It is the condition of being an atheist, not the *word* "atheist," that is specified. (Some philosophers have called this giving a definition in the "material mode.")

Third, you can state *what a word or term means*, this case, by completing this sentence:

`"Atheist" means . . .`

The words that follow will be (or purport to be) synonymous with "atheist." (This is sometimes called giving a definition in the "formal mode.")

Note: Here and elsewhere, when you want to *mention,* or set off a word referred to as a word, you should put that word inside quotation marks ("atheist").

Finally, you can state the *necessary and sufficient conditions* for something to be what it is. A definition of this sort is formulated by means of the biconditional phrase "if and only if." For example:

`A person is an atheist if and only if . . .`

Recall that Gettier used this approach to formulate the three definitions of "knowledge" that he criticized in his essay reprinted in chapter 2 (pp. 34–35). A definition framed in this manner is also called a **contextual** definition, because the term being defined is imbedded in the context of a sentence ("A person is an atheist . . ."), rather than presented as a single word or term ("Atheism is . . ."). The definition on the right-hand side of the biconditional, then, appears in the form of another sentence.

Is choice among these four styles of definition purely a matter of taste? Not entirely. The fourth form is by far preferable to the others. For one thing, this style of definition discourages you from thinking that only *nouns* (or what they refer to) can be defined. Anything, no matter how complex or abstract, can be mentioned to the left of the biconditional and then defined. For example, if you wanted to define what it is to be *causally dependent upon*, you would set up your biconditional like this: "Something (call it X) is causally dependent upon something else (call it Y) if and only if. . . ." Then you would fill in the blanks according to your best understanding of the sufficient and necessary conditions of causal dependency.

Furthermore — and this is of the greatest importance — thinking in terms of sufficient and necessary conditions helps you keep in mind that your definition (that is, what follows "if and only if") must be *neither too broad nor too narrow.* In defining "atheist" from the Nagel passage, you are going to try to state exactly the conditions under which a person is (and by implication, is not) an atheist. And your definition will fail if it doesn't account for some persons who are atheists, just as it will fail if it does include some persons who are not atheists.

One further thought: Because the definition you are about to give is based on *Nagel's* views on atheism, you might wish to leave it open whether you agree or disagree with him, keeping your own views about how to define "atheism" to yourself. If so, the beginning of your definition of "atheist" might read like this:

    A person is an atheist, according to Nagel, if and only
    if . . .

Before reading on, you might want to take out a pencil and a sheet of paper and write your own definition of "atheist" based on Nagel's text. When you're done, compare it with the following student definition:

    A person is an atheist, according to Nagel, if and only
    if she or he rejects the major claims of all varieties of
    theism.

Reviewing the Student's Definition   The student obviously borrowed the phrase "the major claims of all varieties of theism" directly from Nagel's paragraph. That's all right, since it clearly states the essential idea of Nagel's definition. However, the borrowed phrase ought to be in quotation marks, lest a reader unfamiliar with Nagel's remarks be misled into thinking that the borrowed words are the student's. (For more information on citing sources and avoiding plagiarism, see chapter 6.)

Now let's assess whether the student's definition is a good one. What objections might be raised to it? Here are three worth considering.

First, you might complain that the definition is somewhat *vague*, since it uses the term "theism" from Nagel's text; all readers may not understand what that term means. This is a chronic problem in definitions — defining a term by means of its opposite or through other terms that are themselves not precise, clear, or familiar. However, another glance at the original paragraph shows that Nagel has anticipated this problem. For he tells readers what "theism" means — or at least what he means by that term — in the very next sentence, where he quotes an unnamed writer. While it is true that Nagel's account of atheism is explained by reference to its opposite, theism, he in effect defines that term promptly so that readers are in no real doubt as to what theism is.

Second, you might think the definition *too broad* because it blurs the difference between being an *atheist* and being an *agnostic*. An agnostic is one who doubts God's existence and nature, believing there is too little evidence to settle the matter one way or the other ("agnostic" is derived from the Greek and means "without knowledge"). Nagel might reply, however, that his account of atheism implies that the atheist *rejects* or *denies* theism, rather than merely *doubting* its claims. Thus his account of atheism really does not blur the difference between atheism and agnosticism.

Finally, you might think that the definition is *too narrow* because it doesn't address the perception that an atheist is an *irreligious* person, one with no interest in or concern about religious practices or belief — or perhaps even one who is hostile to religion. However, in the paragraphs that immediately follow the one quoted here, Nagel directly addresses this issue, making it clear that what *he* means by the term "atheism" concerns only *philosophical* beliefs, not "religious practices" or "religious attitudes."

In the end, it's probably not possible to fix the definition of "atheist" once and for all, as a history of the term will show. The English philosopher Thomas Hobbes (1588–1679), for example, was denounced in his day as a "damned atheist" despite his professed (and probably sincere) belief in God. The problem was that Hobbes's God was not the God of the prevailing theistic orthodoxy. Hobbes was at best a deist (as were Benjamin Franklin and Thomas Jefferson a century later), believing that God exists independently of the world and does not intervene in its affairs. (In other words, God doesn't perform miracles or answer prayers.) Theism, in contrast, has always accepted God as both transcendent (outside the world) and immanent (intervening in affairs of the world). Hobbes and deism aside, it is enough to note that Nagel, like the rest of us, has some (but not unlimited) freedom to use "atheism" as he wishes, just so long as he makes it clear to readers how he is using the term — as he does in the paragraph quoted here.

EXERCISE 6: Explaining a Definition by Exclusion and Contrast

Some classroom writing assignments in a philosophy course may require the student to *explain* a definition of some key concept. Here the task is not to create the definition, for the definition is given to you from the start. Rather, your task is to show that you understand it. Now one way to do that is to take the definition apart, phrase by phrase, to see what is being *excluded* by each phrase. For example, here's a model assignment of this sort:

> St. Thomas Aquinas (1225–1274) defined "law" as follows: "Law is nothing other than an ordinance of reason directed toward the common good, promulgated by one who has responsibility for

the community." Explain this definition by reference to the implied contrasting ideas that it excludes.

As you think about this assignment, you might jot down your thoughts in this manner.

There seem to be five distinguishable elements in this definition: <u>an ordinance, of reason, directed toward the common good, promulgated, by one who is responsible for the community.</u>

An <u>ordinance</u> is a command, rule, or directive. In this context the term excludes less stringent considerations, such as recommendations, advice, exhortations, or counsel. The imperative feature of an ordinance is missing from these ideas; all are too weak.

To say that the ordinance is from <u>reason</u> evidently excludes other possible sources, such as desire, volition, sensation, feeling, or any other of our noncognitive capacities.

A rational ordinance directed toward <u>the common good</u> excludes a design or intention to serve some private, narrow, or parochial good. To say that it is <u>directed</u> toward the common good, however, does not imply that it succeeds in this direction. It does imply that we can evaluate a law by reference to its success in serving the common good.

To say that law is <u>promulgated</u> is to say that it is made public, announced, posted. This excludes secret ordinances from the status of law — obvious enough, since how could one guide one's conduct by reference to the law if the law remains unknown?

Finally, the source of the promulgation — one who is <u>responsible for the care of the community</u> — excludes unofficial or nongovernmental bodies from the capacity to make law. These bodies may have their rules, but those rules will not have the force of law. Also excluded are ordinances that issue from selfish

St. Thomas Aquinas (1225–1274) is generally regarded as the greatest among the many outstanding Christian, Jewish, and Muslim medieval thinkers. A Neopolitan by birth, he entered the Dominican order in 1242, studied in Cologne, and taught in Paris and at several Italian colleges. His interests in philosophy covered virtually the entire range of topics found in the discipline: logic; metaphysics; epistemology; moral, legal, and political theory; plus the many topics of special concern to Christian theologians. An indication of the respect with which the Church held him and his views was his canonization fifty years after his death. In 1567 Pius V conferred on Aquinas the honorific title, "the Angelic doctor." Despite his enormous contributions to philosophy, after a religious experience during the celebration of Mass, Aquinas is reported to have said, "All that I have written seems to me like straw compared to what has now been revealed to me." His greatest work is his *Summa theologiae,* a multivolume treatise that he did not live to finish. A brief extract from one of its several parts, known as "The Treatise on Law," is reprinted here.

or tyrannical sources, persons or groups who have no interest in what is good for the community whose laws are in question.

By unpacking a definition, piece by piece, looking for what it includes and what it excludes, one develops a good grasp of the concept being defined. Notice, finally, that in this exercise, we are not criticizing or endorsing Aquinas's definition; that is a separate task. All we are trying to do (to borrow a phrase from Peirce) is to make his ideas clearer.

EXERCISE 7: Evaluating an Argument by Analogy

Philosophical arguments frequently make use of *analogy*; one of the most famous such arguments is the so-called argument from analogy for the nature of God, popular among many eighteenth-century European philosophers. David Hume's version of this argument was reprinted in chapter 2 (pp. 11–13). Philosophers are also adept at inventing *hypothetical cases*, thought experiments involving purely imaginary circumstances that are possible but not actual; sometimes they even invent cases to show what is impossible. Such inventions help us think more clearly about real cases by highlighting their important features. Sometimes, as discussed here, a hypothetical case is used as part of an analogy.

Analogies involve comparison between two admittedly different things in the belief that the similarities are more important than the differences. Two illustrations may prove useful.

Around 1955 or so, near the beginning of the computer age, the basic electronic power unit — prior to the invention of the transistor — was the four-inch vacuum tube. John von Neumann (1903–1957), an eminent mathematician and logician, suggested at the time that producing a computer with "computing power" roughly comparable to that of the human brain would require three things: a mass of electron tubes the size of the Empire State Building, all the electricity generated by Niagara Falls to power these tubes, and all the waters of the Niagara to keep the whole thing cool. In effect, von Neumann was offering an analogy between the human brain and this gigantic mass of pulsating electron tubes.

Von Neumann's analogy was not intended to be used as part of an argument, for example, to show that it would be physically impossible to build an artificial intelligence machine with "brain power" comparable to that of the human brain. Rather, his purpose was to illustrate the enormous complexity of the brain and the challenge that technology would face in attempting to duplicate it.

Now for a more recent example. Within the past decade, contemporary philosophers of science, along with biologists and systems analysts, have begun to explore the idea of "artificial life," or "ALife." ALife is a product of certain computer programs; the things artificially alive are called "bugs." The behavior of these bugs is governed by laws in the program akin to the laws of natural selection (evolution). Thus, the study of ALife is the study of behaviors analogous to the behavior of very simple natural organisms. Just how close the analogy is between the evolution of the things studied in ALife and the evolution of living things studied in biology is itself a matter of great interest and some controversy.

Some Guidelines for Evaluating an Analogy

There are no precise rules for evaluating analogies. However, some questions can help you to frame your analysis:

- How different are the two things being compared? Often, the greater the differences, the more dubious the analogy.
- Does the writer overextend the analogy? The fact that an analogy applies to certain aspects of the things being compared doesn't mean it applies to all aspects.
- Can you think of counterexamples or other hypothetical cases that weaken the analogy?

Evaluating an Argument by Analogy

Introduction   A now-famous analogy, in the form of a hypothetical case, is a prominent feature near the beginning of the widely discussed essay "A Defense of Abortion," by the American philosopher Judith Jarvis Thomson (b. 1929). Her essay was originally published in 1971, just two years before the Supreme Court's decision in Roe v. Wade upholding a pregnant woman's right to have an abortion.

Crucial to the abortion debate are the *rights* of those involved — particularly the *right to life*, which antiabortionists are likely to attribute to the unborn, and the woman's *right to autonomy*, a right of a woman to decide for herself what to do and not do with her own body and her life. In the following extract, Thomson assumes for the sake of argument that the human fetus has a right to life just as children and adults do. Her purpose is not to challenge that right but to test its stringency in settling the question of whether abortion is always morally wrong. Does the fetus's right to life — or its needs — always override the pregnant woman's right to autonomy, including the right to terminate her own pregnancy? To carry out this test, Thomson constructs a purely hypothetical example and uses it as an analogy in the paragraphs excerpted here.

After reading Thomson's excerpt, you might want to try writing an essay in which you evaluate her analogy between a plugged-in violinist and a pregnant woman who wants an abortion. When you're done, take a look at the sample paper on pages 67–69 to see how another student approached this assignment. (As you read the excerpt, you might find it helpful to jot your reactions to Thomson's analogy on a separate sheet of paper.)

JUDITH JARVIS THOMSON
from *A Defense of Abortion*

I propose, then, that we grant that the fetus is a person from the 1
moment of conception. How does the argument go from here? Something like this, I take it. Every person has a right to life. So the fetus
has a right to life. No doubt the mother has a right to decide what
shall happen in and to her body; everyone would grant that. But
surely a person's right to life is stronger and more stringent than the
mother's right to decide what happens in and to her body, and so
outweighs it. So the fetus may not be killed; an abortion may not be
performed.

It sounds plausible. But now let me ask you to imagine this. You 2
wake up in the morning and find yourself back to back in bed with
an unconscious violinist. A famous unconscious violinist. He has
been found to have a fatal kidney ailment, and the Society of Music
Lovers has canvassed all the available medical records and found
that you alone have the right blood type to help. They have therefore kidnapped you, and last night the violinist's circulatory system
was plugged into yours, so that your kidneys can be used to extract
poisons from his blood as well as your own. The director of the
hospital now tells you, "Look, we're sorry the Society of Music Lovers did this to you — we would never have permitted it if we had
known. But still, they did it, and the violinist now is plugged into
you. To unplug you would be to kill him. But never mind, it's only
for nine months. By then he will have recovered from his ailment,
and can safely be unplugged from you." Is it morally incumbent on
you to accede to this situation? No doubt it would be very nice of
you if you did, a great kindness. But do you *have* to accede to it?
What if it were not nine months, but nine years? Or longer still?
What if the director of the hospital says, "Tough luck, I agree, but
you've now got to stay in bed, with the violinist plugged into you,
for the rest of your life. Because remember this. All persons have a
right to life, and violinists are persons. Granted you have a right to
decide what happens in and to your body, but a person's right to
life outweighs your right to decide what happens in and to your
body. So you cannot ever be unplugged from him." I imagine you

Judith Jarvis Thomson was educated in New York City and earned her Ph.D. at
Columbia in 1959. After brief stints teaching at Barnard College and Boston University, she joined the philosophy faculty at the Massachusetts Institute of Technology
in 1964, where she continues to teach. She is a past president of the American
Philosophical Association and has worked with the American Association of University Professors to protect academic freedom and tenure. An editor and author of
several books and many articles, the collection of her essays, *Rights, Restitution,
and Risks* (1986), and her treatise, *The Realm of Rights* (1990), have been very influential. Her "A Defense of Abortion" (1971), an excerpt from which is reprinted here,
is probably the most widely discussed and reprinted essay so far published on the
topic.

would regard this as outrageous, which suggests that something really is wrong with that plausible-sounding argument I mentioned a moment ago.

Sample Student Essay

Thomson's Plugged-in Violinist

and the Problem of Abortion

by

Steven Calcote

Though Judith Thomson's example of the plugged-in violinist is captivating, one must remember that a clever thought experiment can be devised for nearly any problem without actually solving it. I will evaluate her use of this hypothetical case as an analogy to the woman considering abortion in three respects: the scope of abortion cases to which it applies, the kind of entrapment that pregnancy involves, and the obligations of the parties.

First, the violence of the kidnapping in the hypothetical case and the forced connection of the violinist to the captive person seem to fit best the case of rape, where a woman is impregnated against her will. Although it may seem within the rights of the kidnapped person to disconnect from the violinist when the opportunity to do so arises, the case is less clear if we consider someone who volunteered to be connected to the violinist. Would it be within the rights of a volunteer to renege on the agreement and disconnect herself? Similarly, would it be within her rights for a woman to abort after a voluntary pregnancy? The case of a woman who "accidentally" becomes pregnant can be related to Thomson's hypothetical case by imagining that she has been frequenting the area where there is a possibility of being drafted to care for the violinist. If she

believed the likelihood of coerced connection was
small, yet she finds herself connected to the violinist against the odds, her right to disconnect is not
as clear as in the case where she was kidnapped without any prior warning, etc.

   The degree of entrapment in the pregnancy needs
to be contrasted with that of the captive in
Thomson's example. A pregnancy on average requires
only nine months of gestation within the mother.
Thomson asks the reader to consider the effects of
extending this period to nine years or even longer.
She makes an important move here. If Thomson can
show there is something wrong with entrapment for a
lifetime, then there is probably something wrong as
well by a much briefer amount of entrapment. After
all, in the case of the mother, a commitment of eigh-
teen years and beyond is most likely required as the
child matures and completes schooling. However, the
mother is certainly not trapped for those years, and
she is not even completely trapped by her pregnancy
for nine months. She can, normally, do pretty much
what she wants to do during pregnancy; and after
birth she could give up the child to adoption. So
the drastic picture of being immobilized through an
external tie (the tubing) to a completely independent
creature (the violinist) exaggerates the situation of
the pregnant mother. Surely, helping someone who is
inside one's body and requires no further assistance
beyond being toted around for nine months seems far
less burdensome than being bedridden with tubes con-
necting one's body to a full-grown stranger for nine
months.

   Finally, we need to compare the rights and obligations in the two cases, which is the crucial issue
for Thomson. The power of her analogy hinges on her
belief that her readers find it "outrageous" to imagine being kidnapped and trapped, perhaps for years,

and to have that justified by appeal to the
violinist's "right to life." Imagine, however, a
different case. While hiking in the woods, you find
an abandoned baby. Surely, you would not say that
your right to autonomy--"your right to decide what
happens in and to your body"--outweighs your obligation to care for the infant, if all that involves is
ending your hike and walking a few hours through the
woods back to civilization. Thomson gives us an
extreme example (being trapped forever) to push the
reader to consider that one person's right to life
does not outweigh another person's right to freedom.
While this may be true in some cases, it does not
seem to be true in all. In some cases, as I have
attempted to show with my hypothetical example, the
demand of another's needs over our freedom to act as
we please seems quite reasonable.

My purpose has not been to defend a pro-life
stance but to demonstrate that Thomson's example is
not as powerful as it seems at first glance. Perhaps
the best one can expect from any given thought experiment, such as hers or mine, is to get the reader
to consider the problem in a new light.

Discussion   As a piece of writing, Calcote's paper is effective. He sticks
to the assigned topic, uses a clear and concise style, and follows proper
conventions for grammar, spelling, punctuation, and integrating quotations. In addition, his paper is carefully organized: Note how his introduction prepares readers for the three ways in which he will evaluate
Thomson's analogy. One somewhat long paragraph is then devoted to
each of these ways. Calcote concludes his essay by again considering
the usefulness of thought experiments, an issue first raised in his introduction. His title, though not especially exciting or provocative, is certainly adequate (for suggestions on choosing titles, see
p. 125). In short, readers are not going to be distracted from Calcote's
argument by careless writing.

As a philosophical work, his paper also has strong merit, and he
does a good job of challenging the point of Thomson's hypothetical
case with a hypothetical case of his own. He sees that Thomson's anal-

ogy is most suitably applied to the predicament of the woman whose pregnancy was caused by rape and is less applicable to other cases, such as fully voluntary pregnancy or accidental pregnancy despite known risk. In essence, Calcote tests the adequacy of Thomson's analogy by bringing out differences between the actual situation of pregnancy and the predicament of the person hooked up to the violinist. He also shows appreciation of the way Thomson appeals to the reader's intuition (as when she writes, "I imagine you would regard this as outrageous"), an intuition she seems to share. Though Calcote's essay is generally effective, there may still be room for further improvement, and you may have thought of some ways in which it falls short of fully recognizing and challenging Thomson's argumentative analogy. (Later, in chapter 5, we'll take a closer look at how to improve essays through revision.)

EXERCISE 8: Evaluating a Formal Argument

The term "formal argument" is used here to refer to any argument whose premises and conclusion are set out explicitly, step by step, with each step of the argument usually numbered in sequence for ease of reference in discussion. The great philosophers from Plato to Ludwig Wittgenstein (1889–1951) rarely if ever presented their views in this manner, though the medieval Scholastic thinkers, such as St. Thomas Aquinas, often came close.

Writing out the steps of an argument is hard work; it's much easier — and perhaps less tedious for readers — to present the argument in a less exact and detailed manner. However, only by writing out the steps can one actually see each element of the argument clearly and distinctly (as René Descartes famously put it) and be sure no hidden assumptions escape notice or faulty inferences remain undetected. In the next chapter, in the writing exercise that begins on page 73, you will have an opportunity to examine a formal argument extracted from the prose in which it is embedded. Our concern here is the easier task of evaluating an argument already formalized for us.

Some Guidelines for Evaluating a Formal Argument

When evaluating formal arguments, you need to ask two questions:

* Is the argument *valid?*
* Are all the premises (and assumptions) *true?*

Let's take a closer look at both of these criteria.

Validity. Philosophers and logicians say that an argument is *valid* if and only if granting its premises requires one to accept the conclusion. In the case of the Serbia-Bosnia-Croatia argument (p. 57), is it possible without self-contradiction to grant the two premises ("Bosnia was destroyed by Serbia and Croatia in 1993" and "Bosnia did not deserve to be destroyed") and yet deny the conclusion ("The destruction inflicted on Bosnia in 1993 by Serbia and Croatia was undeserved")? No, it isn't. This shows that the argument is a valid (or, more precisely, a valid deductive) argument. In still another definition, we can say that any argument is valid if and only if asserting the premises and denying the conclusion result in a self-contradiction.

How in general can one tell whether an argument is valid or invalid? The answer is too complex to try to address in a book focused on writing. Suffice to say that systems of formal deductive logic since the time of Aristotle (384–322 B.C.), its great pioneer, have been developed to answer this question; one cannot appreciate what is involved in testing the validity of arguments without some training in formal deductive logic.

Truth of conclusions. If all we know about an argument is that it is valid, as just defined, we do not know enough to know whether its conclusion is true. The proof lies in the fact that it is quite possible to have a valid argument with a *false* conclusion. Here's an example:

Kant was born before Descartes died.

Mill was born before Kant was born.

Therefore, Mill was born before Descartes died.

One must grant the third statement if one accepts the first two; so the argument is valid. But this argument cannot prove its conclusion, because the conclusion is *false*. And it is false because both premises (assumptions) are false: Kant was born in 1724 and Mill was born in 1806. Descartes died in 1650, long before both their birth dates.

It is also possible to have all true premises in an argument and infer a false conclusion from them, as in this example:

Plato was a student of Socrates.

Aristotle was a student of Plato.

Therefore, Aristotle was a student of Socrates.

Though history fully confirms the truth of each premise, the conclusion of this argument must be false since Aristotle didn't even arrive in Athens until many years after Socrates's death. So the argument must be invalid, since we cannot have a valid argument whose premises are true but whose conclusion is false.

So what has gone wrong? We can see the problem more clearly if we construct another argument superficially of the same form, such as this:

Plato was born after Socrates.

Aristotle was born after Plato.

Therefore, Aristotle was born after Socrates.

This argument is valid, and its premises and conclusion are true. But what is the difference between this argument and the one before it? The difference must be in the relations "was a student of" and "was born after," which are central to the two arguments. These two relations do not have the same logical structure; "was born after" is what logicians call a *transitive* relation, whereas "was a student of" is not a transitive relation.[1]

Finally, there are plenty of *invalid* arguments with true premises and a true conclusion, such as this syllogism:

Some modern philosophers are rationalists.

Some rationalists are materialists.

Therefore, some modern philosophers are materialists.

This argument isn't valid because even if its premises were true (as they are), its conclusion could still be false. For all we know — given only the information contained in the two premises — none of the rationalists who are materialists are among the rationalists who are also modern philosophers.

The preceding examples of unacceptable arguments are designed to teach but one point: The truth or falsehood of an argument's premises and conclusion is completely independent of whether the argument is valid or invalid. What we want from a deductive argument, of course, is *proof* of its conclusion, and an argument proves its conclusion if and only if it is valid and has true premises. Philosophers typically call a valid argument with true premises a *sound* argument. Only sound arguments prove their conclusions. And an argument can be *un*sound for one or both of two reasons: It is invalid or at least one of its premises is false.

Truth of premises. How in general can you tell whether the reasons used as premises in a given argument are true? There are no foolproof methods. About all you can do is evaluate the reasons based on available evidence and resources and then decide for yourself.

Reconsider for a moment the argument on page 71 involving the birth dates of Kant and Mill and the death date of Descartes. How could we have verified those dates? By checking with a suitable reference book, say, the one-volume *Columbia Encyclopedia* or a good dictionary or encyclopedia of philosophy (see chapter 7). Are these infallible sources? Of course not. But they are the best we have, and they are especially reliable for verifying simple facts.

When confronted by *empirical* assertions in particular disciplines — geography, sociology, chemistry, astronomy, and so on — philosophers, like everyone else, must turn to experts and the resources of those disciplines to determine whether the assertions are true. (Assertions are

---

1. The idea of transitivity is intuitively clear and familiar. We can define it precisely as follows: Any relation, R, is *transitive* just in case if something, X, bears R to something else, Y, and if Y bears R to something else. Z, then necessarily X bears R to Z. "Was born after" satisfies this definition; so do many other relations, such as "is bigger than," "is balder than," and "is smarter than." But "Was a student of" does not satisfy this definition, nor do many other relations, such as "is in love with," "is a friend of," and "is next to."

empirical if and only if they are testable and verifiable or falsifiable by observation or experimentation.)

Not all assertions are empirical, however. Some are *normative*, involving ethical, legal, or religious norms, standards, or laws. Can such assertions be true or false? If so, how can we tell? Can norms be used as premises in arguments to defend judgments about what is right or wrong, much as premises establish other types of conclusions in arguments such as described earlier? These questions are central to the study of normative issues, especially in ethics, philosophy of law, and aesthetics. Such issues are too complex and remote from our chief concerns to be addressed here. However, some light is shed on them by this chapter's writing exercise involving a formal argument in which one of the premises is a normative proposition.

A Checklist for Evaluating Arguments

Let's recap five of the main questions you will want to raise as you evaluate any argument (especially a formal one):

- Is the argument *valid* as it stands?
- If you think it is invalid, can you make it valid by adding one or more plausible premises? If so, formulate those premises and be prepared to explain why the argument with them is now valid.
- Are there key terms in one or more of the premises whose meaning or logic puts the validity of the argument in doubt? Or does a given term used in two or more steps of the argument seem to change its meaning, so that there is a subtle equivocation in the reasoning?
- Are all the premises *true?* On what basis are you willing to accept them? Can you think of confirming examples? Can you think of effective tactics to disarm troublesome counterexamples?
- After considering all of these questions, how adequate is the argument, in your judgment?

Evaluating an Argument

Introduction   Consider now an argument by abortion opponents to the effect that abortion is morally wrong. How can we evaluate such arguments, which are based on normative assertions? See if you can answer that question by evaluating a version of the antiabortion argument, adapted from a discussion by the American philosopher Morton White (b. 1917) in his book *What Is and What Ought to Be Done* (1981). Try to keep your evaluation to two or three double-spaced, typed pages. When you're done, you might want to compare your evaluation with the sample student paper that follows.

MORTON WHITE
from *What Is and What Ought to Be Done*

(1) No one ought to take the life of a human being.
(2) The mother took the life of a fetus in her womb.
(3) Every living fetus in the womb of a human being is a human being.
Therefore,
(4) The mother took the life of a human being.
Therefore,
(5) The mother did something that ought not to be done.

Sample Student Essay

An Antiabortion Argument Evaluated

by

David Hoberman

An examination of the argument shows that it is actually two nested arguments, one inside the other. Statements 2 and 3 are the inner premises, and their conclusion is statement 4; the surrounding argument consists of statements 1 and 4 as its premises, and the conclusion is statement 5. Thus statement 4 is both a premise and a conclusion.

The outer argument proves statement 5 if and only if all the premises are true and 5 follows from

---

Morton White grew up in New York and received his Ph.D. from Columbia in 1942 after completing a dissertation on the early philosophy of John Dewey. His career took him to the University of Pennsylvania and then to Harvard, where he taught for more than two decades. At Harvard he was principally responsible for introducing students to the analytic philosophy then prevailing at Oxford and Cambridge. His most widely read book is a compact volume he edited, *The Age of Analysis* (1955). In 1970 he resigned from the Harvard faculty and took up a research professorship at the Institute for Advanced Study in Princeton, New Jersey. Probably his most enduring legacy as a scholar will be the series of books he has written on American philosophy, from the colonial period to the recent past — described by one reviewer as "A landmark in the writing of the history of American philosophy." His autobiography, *A Philosopher's Story* (1999), gives a vivid portrait of his life and career, which spanned most of the previous century.

its premises as a valid inference. Statement 4 val-
idly follows from its premises, 2 and 3; and statement 5 is also valid given its premises, 1 and 4. So
both the inner and outer arguments are valid. Further evaluation of the argument therefore must focus
on the status of the premises of both arguments.

Statement 2 is an assumed statement of fact,
while 3 is a truth of human biology. It is hard to
see how any problems in this argument could arise
from either of these premises. Criticism of the
argument is therefore likely to concentrate on statements 1 and 4.

Statement 1 is rooted in the Old Testament commandment "Thou shalt not kill." Few of us would object to that. But there are problems. The commandment really is a prohibition against murder; the
rights of persons to protect their own lives by the
use of deadly force is not in question. With this in
mind, we might revise statement 1 by adding the word
"innocent"--surely the unborn human is innocent. Yet
there are cases involving pregnancy where the development of the fetus threatens the life of the mother,
as in ectopic pregnancy. Such a fetus is clearly
innocent but is still a threat to its mother. Very
few would argue against the mother's right to life
over that of her fetus, if both cannot live. So
statement 1 may have to be rephrased to read: "No one
ought to take the life of an innocent human being
unless there is no alternative."

This brings us to the crux of the entire argument: the definition of a human fetus as a "human
being." The sense in which this term is used in step
1 and in step 4 is not quite the same as the sense it
has in step 3. In 1 and 3, the term implicitly refers to adults, children, and infants, all able to
survive without any biological connection to the
mother. Each is an independent human creature. They
may be dependents, with physical and emotional needs,

of their mothers; but this is quite different from
the absolute biological dependence that a human fetus
has on its mother. The term "human fetus" in this
argument refers to a fertilized ovum or to a mass of
cells, and thus only to a potential human being dependent on its mother, not to a human being actually
developed and independent.

In short, this pro-life argument categorically
grants to the fetus the status of a human being,
regardless of its development, on the basis of its
potentiality. This implicit equivalence of potential
humanity with actual humanity is the true point of
contention between the two sides in the abortion
debate

Discussion   Hoberman's evaluation is thorough, yet within the length limits, and well written. Hoberman succinctly addresses each aspect of the argument — each premise, each conclusion, each inference; his paragraphs effectively break up his essay into distinct parts; and he follows conventions of grammar, spelling, and punctuation. His tone throughout is respectful, even though he clearly thinks the argument is flawed.

His opening and closing paragraphs deserve special notice. Hoberman's introduction does not so much set the stage as directly tackle the logic of the argument he is evaluating. His closing paragraph, however, shows how his analysis of the argument opens up some new horizons. Of the two paragraphs, the closing is the more interesting.

As a piece of philosophical writing, the essay shows a good grasp of a fundamental point: A deductive argument can be valid without proving its conclusion (recall p. 71). Hoberman is right that the two arguments (steps 2 and 3, therefore 4; and steps 1 and 4, therefore 5) are valid. One line of criticism he touches on but does not develop is that the key term "human being" seems to be used equivocally in the premises. That is, it has one meaning in steps 1 and 4 (human being = a creature with moral worth) but a different meaning in step 3 (human being = a biologically defined creature). Therefore, the argument leading to the conclusion in step 5 cannot be valid, since its validity depends on this key term being used in the *same* sense throughout.

That issue aside, Hoberman correctly points out that the moral principle in statement 1 has several exceptions that even many abortion opponents would allow. What he doesn't make explicit is that when this moral principle is restated to reflect the qualifications he raises ("No one ought to take the life of an innocent human being unless there is no alternative"), the whole argument changes. First, the main argument is no longer valid unless the qualifications used to revise statement 1 ("an innocent human being," "unless there is no alternative") are also used to revise statements 3, 4, and 5; without such revisions, the argument ceases to be valid. Second, once these revisions have been made, at least some abortions will turn out *not* to be the wrong thing to do — everything now depends on whether there is any "alternative" to the abortion. In cases of ectopic pregnancy, especially, there may be no alternative. What about unwanted pregnancies — is abortion the only alternative in such cases? As soon as the moral principle laid down in statement 1 is revised, as Hoberman recommends, the entire revised argument will raise new questions like these, questions his essay does not address. But then how could it, given the length restriction?

Undoubtedly the best aspect of Hoberman's critique is his suggestion that what really underlies the dispute between the two sides of the abortion debate is whether unborn but potentially normal human beings have the same moral status — the same rights and worth — that we accord to humans who are already born. He ends his essay by bringing this point to the surface, thereby pointing to a direction in which further debate on the subject could profitably move.

4. Putting It All Together: The Philosophical Essay

> The light of human minds is Perspicuous Words, but
> by exact definitions first snuffed and purged from
> ambiguity; Reason is the pace, Increase the way; and
> the Benefit of mankind the end.
>
> — Thomas Hobbes

The writing assignments discussed in chapters 2 and 3 — summarizing, abstracting, and formulating and evaluating a definition or outlining a philosophical essay, extracting an author's thesis — are aimed largely at helping you to *read* better, thus helping you *write* more effectively about what you have read. But none of those exercises taken individually results in a philosophical essay. The reason is that the exercises omit two prominent and distinctive features of most philosophical writing: *Evaluation of the views of others* and *development of one's own ideas*. In chapter 3 we discussed the basic elements of argument and we put some of those tools to work in evaluating a sample formal argument. Now it is time to put together what we've learned in chapters 2 and 3 and turn to the kinds of essays typical of philosophy courses, essays that require you to develop and write out your own thoughts in response to an assignment based on philosophical readings. In this chapter we will discuss some general strategies for developing a paper based on a specific assignment and then look at two papers produced by applying such strategies. In the next chapter, we will examine the writing process in more detail, considering all the steps of *drafting* and *revising* the philosophical essay.

GETTING STARTED

Bertrand Russell once told how he wrote his book *Our Knowledge of the External World* (1914). He had committed himself to give a series of lectures at Harvard and to turn over the lectures to his London publisher right away for printing in book form. But as the date for his departure to America loomed, Russell continued to dither. He couldn't seem to get his lectures down on paper, as he had hoped to do. Time was running out; in a few weeks his ship was scheduled to leave and he hadn't written a thing. With little time left, he pulled himself together and hired a stenographer who could take shorthand. With intense concentration on his philosophical ideas, he proceeded to dictate to her, hour after hour, day after day, without pauses or revisions, all of his intended Harvard lectures. With the dictation transcribed and typed, Russell had the text of his lectures finished just in time to catch his ship. He'd finished his book as well because he made no revisions (or so he said) in his lectures before sending them off to the publisher.

Only someone like Russell could write a book — or even a five-page essay — in this way. Most of the rest of us must learn to work at our writing if it is to advance our understanding of what we have read and to help us think critically and constructively about the philosophical problems before us. Often we must *rethink* and *revise* what we have written several times before it clearly makes all the points we want it to make.

Your first philosophy paper may well be the most difficult one you have to write because you are being asked to write in a style and on a subject that may be entirely new to you — it will have little or no connection to what you have written in high school or even college for English, history, or social science classes. Fortunately, several tactics can help you get from a blank sheet of paper to a first draft.

THE EIGHT-STEP SEQUENCE

The following eight-step sequence assumes that you are writing in response to a specific assignment, but you can use much of the advice for writing a paper on a topic of your own choice. Several of the steps will also prove useful in writing answers to essay examinations and in writing essays for courses other than philosophy. (Keep in mind that this advice is presented as an eight-step sequence for the sake of clarity. You may find that you return to certain steps more than once or that you can skip over one or two of the steps.)

1. *Examine the assignment carefully.* What exactly does the assignment ask you to do? *Define* two or three key ideas from the assigned reading? *Explain* a paradox or *solve* a puzzle or problem? *Compare* the different views of two philosophers on the same topic? You want to be sure that what you write responds directly to the assignment. Of course, a good paper is not guaranteed by your thoughtful and analytic attention to the assigned or chosen topic. But a mediocre paper (or worse) *is* guaranteed if you neglect to focus on the topic.

2. *Break the assignment into parts.* Be guided by the maxim of the ancient Romans "Divide and conquer." It is possible, of course, that the

assignment will be very abstract and not suggest specific steps, as in this paper topic:

> Write a 500-word essay on what truth is.

If you were working on this assignment, you would need to break it into appropriate subtopics that could be developed with evidence and examples into somewhat discrete parts of your essay. Such a vague topic, however, would be a tough challenge for a beginner. In an introductory course, it is more likely that your assignment will specify two or three aspects of the whole topic, as in this example:

> Write a 500-word paper in which you define truth, explain the difference between truth and falsehood, and explain whether there are or could be any truths that nobody knows.

This assignment specifies three somewhat independent subtopics in the overall topic to help you break up the assignment into more manageable parts. So far so good. But you will probably have to break down the topic even further. To do this, you will have to ask questions about each part of the assignment, which brings us to the next step.

3. *Ask yourself questions about each subtopic.* In general, as soon as you can formulate a question, you can probably say something by way of an answer — assuming, of course, that you have done the assigned reading on the topic (if any) and have been attentive to relevant classroom discussions. What might such questions be? Here are some questions that could be posed about the second version of the hypothetical paper topic on truth:

- How does one define a concept anyway?
- What might truth be contrasted with to bring out its defining features? (For example, what does it mean for something to be true in contrast to being false or to being neither true nor false?)
- What makes a belief or hypothesis false?
- What is knowledge, as opposed to a lucky guess, or a firm belief that turns out to be true, or a hypothesis for which there is some but not conclusive evidence?
- Could a belief be true even if no one is able to verify it? (For example, consider this assertion: "There are more than 100,000 but fewer than 1 million asteroids circling the earth." Could that be true even if no one can verify it?)

4. *Turn to your class notes, assigned readings, and other sources to help you answer your questions.* In addition to taking notes on lectures, you might keep a journal of reactions and ideas stimulated by class discussions and readings. Or you might highlight or annotate passages in your readings to point out a thesis, a decisive argument, key evidence, and so on. Once you have formulated questions based on your assignment, you can return to your notes and your journal, if you are keeping one, to answer them.

**5. *Jot down your answers and any other reactions and ideas; let
your thoughts flow freely.*** On paper or a computer, try to answer the
questions you have posed. You might also copy relevant quotations that
support the answers or record any reactions to readings or lecture notes
that have arisen in light of your assignment (for example, "This argument isn't convincing" or "I don't understand why the author believes
this"). Don't be afraid to admit that you don't understand something;
such an admission may be the first step to getting the information you
need. Or it may indicate that the author hasn't made his or her point
clearly — a problem you might want to address in your paper.

Above all, at this stage, *do not try to criticize your thoughts.* What
you are trying to do now is get something — *anything* — down on paper. Don't be afraid to write half-formed thoughts, first reactions, and
tentative connections between ideas. Generating a lot of ideas at this
stage will help you develop a richer, more thoughtful paper. You can
always discard irrelevant material later. (If your assignment requires you
to evaluate an argument, keep the guidelines outlined in chapter 3 in
mind as you jot down reactions and ideas.)

At this stage, you might want to keep each question and your responses to it on a separate sheet of paper so that you can arrange and
rearrange ideas easily. If you are using a computer, you might rearrange
material using cut and paste functions or similar commands. Even when
using a computer, you might find it easier to work with hard copy on
separate sheets of paper, physically rearranging material that you have
printed out.

6. *Focus and structure your thoughts; devise a tentative thesis.* Now
that you've carefully considered your assignment and generated a lot of
ideas about it, it's time to focus your thoughts so that you can write the
first draft of your paper. To do this, you need to ask two questions:

- What is the main point I want to make about the topic?
- How should I structure evidence and examples to support this
  point?

The first question describes your *thesis,* the main point or argument
that you want to make in your paper. Because the thesis determines the
organization of the rest of the paper, try to come up with it first. Don't
worry if the exact wording is a little rough at this point; you can always
revise it later, after you have developed a more detailed outline or written the first draft. (For more advice on the thesis, see p. 109.)

After you've come up with a working thesis, you might find it helpful to sketch out an outline of various points of support for the thesis.
This outline can be rough, or it can be a formal outline of the type
discussed in chapter 2 (pp. 38–39). (For more advice on using outlines
to help you develop your paper, see pp. 39–40.) Grouping together
notes that deal with roughly the same question or subtopic can help you
come up with your outline. You can rearrange material using the strategies suggested in step 5.

In addition to helping you structure ideas to support the thesis, an outline can point out places where you need more evidence or examples. By providing an explicit structure, your outline can also help you eliminate irrelevant material.

7. *Write the first draft of your paper.* Working from your outline and notes, write your first draft by hand or on a typewriter or computer. Try to stay focused on your assignment — and the thesis you developed in response to it — as you write. (For more advice on drafting, including developing an introduction, supporting paragraphs, and a conclusion, see chapter 5.) Be sure to double-, or even triple-, space your draft for ease of revision.

8. *Revise your essay and prepare it for submission.* After you've gotten some distance from your paper — and, depending on circumstances, gathered comments from your instructor or your peers — figure out how you could strengthen your paper by further refining the focus, providing additional examples and evidence, and reorganizing material. (Computers are especially helpful at this stage because they allow you to insert, delete, and move blocks of text quickly and easily.) After you have completed major revisions, edit your paper to correct errors in grammar, punctuation, and spelling. Finally, prepare your paper for submission according to your instructor's specifications. (For more information on revising your paper and preparing it for submission, see chapter 5.)

Now let's take a closer look at how a complete paper can be developed from preliminary notes.

EXERCISE 9: Writing an Essay on a Definition and a Counterexample

To illustrate how to move from notes on an assignment to a completed essay, we will focus on a classic text that presents us with an opportunity to examine a definition of an important concept and what we should think when that definition collides with a counterexample.

Introduction   The great dialogue *Republic*, written in the fourth century b.c. by the Greek philosopher Plato (c. 427–347 b.c.), is ostensibly devoted to answering the question, "What is justice?" But only ostensibly, one must say, because the dialogue is very long, and before it is over, Plato has discussed a wide range of issues in education, epistemology, and metaphysics that have only an indirect connection to the nature of justice. Book 1 of the dialogue opens with a brief exchange (whether imaginary or historically genuine, we do not know) between Socrates, Plato's famous teacher, and Cephalus, one of Athens's distinguished elder citizens. Their conversation proceeds amiably until Socrates asks, "What is the greatest benefit you have received from the enjoyment of wealth?" That provocative question begins the following excerpt, translated by G.M.A. Grube. Scholars have assured us that

Cephalus's answer is pretty much what any Athenian nobleman of the day would have said in similar circumstances — nothing idiosyncratic or culturally deviant emerges in Cephalus's remarks. Nevertheless, what he says provokes Socrates to raise doubts about the adequacy of his answer. And that suggests the following assignment for an essay:

> In an essay of not more than 500 words, state Cephalus's view of right conduct. What is Socrates's objection to that account? Does Socrates show that Cephalus's view is wrong?

Following the excerpt are guidelines for evaluating and taking notes on the discussion between Cephalus and Socrates. As you read the text and guidelines, you might want to make some notes of your own. Then try your hand at writing an essay, perhaps outlining it first. A sample essay written in response to this assignment appears on pages 87–89.

PLATO
from *Republic*

[Socrates:] Now tell me this much more: What is the greatest 1 benefit you have received from the enjoyment of wealth?

[Cephalus:] I would probably not convince many people in say- 2 ing this, Socrates, but you must realize that when a man approaches the time when he thinks he will die, he becomes fearful and concerned about things which he did not fear before. It is then that the stories we are told about the underworld, which he ridiculed before — that the man who has sinned here will pay the penalty there — torture his mind lest they be true. Whether because of the weakness of old age, or because he is now closer to what happens there and has a clearer view, the man himself is filled with suspicion and fear, and he now takes account and examines whether he has wronged anyone. If he finds many sins in his own life, he awakes from sleep in terror, as children do, and he lives with the expectation of evil. However, the man who knows he has not sinned has a sweet and good hope as his constant companion, a nurse to his old age, as

Plato is perhaps the greatest philosopher — and second to none as a writer — in Western civilization. One admirer, the philosopher Alfred North Whitehead, once wrote that the briefest way to characterize Western philosophy is as "a series of footnotes to Plato." Plato began his career as a student of Socrates (470–399 B.C.), and it is thanks to Plato's dialogues (in which Socrates figures as the main character) that we have a fairly clear picture of Socrates as a philosophical thinker. But Plato's philosophical interests were far wider than Socrates's. Scholars agree that most of Plato's writings (some twenty-six dialogues) are devoted to using Socrates as a mouthpiece for Plato's own views on metaphysics, eistemology, philosophy of mind, and other topics foreign to Socrates. Perhaps the most widely read of Plato's dialogues and one of the longest is his *Republic,* probably written in mid-career. Under the guise of defining justice and discussion related issues, the dialogue in fact ranges widely over virtually the entire philosophical landscape. An excerpt is reprinted here.

Pindar too puts it. The poet has expressed this charmingly, Socrates, that whoever lives a just and pious life

> Sweet is the hope that nurtures his heart,
> companion and nurse to his old age,
> a hope which governs the rapidly changing thoughts of mortals.

This is wonderfully well said. It is in this connection that I would 3 say that wealth has its greatest value, not for everyone but for a good and well-balanced man. Not to have lied to or deceived anyone even unwillingly, not to depart yonder in fear, owing either sacrifices to a god or money to a man: to this wealth makes a great contribution. It has many other uses, but benefit for benefit I would say that its greatest usefulness lies in this for an intelligent man, Socrates.

Beautifully spoken, Cephalus, said I [Socrates], but are we to say 4 that justice or right[1] is simply to speak the truth and to pay back any debt one may have contracted? Or are these same actions sometimes right and sometimes wrong? I mean this sort of thing, for example: Everyone would surely agree that if a friend has deposited weapons with you when he was sane, and he asks for them when he is out of his mind, you should not return them. The man who returns them is not doing right, nor is one who is willing to tell the whole truth to a man in such a state.

What you say is correct, he [Cephalus] answered.   5

This then is not a definition of right or justice, namely to tell the 6 truth and pay one's debts [Socrates said].

It certainly is, said Polemarchus[2] interrupting, if we are to put 7 any trust in Simonides.[3]

And now, said Cephalus, I leave the argument to you, for I must 8 go back and look after the sacrifice.

Do I then inherit your role? asked Polemarchus.   9

You certainly do, said Cephalus laughing, and as he said it he 10 went off to sacrifice.

Guidelines for Preliminary Notes   Before you start writing your essay, you will want to make some preliminary notes based on reading and rereading the excerpt, notes that will guide you in writing the essay itself (a strategy suggested in the eight-step sequence described on pp. 79–82). What are some features of this text that you ought to focus on because they are relevant to the assignment? To help pinpoint relevant

---

1. It should be kept in mind throughout the *Republic* that the Greek word *dikaios* and the noun *dikaiosyne* are often used, as here, in a much wider sense than our word "just" and "justice" by which we must usually translate them. They then mean "right" or "righteous," i.e., good conduct in relation to others, and the opposite *adikia* then has the general sense of wrongdoing. [Trans.]

2. An Athenian nobleman presumably a contemporary of Socrates. [Ed.]

3. Simonides of Ceos (c. 556–468 B.C.), a lyric poet whose apothegms were regularly invoked in later centuries. [Ed.]

features, it's helpful to make notes according to the sequence of topics suggested by the assignment: Cephalus's view, Socrates's objection to Cephalus's view, and what Socrates has proved. The following discussion is intended to help guide your note taking on each of these elements. (If this exercise were actually assigned in your class, your instructor would probably preface it with a class discussion of the text, and some of the points made here would probably emerge in that discussion.)

Cephalus's view. You might start by realizing that you have to be clear about what is meant by the phrase in the assignment "Cephalus's view of right conduct." Careful rereading of the passage will convince you that nowhere does Cephalus himself offer any such "account"; that is, nowhere does he say anything like this: "Socrates, in my view right conduct is . . ." or "My account of right conduct is this. . . ." Cephalus never explicitly *generalizes* about right conduct — that is, he never tries to state what right conduct *is*, to define the term. All he says is that he expects to die content because he has not "lied to or deceived anyone even unwillingly" and does not owe "either sacrifices to a god or money to a man" (paragraph 3).

Does this mean that your paper assignment has been badly formulated or that it involves a trick question because there really is no such thing as "Cephalus's view of right conduct"? No. Rather, Socrates has inferred Cephalus's definition of right conduct from Cephalus's remarks about the benefits of a "just and pious life" (paragraph 2). Socrates concludes that, given what Cephalus has said, he *must* believe that "justice or right is simply to speak the truth and to pay back any debt one may have contracted" (paragraph 4).

So far so good. By closely rereading the text in light of the assignment, you have discovered something: Socrates, not Cephalus, formulates the definition of right conduct that purports to express Cephalus's view. In your paper you will have to treat this as "Cephalus's view of right conduct" — whether Cephalus would approve or not!

Now, another question might occur to you: Is Socrates being fair to Cephalus to infer what he has from Cephalus's comments? He isn't being fair, you might think, to the extent that you believe Cephalus has spoken somewhat in haste. After further reflection, Cephalus might have preferred to express his views some other way. Or you might think that Cephalus is telling Socrates only what he believes right conduct is for *him*, not for everyone. Or, alternatively, you might well believe that Socrates *is* treating Cephalus fairly, since what Cephalus has said, if it is to be taken seriously, invites just the kind of inference that Socrates makes.

Though further questions such as these are thought-provoking, they are not directly relevant to the assignment; thus, you probably would not want to address them in your essay. Knowing when to leave out irrelevant ideas — even if they are good ones — is an important part of your job.

Socrates's objection. Now you are ready to address the next part of the paper topic, Socrates's objection to Cephalus's view. You can see immediately that this objection consists of a *counterexample* that challenges Cephalus's account of justice and shows him that there is a *contradiction* in his professed beliefs. To see Socrates's objection more clearly, it would help you to restate his argument step by step. (For more advice on evaluating and restating arguments, see chapter 3.)

As a first step in restating Socrates's argument, you would identify its *conclusion*: Cephalus has contradicted himself, according to Socrates, because he believes that right conduct is paying one's debts and never deceiving others, yet he also agrees that it would be wrong to return a weapon to its owner if the owner became insane. Then — and this is the hard part — you would have to identify the assumptions on which Socrates relies and without which he doesn't have a rigorous or conclusive argument. Here's what Socrates's reconstructed argument might look like:

(1) Cephalus believes that <u>right</u> conduct is essentially paying your debts and never intentionally deceiving anyone.

(2) However, Cephalus also agrees that it would be <u>wrong</u> (because it is too dangerous) to return a weapon to its owner if the owner is insane when he asks for it.

(3) But to be consistent with (1), Cephalus ought to believe that it is right to return the weapon to its owner.

(4) Now, the same act (such as returning a weapon to its owner) cannot be both <u>right</u> and <u>wrong</u> at the same time; that would be a <u>contradiction</u>.

(5) Nevertheless, Cephalus does believe both (1) and (2) --and so he appears to have contradicted himself.

Notice how the statement of Cephalus's self-contradiction, step 5, relies on step 4 — a proposition neither Cephalus nor Socrates explicitly asserts. Yet this step is crucial; if you do not *think* of this step, you cannot believe that Socrates's counterexample has really challenged Cephalus's account. Furthermore, if you think of step 4 but do not *believe* it — if you think it is possible for a given act to be both right and wrong at the same time — then, again, you cannot believe that Socrates has pointed out a real problem in Cephalus's definition of justice. (Although it is not directly relevant to your paper topic, you might well wonder whether, in general, a proposition such as step 4 is true. Is it really true that a given act cannot be both right and wrong at the same time? And if it is true, why is it true?)

What has Socrates proved? Now for the last and most challenging part of the assignment: What does the incompatibility in Cephalus's beliefs show or prove? Specifically, does it show that one of his beliefs must be false? That is, if Socrates has shown that Cephalus believes it would be wrong to return a weapon to a madman, which is inconsistent with Cephalus's prior definition of right conduct, has Socrates disproved that definition?

We may be inclined to think that he has if we believe that it would be wrong to return the weapon to a madman. In effect, we might reason, "If I accept the counterexample, and I do, and if Cephalus's definition and the counterexample are logically inconsistent, and they are, then I must give up my belief in Cephalus's definition because it must be false." (Such inconsistency is not troubling to everyone. The poet Walt Whitman once made the memorable remark "Do I contradict myself? Very well then I contradict myself. . . . I contain multitudes.")

Nevertheless, we are not forced to infer that Cephalus's definition is false because we cannot claim to *know* that the counterexample is an example of right conduct (though it certainly seems to be). Pure logic allows us to say no more than this: If someone holds two beliefs, one of which contradicts the other, then *one* of the beliefs *must* be false. *Which* one is false can be determined only by further analysis.

This is crucial to understanding the outcome of the exchange between Socrates and Cephalus. Socrates has successfully shown that Cephalus holds contradictory beliefs about right conduct; thus, Cephalus cannot reasonably claim to know what right conduct is. But Socrates has *not* shown that right conduct is something other than paying our debts and never deceiving others. In short, proving that two of Cephalus's beliefs are logically incompatible is enough to prove that Cephalus contradicts himself, but it is not enough to prove that any particular one of his beliefs — especially his view of right conduct — is false.

This conclusion might be your thesis, the particular stand that you take on the paper topic (see p. 109). Though the thesis frequently appears at the beginning of a paper, it is sometimes more effectively presented later, after you have carefully prepared readers for your position by using evidence and examples from the text. The student who wrote the following paper decided to use the latter strategy.

Sample Student Essay

Cephalus's Self-Contradiction

by

Stacey Schmidt

In Book 1 of Plato's <u>Republic,</u> there is a brief argument between Cephalus and Socrates regarding justice and right conduct. Cephalus says he believes he has led a just life because he never "lied to or deceived anyone even unwillingly," and he does not

owe "either sacrifices to a god or money to a man."
Socrates sums this up into the view that, according
to Cephalus, one is just if and only if he is truthful and pays his debts; and he treats this as a
statement of what Cephalus believes to be the nature
of justice and right conduct.

Socrates then objects to this generalization and
offers a hypothetical counterexample. Suppose, he
says, a friend asks Cephalus to look after his weapons. The friend later returns to collect them, but
the friend is now insane. Socrates says that "everyone would surely agree" that it would not be right to
return the weapons to the insane man, presumably
because he might use them irrationally. For the same
reason, Cephalus ought not to tell the insane man the
"whole truth," in this case perhaps making up a reason why the weapons cannot be returned.

Cephalus agrees with Socrates's objection but is
never given the chance to say whether the definition
he is credited with really expresses what he believes
to be the correct definition of right conduct. However, for the purpose of this essay let us accept the
definition as Cephalus's position. On this assumption, it seems that Socrates does not prove that
Cephalus's definition is wrong.

Socrates's objection, based on his
counterexample of the insane man, proves there is a
contradiction in Cephalus's beliefs. But that is all
it proves. Socrates has not shown that his
counterexample to Cephalus's idea of right conduct is
correct. All he has done is to rely on what "everyone would surely agree." But everyone could be wrong;
the fact (if it is a fact) that everyone holds the
same opinion on a matter of this sort is no proof
that the opinion is true.

So what has come out of the argument between
Socrates and Cephalus? Not very much. We are no
closer to knowing the nature of justice and right

```
conduct than when we started. We know only that
Cephalus has contradicted himself, that he doesn't
seem very interested in straightening out his beliefs
to avoid this contradiction, and that most people
would think it wrong in certain circumstances to
"tell the whole truth" and to "pay back any debt one
. . . [has] contracted."
```

Discussion   Schmidt addresses all three parts of the assignment (p. 83), and her summary of the text would convince most readers that she understands what Plato has written. (Note, too, that she is able to step back from the text and point out that Socrates, not Cephalus, frames Cephalus's view of right conduct as a definition.) What about the third and most important part of the assignment? Stacey devotes three paragraphs (including her closing paragraph, which contains the thesis) to this important question, and what she writes is clear and correct. She seems to have fully grasped the basic logical point needed to assess the force of Socrates's counterexample: Proving that someone holds inconsistent beliefs does not show *which* of those beliefs is false. So she answers the key question in the assignment, and she answers it correctly.

The paper is well written and logically structured, and it follows conventions of grammar, diction, punctuation, spelling, and use of quotations. Could its content be improved? Perhaps the first two paragraphs could be condensed, leaving a bit more room for more detail on the third part of the assignment. That's the only part of the paper worth developing at greater length, since the analysis of self-contradiction is the most philosophically interesting aspect of the assignment. (It could be argued that an important challenge in this assignment is covering the third part adequately within the length limit.) You might want to review the preliminary discussion (pp. 84–87) to see if you can point out other strengths or weaknesses in the paper.

EXERCISE 10: Writing an Essay on Divergent Views of Criteria and Evidence

For the previous assignment, writing an essay on a definition and a counterexample, we went step by step through the process of thinking and writing about the topic, from breaking down and analyzing its separate parts to forming the thesis that would guide the essay. For the next and most challenging writing exercise in this book, try to go through this process on your own and write an essay on the excerpts by René Descartes and Alan M. Turing reprinted here. This is the assignment:

From Turing's argument in "Computing Machinery and Intelligence" and Descartes's remarks in his *Discourse on Method,* it appears that the two writers disagree over whether any machine or artifact can think. In a 1,000 to 1,500-word essay (four to six double-spaced, typed pages), explain exactly where their disagreement lies and which philosopher you think has the better argument.

After reading the excerpts, you should review the eight-step sequence described at the beginning of this chapter (see pp. 79–82) to help you complete the assignment. When you have finished your essay, compare it with the sample student paper that begins on page 100.

Introduction   The following excerpts, both from classics in philosophy, were written some three centuries apart. The first is from *Discourse on Method* (1636) by René Descartes (1596–1650), in the translation by E. S. Haldane and G. R. T. Ross; the second is from "Computing Machinery and Intelligence" (1950) by the English mathematical logician Alan M. Turing (1912–1954). Descartes and Turing address perennial philosophical questions: What is consciousness, and is it unique to humans?

Descartes is famously associated with the belief that human *minds* are distinct from (although causally interactive with) human *bodies.* Further, he argued, lesser creatures — household pets and animals generally, including porpoises, whales, and the like — have no mental life, or at least no mental life remotely like ours; in particular, they lack consciousness and self-consciousness. To put the point bluntly another way: We are *persons*, and they are not.

By Descartes's day, skilled craftsmen in many parts of Europe had been able to fabricate intricate clocklike mechanisms that could be fitted inside puppets or figurines. Such mechanical puppets, when viewed from a distance, might be mistaken for humans. These figures can be seen even today in the clock towers of many European cities, for example in Munich, the capital of Bavaria, and in Prague, the capital of Bohemia. On the chiming of each hour, half a dozen or so figures, clothed and painted to resemble humans, emerge from a little door to the side of the large clock. They march out single file around a semicircular track, playing tiny musical instruments or waving symbols of their craft or trade, and then disappear through another door — until the next hour, when they repeat their performance.

Whether inspired by such figures or by something else, Descartes was led to ask the following question: How can we tell — indeed, *can* we always tell — whether what appears to be a human is just an artifact cleverly designed to mimic human behavior or whether it is indeed a person with an inner conscious life whose actions are typically governed by conscious intentions and deliberation? Descartes believed he had an answer to this question, and he stated it in a succinct passage near the end of his *Discourse,* his first philosophical treatise — and a text of enormous influence in its day. In this passage he offers two criteria he believes all and only humans can satisfy.

Following the excerpt from Descartes are selected excerpts from Turing's essay, published only a few years into the computer era and before the concept of "artificial intelligence" was in vogue. Although Descartes goes unmentioned in the essay, Turing in effect directly challenges Descartes's argument by means of an ingenious proposal he calls "the imitation game." Turing's essay has become a modern classic and has had enormous influence.

If you were assigned to read these texts from Descartes and Turing with the expectation that you would write a short essay based on them, your instructor would certainly have helped prepare you for the material through lectures or class discussion, since there is much to think about in what these two philosophers have written. Indeed, in recent years whole books have been devoted to discussing the implications of their views. For example, Hubert L. Dreyfus, in *What Computers Still Can't Do* (1991), and John R. Searle, in *Minds, Brains, and Science* (1984), argue for a version of Descartes's views, and Daniel C. Dennett argues for a version of Turing's views in *The Intentional Stance* (1987) and in *Consciousness Explained* (1992).

RENÉ DESCARTES
from *Discourse on the Method of Rightly Conducting the Reason*

If there were machines which bore a resemblance to our body 1
and imitated our actions as far as it was morally possible to do so, we should always have two very certain tests by which to recognize that, for all that, they were not real men. The first is, that they could never use speech or other signs as we do when placing our thoughts on record for the benefit of others. For we can easily understand a machine's being constituted so that it can utter words, and even emit some responses to action on it of a corporeal kind, which brings about a change in its organs; for instance, if it is touched in a particular part it may ask what we wish to say to it; if in another part it may exclaim that it is being hurt, and so on. But it never happens that it arranges its speech in various ways, in order to reply appro-

René Descartes has been rightly described as "the chief architect of the seventeenth-century intellectual revolution" that dethroned medieval Scholasticism and laid the basis for modern science. Although educated by the Jesuits, Descartes discarded the metaphysics and epistemology they taught him. He suppressed his first book, on physics and cosmology, when he learned of Galileo's ordeal before the Inquisition, lest he suffer the same fate. His collected writings in French and Latin fill fourteen large volumes. Descartes's philosophical views are best presented in three books: *Discourse on Method* (1637), *Meditations on First Philosophy* (1641), and *Principles of Philosophy* (1644). Descartes did not limit his interests to science and philosophy; his legacy includes analytic geometry, and what we know as "Cartesian coordinates," which prefaced calculus, invented a few decades after Descartes's death by Isaac Newton (1642–1727) and Gottfried Leibniz (1646–1716).

priately to everything that may be said in its presence, as even the lowest type of man can do. And the second difference is, that although machines can perform certain things as well as or perhaps better than any of us can do, they infallibly fall short in others, by which means we may discover that they did not act from knowledge, but only from the disposition of their organs. For while reason is a universal instrument which can serve for all contingencies, these organs have need of some special adaptation for every particular action. From this it follows that it is morally impossible that there should be sufficient diversity in any machine to allow it to act in all the events of life in the same way as our reason causes us to act.

By these two methods we may also recognize the difference that 2 exists between men and brutes. For it is a very remarkable fact that there are none so depraved and stupid, without even excepting idiots, that they cannot arrange different words together, forming of them a statement by which they make known their thoughts; while, on the other hand, there is no other animal, however perfect and fortunately circumstanced it may be, which can do the same. It is not the want of organs that brings this to pass, for it is evident that magpies and parrots are able to utter words just like ourselves, and yet they cannot speak as we do, that is, so as to give evidence that they think of what they say. On the other hand, men who, being born deaf and dumb, are in the same degree, or even more than the brutes, destitute of the organs which serve the others for talking, are in the habit of themselves inventing certain signs by which they make themselves understood by those who, being usually in their company, have leisure to learn their language. And this does not merely show that the brutes have less reason than men, but that they have none at all, since it is clear that very little is required in order to be able to talk. And when we notice the inequality that exists between animals of the same species, as well as between men, and observe that some are more capable of receiving instruction than others, it is not credible that a monkey or a parrot, selected as the most perfect of its species, should not in these matters equal the stupidest child to be found, or at least a child whose mind is clouded, unless in the case of the brute the soul were of an entirely different nature from ours. And we ought not to confound speech with natural movements which betray passions and may be imitated by machines as well as be manifested by animals; nor must we think, as did some of the ancients, that brutes talk, although we do not understand their language. For if this were true, since they have many organs which are allied to our own, they could communicate their thoughts to us just as easily as to those of their own race. It is also a very remarkable fact that although there are many animals which exhibit more dexterity than we do in some of their actions, we at the same time observe that they do not manifest any dexterity at all in many others. Hence the fact that they do better than we do, does not prove that they are endowed with mind, for in this case they would have more reason than any of us, and would surpass us in all other things. It rather shows that they have no reason at all, and that it is nature which acts in them according to the disposition of their organs, just as a clock, which is only composed of wheels and weights is able to tell the hours and measure the time more correctly than we can do with all our wisdom.

ALAN M. TURING
from *Computing Machinery and Intelligence*

THE IMITATION GAME

I propose to consider the question, "Can machines think?" This 1 should begin with definitions of the meaning of the terms "machine" and "think." The definitions might be framed so as to reflect so far as possible the normal use of the words, but this attitude is dangerous. If the meaning of the words "machine" and "think" are to be found by examining how they are commonly used it is difficult to escape the conclusion that the meaning and the answer to the question, "Can machines think?" is to be sought in a statistical survey such as a Gallup poll. But this is absurd. Instead of attempting such a definition I shall replace the question by another, which is closely related to it and is expressed in relatively unambiguous words.

The new form of the problem can be described in terms of a 2 game which we call the "imitation game." It is played with three people, a man (A), a woman (B), and an interrogator (C) who may be of either sex. The interrogator stays in a room apart from the other two. The object of the game for the interrogator is to determine which of the other two is the man and which is the woman. He knows them by labels X and Y, and at the end of the game he says either "X is A and Y is B" or "X is B and Y is A." The interrogator is allowed to put questions to A and B thus:

C: Will X please tell me the length of his or her hair?

Now suppose X is actually A, then A must answer. It is A's object in the game to try and cause C to make the wrong identification. His answer might therefore be:

Alan Turing, a precocious mathematician and logician, was educated at Cambridge where he received his Ph.D. in 1938 and was elected a Fellow of the Royal Society in 1951. Prior to World War II, he worked to restate the logical discoveries of Kurt Gödel and Alonzo Church in terms that a digital computer could "understand." When the war came, he joined the high-powered team of cryptographers and cryptanalysts that assembled at Bletchley Park in Buckinghamshire and succeeded in breaking the code of the German "Enigma" machine. After the war he invented what came to be called the Turing machine; he also is the father of the Turing test, a thought experiment designed to test whether "machines" can "think." This test, called the Imitation Game, is an excerpt from his pioneering 1950 paper, "Computing Machinery and Intelligence," reprinted here.

"My hair is shingled, and the longest strands are about nine inches long."

In order that tones of voice may not help the interrogator the 3 answers should be written, or better still, typewritten. The ideal arrangement is to have a teleprinter communicating between the two rooms. Alternatively the questions and answers can be repeated by an intermediary. The object of the game for the third player (B) is to help the interrogator. The best strategy for her is probably to give truthful answers. She can add such things as "I am the woman, don't listen to him!" to her answers, but it will avail nothing as the man can make similar remarks.

We now ask the question, "What will happen when a machine 4 takes the part of A in this game?" Will the interrogator decide wrongly as often when the game is played like this as he does when the game is played between a man and a woman? These questions replace our original, "Can machines think?" . . .

THE MACHINES CONCERNED IN THE GAME

The question which we put [in the previous section] will not be 5 quite definite until we have specified what we mean by the word "machine." . . . The present interest in "thinking machines" has been aroused by a particular kind of machine, usually called an "electronic computer" or "digital computer." Following this suggestion we only permit digital computers to take part in our game. . . .

There are already a number of digital computers in working 6 order, and it may be asked, "Why not try the experiment straight away? It would be easy to satisfy the conditions of the game. A number of interrogators could be used, and statistics compiled to show how often the right identification was given." The short answer is that we are not asking whether all digital computers would do well in the game nor whether the computers at present available would do well, but whether there are imaginable computers which would do well. But this is only the short answer. We shall see this question in a different light later.

DIGITAL COMPUTERS

. . . The idea of a digital computer is an old one. Charles Babbage, 7 Lucasian Professor of Mathematics at Cambridge from 1828 to 1839, planned such a machine, called the Analytical Engine, but it was never completed. Although Babbage had all the essential ideas, his machine was not at that time such a very attractive prospect. The speed which would have been available would be definitely faster than a human computer but something like 100 times slower than the Manchester machine,[1] itself one of the slower of the modern

---

1. A computing machine used in the late 1940s at Manchester University in England. [Ed.]

machines. The storage was to be purely mechanical, using wheels and cards. . . .

CONTRARY VIEWS ON THE MAIN QUESTION

We may now consider the ground to have been cleared and we   8 are ready to proceed to the debate on our question, "Can machines think?" . . . We cannot altogether abandon the original form of the problem, for opinions will differ as to the appropriateness of the substitution and we must at least listen to what has to be said in this connection.

It will simplify matters for the reader if I explain first my own   9 beliefs in the matter. Consider first the more accurate form of the question. I believe that in about fifty years' time it will be possible to program computers, with a storage capacity of about 10^9, to make them play the imitation game so well that an average interrogator will not have more than 70 percent chance of making the right identification after five minutes of questioning. The original question, "Can machines think?" I believe to be too meaningless to deserve discussion. Nevertheless I believe that at the end of the century the use of words and general educated opinion will have altered so much that one will be able to speak of machines thinking without expecting to be contradicted. I believe further that no useful purpose is served by concealing these beliefs. The popular view that scientists proceed inexorably from well-established fact to well-established fact, never being influenced by any improved conjecture, is quite mistaken. Provided it is made clear which are proved facts and which are conjectures, no harm can result. Conjectures are of great importance since they suggest useful lines of research.

I now proceed to consider opinions opposed to my own. . . .   10

The Argument from Consciousness

This argument is very well expressed in Professor Jefferson's   11 Lister Oration for 1949, from which I quote.

> Not until a machine can write a sonnet or compose a concerto because of thoughts and emotions felt, and not by the chance fall of symbols, could we agree that machine equals brain — that is, not only write it but know that it had written it. No mechanism could feel (and not merely artificially signal, an easy contrivance) pleasure at its successes, grief when its valves fuse, be warmed by flattery, be made miserable by its mistakes, be charmed by sex, be angry or depressed when it cannot get what it wants.

This argument appears to be a denial of the validity of our test.   12 According to the most extreme form of this view the only way by which one could be sure that a machine thinks is to *be* the machine and to feel oneself thinking. One could then describe these feelings to the world, but of course no one would be justified in taking any notice. Likewise according to this view the only way to know that a *man* thinks is to be that particular man. It is in fact the solipsist point of view. It may be the most logical view to hold but it makes communication of ideas difficult. A is liable to believe "A thinks but B does not" whilst B believes "B thinks but A does not." Instead of arguing continually over this point it is usual to have the polite convention that everyone thinks.

I am sure that Professor Jefferson does not wish to adopt the 13 extreme and solipsist point of view. Probably he would be quite willing to accept the imitation game as a test. The game (with the player B omitted) is frequently used in practice under the name of viva voce[2] to discover whether someone really understands something or has "learnt it parrot fashion." Let us listen in to a part of such a viva voce:

> *Interrogator:* In the first line of your sonnet which reads "Shall I compare thee to a summer's day," would not "a spring day" do as well or better?
> *Witness:* It wouldn't scan.
> *Interrogator:* How about "a winter's day." That would scan all right.
> *Witness:* Yes, but nobody wants to be compared to a winter's day.
> *Interrogator:* Would you say Mr. Pickwick reminded you of Christmas?
> *Witness:* In a way.
> *Interrogator:* Yet Christmas is a winter's day, and I do not think Mr. Pickwick would mind the comparison.
> *Witness:* I don't think you're serious. By a winter's day one means a typical winter's day, rather than a special one like Christmas.

And so on. What would Professor Jefferson say if the sonnet- 14 writing machine was able to answer like this in the viva voce? I do not know whether he would regard the machine as "merely artificially signaling" these answers, but if the answers were as satisfactory and sustained as in the above passage I do not think he would describe it as "an easy contrivance." This phrase is, I think, intended to cover such devices as the inclusion in the machine of a record of someone reading a sonnet, with appropriate switching to turn it on from time to time. . . .

I do not wish to give the impression that I think there is no 15 mystery about consciousness. There is, for instance, something of a paradox connected with any attempt to localize it. But I do not think these mysteries necessarily need to be solved before we can answer the question with which we are concerned in this paper.

Arguments from Various Disabilities

These arguments take the form "I grant you that you can make 16 machines do all the things you have mentioned but you will never be able to make one to do X." Numerous features X are suggested in this connection. I offer a selection:

Be kind, resourceful, beautiful, friendly, have initiative, have a 17 sense of humor, tell right from wrong, make mistakes, fall in love, enjoy strawberries and cream, make someone fall in love with it,

2. By word of mouth; that is, an oral examination. [Ed.]

learn from experience, use words properly, be the subject of its own thought, have as much diversity of behavior as a man, do something really new.

No support is usually offered for these statements. I believe they 18 are mostly founded on the principle of scientific induction. A man has seen thousands of machines in his lifetime. From what he sees of them he draws a number of general conclusions. They are ugly, each is designed for a very limited purpose, when required for a minutely different purpose they are useless, the variety of behavior of any one of them is very small, etc., etc. Naturally he concludes that these are necessary properties of machines in general. Many of these limitations are associated with the very small storage capacity of most machines. (I am assuming that the idea of storage capacity is extended in some way to cover machines other than discrete-state machines. The exact definition does not matter as no mathematical accuracy is claimed in the present discussion.) A few years ago, when very little had been heard of digital computers, it was possible to elicit much incredulity concerning them, if one mentioned their properties without describing their construction. That was presumably due to a similar application of the principle of scientific induction. These applications of the principle are of course largely unconscious. When a burnt child fears the fire and shows that he fears it by avoiding it, I should say that he was applying scientific induction. (I could of course also describe his behavior in many other ways.) The works and customs of mankind do not seem to be very suitable material to which to apply scientific induction. A very large part of space-time must be investigated, if reliable results are to be obtained. Otherwise we may (as most English children do) decide that everybody speaks English, and that it is silly to learn French.

There are, however, special remarks to be made about many of 19 the disabilities that have been mentioned. The inability to enjoy strawberries and cream may have struck the reader as frivolous. Possibly a machine might be made to enjoy this delicious dish, but any attempt to make one do so would be idiotic. What is important about this disability is that it contributes to some of the other disabilities, e.g., to the difficulty of the same kind of friendliness occurring between man and machine as between white man and white man, or between black man and black man.

The claim that "machines cannot make mistakes" seems a curi- 20 ous one. One is tempted to retort, "Are they any the worse for that?" But let us adopt a more sympathetic attitude, and try to see what is really meant. I think this criticism can be explained in terms of the imitation game. It is claimed that the interrogator could distinguish the machine from the man simply by setting them a number of problems in arithmetic. The machine would be unmasked because of its deadly accuracy. The reply to this is simple. The machine (programmed for playing the game) would not attempt to give the *right* answers to the arithmetic problems. It would deliberately introduce mistakes in a manner calculated to confuse the interrogator. A mechanical fault would probably show itself through an unsuitable decision as to what sort of a mistake to make in the arithmetic. Even this interpretation of the criticism is not sufficiently sympathetic. But we cannot afford the space to go into it much further. It seems to me that this criticism depends on a confusion between two kinds of mistake. We may call them "errors of functioning" and "errors of conclusion." Errors of functioning are due to some mechanical or electrical fault which causes the machine to behave otherwise than it was designed to do. In philosophical discussions one likes to ignore the possibility of such errors; one is therefore discussing "abstract machines." These abstract machines are mathematical fictions rather than physical objects. By definition they are incapable of errors of functioning. In this sense we can truly say that "machines can never make mistakes." Errors of conclusion can only arise when some meaning is attached to the output signals from the machine. The machine might, for instance, type out mathematical equations, or sentences in English. When a false proposition is typed we say that the machine has committed an error of conclusion. There is clearly no reason at all for saying that a machine cannot make this kind of mistake. It might do nothing but type out repeatedly "0 = 1." To take a less perverse example, it might have some method for drawing conclusions by scientific induction. We must expect such a method to lead occasionally to erroneous results.

The claim that a machine cannot be the subject of its own thought can of course only be answered if it can be shown that the machine has *some* thought with *some* subject matter. Nevertheless, "the subject matter of a machine's operations" does seem to mean something, at least to the people who deal with it. If, for instance, the machine was trying to find a solution of the equation $x^2 - 40x - 11 = 0$ one would be tempted to describe this equation as part of the machine's subject matter at that moment. In this sort of sense a machine undoubtedly can be its own subject-matter. It may be used to help in making up its own programs, or to predict the effect of alterations in its own structure. By observing the results of its own behavior it can modify its own programs so as to achieve some purpose more effectively. These are possibilities of the near future, rather than Utopian dreams. 21

Lady Lovelace's Objection

Our most detailed information of Babbage's Analytical Engine comes from a memoir by Lady Lovelace (1842). In it she states, "The Analytical Engine has no pretensions to *originate* anything. It can do *whatever we know how to order it* to perform" (her italics). This statement is quoted by Hartree (1949) who adds: 22

> This does not imply that it may not be possible to construct electronic equipment which will "think for itself," or in which, in biological terms, one could set up a conditioned reflex, which would serve as a basis for "learning." Whether this is possible in principle or not is a stimulating and exciting question, suggested by some of these recent developments. But it did not seem that the machines constructed or projected at the time had this property.

I am in thorough agreement with Hartree over this. . . . 23

A variant of Lady Lovelace's objection states that a machine can 24 "never do anything really new." This may be parried for a moment with the saw, "There is nothing new under the sun." Who can be certain that "original work" that he has done was not simply the growth of the seed planted in him by teaching, or the effect of following well-known general principles. A better variant of the objection says that a machine can never "take us by surprise." This statement is a more direct challenge and can be met directly. Machines take me by surprise with great frequency. This is largely because I do not do sufficient calculation to decide what to expect them to do, or rather because, although I do a calculation, I do it in a hurried, slipshod fashion, taking risks. Perhaps I say to myself, "I suppose the voltage here ought to be the same as there: anyway let's assume it is." Naturally I am often wrong, and the result is a surprise for me for by the time the experiment is done these assumptions have been forgotten. These admissions lay me open to lectures on the subject of my vicious ways, but do not throw any doubt on my credibility when I testify to the surprises I experience.

I do not expect this reply to silence my critic. He will probably 25 say that such surprises are due to some creative mental act on my part, and reflect no credit on the machine. This leads us back to the argument from consciousness, and far from the idea of surprise. It is a line of argument we must consider closed, but it is perhaps worth remarking that the appreciation of something as surprising requires as much of a "creative mental act" whether the surprising event originates from a man, a book, a machine, or anything else.

The view that machines cannot give rise to surprises is due, I 26 believe, to a fallacy to which philosophers and mathematicians are particularly subject. This is the assumption that as soon as a fact is presented to a mind all consequences of that fact spring into the mind simultaneously with it. It is a very useful assumption under many circumstances, but one too easily forgets that it is false. A natural consequence of doing so is that one then assumes that there is no virtue in the mere working out of consequences from data and general principles. . . .

The Argument from Informality of Behavior

It is not possible to produce a set of rules purporting to describe 27 what a man should do in every conceivable set of circumstances. One might for instance have a rule that one is to stop when one sees a red traffic light, and to go if one sees a green one, but what if by some fault both appear together? One may perhaps decide that it is safest to stop. But some further difficulty may well arise from this decision later. To attempt to provide rules of conduct to cover every eventuality, even those arising from traffic lights, appears to be impossible. With all this I agree.

From this it is argued that we cannot be machines. I shall try to 28 reproduce the argument, but I fear I shall hardly do it justice. It seems to run something like this. "If each man had a definite set of rules of conduct by which he regulated his life he would be no better than a machine. But there are no such rules, so men cannot be machines." The undistributed middle is glaring. I do not think the argument is ever put quite like this, but I believe this is the argument used nevertheless. There may however be a certain confusion between "rules of conduct" and "laws of behavior" to cloud the issue. By "rules of conduct" I mean precepts such as "Stop if you see red lights," on which one can act, and of which one can be conscious. By "laws of behavior" I mean laws of nature as applied to a man's body such as "if you pinch him he will squeak." If we substitute "laws of behavior which regulate his life" for "laws of conduct by which he regulates his life" in the argument quoted the undistributed middle is no longer insuperable. For we believe that it is not only true that being regulated by laws of behavior implies being some sort of machine (though not necessarily a discrete-state machine), but that conversely being such a machine implies being regulated by such laws. However, we cannot so easily convince ourselves of the absence of complete laws of behavior as of complete rules of conduct. The only way we know of for finding such laws is scientific observation, and we certainly know of no circumstances under which we could say, "We have searched enough. There are no such laws." . . .

We may hope that machines will eventually compete with men 29 in all purely intellectual fields. But which are the best ones to start with? Even this is a difficult decision. Many people think that a very abstract activity, like the playing of chess, would be best. It can also be maintained that it is best to provide the machine with the best sense organs that money can buy, and then teach it to understand and speak English. This process could follow the normal teaching of a child. Things would be pointed out and named, etc. Again I do not know what the right answer is; but I think both approaches should be tried.

We can only see a short distance ahead, but we can see plenty 30 there that needs to be done.

Sample Student Essay

Can Machines Think? Turing vs. Descartes

by

Ellen Wheeler

René Descartes and Alan M. Turing disagree over whether machines can be distinguished from humans and over the criteria by which the issue can be decided, if at all. In this paper I will explicate Descartes's argument in his <u>Discourse</u> and Turing's

argument in his essay "Computing Machinery and Intelligence." I will discuss the "contrary views" to
Turing's argument that are most relevant to the criteria proposed by Descartes: "Lady Lovelace's Objection," "Arguments from Various Disabilities," "The
Argument from Informality of Behavior," and "The
Argument from Consciousness." I intend to show that
although Descartes may have been correct in light of
the evidence available to him that machines were
distinguishable from humans, Turing's responses to
these objections show that his argument to the contrary is stronger.

In the Discourse, Descartes maintains that there
are two criteria by which the human mind and its
ability to reason can be distinguished from mere
animals or machines. First, he grants that a machine
could be "constituted" so that it could in some sense
"speak"; brutes have less reason than we do yet they
can speak, so "very little is required in order to be
able to talk" (para. 2). However, he argues that a
machine "could never use speech or other signs as we
do . . . in order to reply appropriately to everything that may be said in its presence, as even the
lowest type of man can do" (para. 1). In other
words, for Descartes, even if machines could communicate as humans can, they could never be programmed in
such a way that they could respond to humans "appropriately" in every circumstance.

Second, Descartes argues that machines "infallibly fall short" of being able to perform at least
some things as well as we do, and therefore machines
do not "act from knowledge, but only from the disposition of their organs" (para. 1). In other words, a
machine's program will never be sufficiently diverse
to "allow it to act in all events of life in the same
way as our reason causes us to act" (para. 1).
Descartes further asserts that mere physical abilities do not constitute intelligence, for there are

many animals that are more dexterous than many humans.

Turing challenges the claim that machines, in particular computing machines, can always be distinguished from human minds by proposing the "imitation game." The imitation game uses two players, a computing machine and a human, plus an interrogator. The interrogator asks the two players, A and B, a series of questions and tries to tell from their answers whether A or B is the human and B or A the machine. All three participants are separated and they communicate via a "teleprinter"--that is, a computer keyboard (and a screen). Turing's argument is not concerned with possible differences between the processes inside the computer and what we refer to as "human thinking" inside our heads. He argues that it is conceivable to imagine a computing machine, specifically a digital computer with "adequate storage capacity," to be so programmed that its responses to the interrogator could not be distinguished by the interrogator from the responses of the human being. Thus, by using the imitation game, Turing <u>replaces</u> the question "Can machines think?" with a new question, "Can a computer satisfactorily play the imitation game?" (para. 8).

The objection "from various disabilities" states that while machines may have been proved to do some things, they will never be able to do "something really new" (para. 17). Turing argues that this view is a result of "scientific induction" from the observed behavior of existing machines and that these machines have "very small storage capacity" (para. 18) (and they did, in 1950). He suggests that were there machines with "adequate" storage capacity, this objection would not hold. Another objection states that machines cannot make mistakes and therefore could be distinguished from humans by their accuracy. Turing separates errors of "functioning" and errors of "conclusion" and explains that the former are mechanical errors that cannot occur in the "abstract" (that is, in the imaginary and perfect) machines of Turing's argument (para. 20). The latter errors "can only arise when some meaning is attached to the output signals from the machine," and any machine can be programmed to make such errors to confuse the interrogator in the imitation game (para. 20).

Turing also addresses in effect Descartes's second criterion, that machine behavior can never be diverse enough to resemble human behavior, which reflects human reason. In his response to the "argument from informality of behavior," which states that "it is not possible to produce a set of rules purporting to describe what a man should do in every conceivable set of circumstances," Turing reformulates the objection to read: "If each man had a definite set of rules of conduct by which he regulated his life he would be no better than a machine. But there are no such rules, so men cannot be machines." But, as Turing points out, this argument is invalid. Although he admits that it seems "impossible" to provide "rules of conduct to cover every eventuality" in human behavior, perhaps "complete laws of behavior" do exist and might be discovered. Thus, it does not follow from our current inability to predict human behavior, due perhaps to our lack of adequate scientific investigation, that humans are not really well-regulated machines. Besides, he argues, we know that computers are machines, yet he denies that we can always predict what they will do (paras. 23–24).

So how can we decide whether a person or a machine "really understands something or has 'learnt it parrot fashion'" (para. 13)? Here Turing confronts the "argument from consciousness." Turing admits he is interested not in solving the "mysteries of consciousness," but only in persuading us that appropriate verbal behavior by a computing machine should be enough. If the machine could provide "satisfactory and sustained" answers so that the human interrogator could not tell whether he was talking to a machine or to a human, then that ought to be sufficient.

In light of the times in which they lived, Descartes and Turing had very different evidence available to them for what constitutes a "machine." For Descartes, a machine program was no more than the way the various wheels and gears of a clock were set. Computing machines today, fifty years after Turing wrote his essay, come much closer to his idea of a machine that can "think" than anything Descartes or Lady Lovelace ever imagined.

Although Turing does not present a convincing positive argument--he replies to various objections and defends the imitation game as a fair test--he does provide a good reason against the view that computing machines cannot play the imitation game. Thus he shows that it is "conceivable" that a machine might one day satisfy both of Descartes's criteria and therefore be indistinguishable from a human (except in irrelevant physical aspects). However, the implications of Turing's argument give rise to many provocative questions. If humans are merely "learning machines," then what is the difference between the mental capacities of humans and the corresponding capacities of computers, if there is a difference at all? Is the imitation game really an adequate test for determining whether there are any such differences?

Discussion   The Descartes-Turing topic is not an easy one; some beginning students may well find it a bit over their heads. And none of the helpful tactics from the eight-step sequence (see pp. 79–82) were discussed in light of this essay. So we will not explore how Wheeler worked out the preliminary stages of her essay. Instead, let's focus on five features of her essay that make it effective.

1. *Title and thesis*. Wheeler addresses a difficult topic fairly and thoroughly. Her title clearly indicates her general topic, though it doesn't indicate where she stands on the matter. (See pp. 125–27 for a discussion of titling papers.) Her stand, however, becomes immediately clear in the opening paragraph, where she states her thesis at the end.

2. *Use of evidence*. Wheeler supports her thesis effectively, using evidence and examples from both texts. Some instructors might criticize Wheeler's essay on the ground that she quotes too frequently from Descartes and Turing and does not devote enough attention to critical evaluation of their views. In her defense, her quotations are well chosen and clearly support her position. Further, the quotations give readers who might be unfamiliar with the texts of Descartes and Turing enough background to understand her argument.

3. *Tone*. The tone of Wheeler's paper is appropriate and fair. She does not condescend to Descartes just because his views are three and a half centuries old and, if judged by today's standards, perhaps inconclusive. Nor is she unduly respectful of Turing, even though she believes that his argument is more convincing than Descartes's. The reader comes away convinced of Wheeler's earnestness and patience, her desire to understand before she criticizes. The result is that the reader is not put off or distracted by her manner and can thus attend to the content of the essay.

4. *Closing paragraph*. Note that Wheeler's closing paragraph points out some undecided questions that arise from the topic, provoking the reader to further thought. She says in effect that although her essay may be finished, the problems it raises are not all solved. Although Wheeler's conclusion doesn't raise especially novel or surprising issues, it does make explicit some questions that might have been brewing in the reader's mind. (See p. 125 for a discussion of concluding paragraphs.)

5. *Mechanics*. As for more mechanical concerns, Wheeler is careful to observe conventions of grammar, punctuation, and spelling, and she integrates quotations properly. The paper's length (about 1,300 words) is well within the limits set by the instructor.

The most important question to ask is how well Wheeler's essay holds up as a piece of philosophical writing. Does she give evidence that she fully grasped both Descartes's position and the precise points at which Turing would disagree? Does she build a convincing case that Turing has the better of the argument? Not everyone will agree about how good her paper is in these respects; even instructors might have different opinions. But you might attempt your own evaluation, just as you might think of ways to improve Wheeler's essay.

5. Drafting and Revising the Philosophical Essay

> Clarity has been said to be not enough: But perhaps it will be time to go into that when we are within measurable distance of achieving clarity on some matter.
>
> — J. L. Austin

The previous chapter presented some general strategies for developing philosophical essays and provided two sample papers to illustrate how such strategies can be applied. In this chapter we will take a closer look at the process of writing philosophical essays, from developing and supporting a thesis to revising completed drafts and preparing papers for submission.

DRAFTING

Using an Outline to Help Construct Your Paper

The eight-step sequence in chapter 4 (see pp. 79–82) discusses techniques for generating thoughtful responses to particular paper topics. How can you ensure that your paper will present those responses logically, coherently, and comprehensively? Consider drawing up an *outline* as you begin drafting your paper. The outline, as discussed in chapters 2 and 4 (see pp. 38–39 and 81), lays bare the structure of an essay: the main idea (or thesis); the points of support for the thesis, with examples and illustrations to support these points; and the conclusion. Drawing up an outline at an early stage can help you organize your thoughts and determine where support for your thesis is thin or where you might be introducing information that doesn't directly address your topic. It also can give you a sense of control over your essay right from the start.

Keep in mind that it's natural — and often productive — to deviate from your outline once you begin writing. You might find yourself expanding on what you thought was a minor point or even introducing a new line of argument. Don't be concerned about this; when writing the first draft, it's best to let your thoughts and ideas flow freely. You can always refine and refocus your paper later.

Of course, starting off with an outline is not the best strategy for everyone. Some writers prefer to plunge right into a first draft, perhaps working from preliminary notes that they have rearranged to suggest a structure for the paper. (This strategy is discussed on p. 84.)

Whether or not you sketch an outline before you begin writing, you might find it helpful to prepare one *after* you have written your first draft. By using the outline to show the structure of your draft, you can see clearly where the organization is illogical or where you don't provide adequate support. You can then revise your paper more effectively.

Remember: It is not enough that your paper *has* a structure: It ought to *show* that structure. You want to write reader-friendly analytic and argumentative prose, and to achieve that end something of your paper's structure must be visible to your readers. True, if the structure is marked too conspicuously and too frequently, readers may become bored or annoyed, because you are overstating the obvious by tediously shoving under their noses too many transitional phrases ("Now I turn to my second point . . . ", "Three examples to illustrate my thesis are, first . . ."). It takes practice and experience to strike the right balance — avoiding excessive notice to readers, while not burying the paper's structure so deeply that readers have to struggle to find it. If you are in doubt, it is better to err on the side of being explicit. Better to say "Now I turn to my second point" than to have readers suddenly wonder what the connection is between what they are now reading and what they have just read.

Now, we'll take a closer look at the three main elements that will be a part of your outline and completed essay: (1) the introduction and thesis, (2) the supporting paragraphs, and (3) the conclusion.

The Opening Paragraph

Every essay, whatever the subject or length, has to begin somewhere. Experienced news reporters and fiction writers know what a vital role their *opening paragraph* plays in arousing their readers' interest and encouraging them to find out how the story unfolds. Students writing critical, analytic, or argumentative papers in philosophy should think of their opening paragraphs in the same way. No other paragraph in your paper is as important as the opening paragraph for "grabbing" readers' interest, and no subsequent paragraph can be as helpful in sketching the territory ahead or focusing attention on your chosen topic. So it's worth the effort to think about the content and structure of this paragraph above all others — and to anticipate that you might need to rework it right up to the final revision of your paper. In fact, in many good essays the final paragraph written is the opening one.

Here, for consideration, is the opening paragraph of chapter 1 of *The Nature of Rationality* (1993) by the American philosopher Robert Nozick (b. 1938):

> What are principles *for?* Why do we hold principles, why do we put them forth, why do we adhere to them? We could instead simply act on whim or the passion of the moment, or we could maximize our own self-interest and recommend that others do the same. Are principles then a constraint upon whim and self-interest, or is adherence to principles a way of advancing self-interest? What functions do principles serve?

By asking these four questions, Nozick not only indicates what is to follow (it will be his answers to these questions) but he engages his readers' interest, encouraging them to consider the role of principles in their conduct.

Here's an example of a very different opening paragraph, from the essay "On Bullshit" (in *The Importance of What We Care About,* 1988) by the American philosopher Harry G. Frankfurt (b. 1929):

> One of the most salient features of our culture is that there is so much bullshit. Everyone knows this. Each of us contributes his share. But we tend to take the situation for granted. Most people are rather confident of their ability to recognize bullshit and to avoid being taken in by it. So the phenomenon has not aroused much deliberate concern, nor attracted much sustained inquiry.

The topic of the essay is clear enough, and the reader is amply forewarned: Bullshit is about to receive an overdue examination. Finally, notice how the brief and direct opening sentences fit the vulgarity of the topic itself. No embellishments or verbal filigree here!

And here is yet another opening paragraph, from "Indispensability and Practice" (1992) by the British philosopher Penelope Maddy (b. 1950):

> For some time now, philosophical thinking about mathematics has been profoundly influenced by arguments based on its application in natural science, the so-called "indispensability arguments." The general idea traces back at least to Gottlob Frege, but contemporary versions stem from the writings of W. V. Quine, and later, Hilary Putnam. Much contemporary philosophy of mathematics (including my own) operates within the parameters of the indispensability arguments; they are called upon to motivate various versions of nominalism, as well as to support various versions of realism. Still, attention to practice, both scientific and mathematical, has recently led me to doubt their efficacy. I shall try to explain these doubts in what follows. If they are legitimate, we will be forced to rethink much of current orthodoxy in the philosophy of mathematics.

This long and difficult paragraph is virtually unintelligible to the uninitiated. Nevertheless, it clearly indicates that the author is going to focus on the adequacy of certain arguments ("indispensability arguments"), which she once accepted herself but about which she now has "doubts." Readers have been told the essentials, enough to arouse or squelch further interest.

Introducing the Topic

By the time readers have finished your opening paragraph, they ought to have a reasonably clear idea about what the *topic* of your paper is. If it's about some issue in Plato, then by all means mention Plato's name. If it's on a topic in ethics, but not epistemology, then make that clear. Don't count on your paper's title to do this job alone; use the initial paragraph as well.

Stating Your Thesis

Think of your opening paragraph as the statement of an implicit criterion by means of which readers can assess the relevance and cogency of the rest of the paper. One sure way to accomplish this purpose is to *know* what your thesis is and then *state* it succinctly — or, if explicit statement strikes you as too obvious and uninteresting, then hint at it. Thus, instead of writing "My thesis is that Socrates in Plato's *Republic*, contrary to what he thinks, fails to refute Thrasymachus," you might write "Does Socrates really succeed in refuting Thrasymachus in Plato's *Republic?* I think not, and I shall try to show why."

Of course, readers of your paper who do not know who Thrasymachus is and what his views in the *Republic* are will find both of the foregoing versions of your thesis too obscure. Very well, if you think you cannot or should not take such knowledge for granted, revise the thesis by describing Thrasymachus's views; for example, "In Plato's *Republic,* does Socrates really succeed in refuting Thrasymachus's thesis that justice is whatever is in the interest of the stronger? I think not, and shall try to show why."

Throughout every paper, this kind of problem will need to be faced: Could a reader — for instance, your college roommate — who is (presumably) uninformed about the precise language of your paper topic still read your paper and make sense of it? Or are there too many cryptic allusions? too much undefined jargon? too little explanation? If so, then introduce whatever further information is necessary to provide the proper context. Remember, *your aim is to write reader-friendly prose,* and the opening paragraph is the place to show readers that this is your intention. This doesn't mean you should condescend or give simpleminded and obvious explanations — just that you shouldn't assume your readers (and your instructor) know what you're getting at. Be direct and clear! No reader should finish the first paragraph of your essay and remain in doubt about what you as the author are going to assert, defend, criticize, explain, or analyze.

Sketching Your Argument

Having indicated the general topic and your specific thesis, you can further help readers by alerting them to how your argument will unfold. (If your topic and thesis are complex, or their statement takes more than half a dozen lines, you may need to begin a new paragraph to sketch out your arguments. But remember, one goal of the paper's opening should be to get to the point briskly. Beware of belaboring your opening remarks.)

A good example of an opening paragraph that achieves these purposes can be found in Ellen Wheeler's essay on Descartes and Turing (p. 100). Here is what she wrote, with a few omissions:

> René Descartes and Alan M. Turing disagree over whether
> machines can be distinguished from humans and over the
> criteria by which the issue can be decided, if at all.
> In this paper I will explicate Descartes's argument in
> his <u>Discourse</u> and Turing's argument in his essay "Comput-
> ing Machinery and Intelligence." I will discuss the
> "contrary views" to Turing's argument that are most
> relevant to the criteria proposed by Descartes. . . .   I
> intend to show that although Descartes may have been
> correct in light of the evidence available to him . . . ,
> Turing's responses to [the] . . . objections show that
> his argument to the contrary is stronger.

In her opening paragraph, Wheeler spells out for readers her topic and her position on it (her thesis), and she sketches how she will develop her argument. If you have done all of that in your opening paragraph, you have probably written a satisfactory introduction.

Putting First Things Last

Somewhat paradoxically, as noted earlier, even though the introductory paragraph is by definition the *first* paragraph of your paper, it may well be the *last* paragraph you write. The reason is that it is rare for writers to know at the start of a first draft exactly what they are going to argue and how the general lines of argument will unfold and interconnect. Most writers, therefore, cannot confidently write the best opening paragraph until they have written and rewritten the rest of their paper. Of course, a writer can make a rough sketch of the opening paragraph early on, knowing that it will probably need revision later. Once the whole paper is drafted, the thoughtful writer will then review that sketchy initial paragraph and refine it so that it more precisely and effectively describes what lies ahead. And when the final rewriting and polishing are done, a good writer will take one more look at how he or she began what is now finished.

If the expectations raised in the opening paragraph are to be fulfilled in the subsequent paragraphs, these paragraphs will need to be drafted with that purpose in mind. We will now consider how to develop the supporting paragraphs.

Paragraph Structure

Elementary composition books tell us that the purpose of a paragraph is to *develop one idea* and that the boundaries of the paragraph are intended to help readers focus on that idea. Less frequently stressed is the way in which each paragraph has, or ought to have, its own *logic* — a structure, built out of an orderly sequence of sentences, that helps readers follow the line of reasoning presented in the paragraph. This is especially important in critical, analytic, argumentative prose, in which there is usually no narrative, time sequence, or dialogue to shape and advance paragraphs. As you write such prose, don't let any of your paragraphs be just a bunch of sentences with a common topic but without any visible connection and sequence. To be sure, a paragraph can be just a hunk of prose created by hitting the tab key at the beginning of an arbitrary line of text. And for ease of reading one might turn every sentence into a paragraph, as newspapers often do. But no good paragraph results from such techniques.

Good writers give *internal organization* to their paragraphs by using structural clues, or transitions. Transitions such as "also," "in addition," and "moreover" indicate that you are introducing information that will expand on a previous point. Expressions like "for instance" and "for example" prepare readers for illustrations and examples. "On the one hand, . . . on the other hand," "however," "on the contrary," and similar expressions indicate contrast. Philosophers and others arguing a point depend especially on *transitions of conclusion,* such as "therefore," "in conclusion," and "as a result of."

Not to be overlooked is the role the *pronoun* can play in tying sentences together — as long as the reference to antecedents is clear: "Rationalists believe that. . . . *They* also argue . . ."; ". . . but not Plato or Aristotle. *Neither* would have. . . ."

EXERCISE 11: The Internal Logic of the Paragraph — Unscrambling the Elements

Introduction   Not all devices used by writers to give internal structure to their paragraphs are as obvious as those just mentioned. What we might call the *logic* of a paragraph is built out of many different signs and cues; some rather subtle devices are difficult to notice — unless a paragraph is taken apart, sentence by sentence, for close inspection. A revealing exercise that forces you to look closely for these logical cues to paragraph structure is to choose some paragraph, isolate each of its sentences (cut them out, if you have a pair of scissors handy), scramble their original sequence, and then — using whatever cues you can find — reestablish the original sequence. Here is an exercise of this sort, based on a paragraph by the American philosopher Mary Anne Warren (b. 1946) in her essay "Future Generations," which originally appeared as a chapter in the book *And Justice for All* (1982). The italics are in the original.

Following are seven sentences from a paragraph in Warren's essay. See if you can reconstruct the order in which these sentences originally appeared. Be prepared to explain why you propose the order you have decided upon.

A Scrambled Paragraph of Text

MARY ANNE WARREN
⟨ from *Future Generations*

1. Either the *contingency* of future generations or our *ignorance* about them might be thought to defeat any claim that we have specific moral obligations regarding them.

2. Second, the very existence (in the future) of future generations is in doubt.

3. Those who doubt that we have *any* moral obligations with respect to future generations may doubt this because they are troubled by a number of peculiar features about the relationship between ourselves and not-yet-existent people.

4. I would argue, on the contrary, that, as important as these facts are, they do not show that we lack moral obligations with respect to future generations.

5. It may seem odd to claim that we have moral obligations to *presently nonexistent people.*

6. Not only do we not know whether or not there will be human beings one hundred or one thousand years from now, or how many of them there will be, but the existence or nonexistence of future persons, as well as *which particular individuals* will exist in the future, is to some extent contingent upon our own actions.

7. First, there is the fact that future people (by definition) do not exist *now.*

Discussion   At first glance, the most obvious structural devices used in this paragraph are the transitions at the beginning of sentences 7 and 2: "First" and "Second," respectively. Clearly, sentence 7 precedes sentence 2. From here on, however, the going is a bit tougher.

Mary Anne Warren (b. 1946) earned her Ph.D. from the University of California at Berkeley in 1975. For some years she has been a professor of philosophy at San Francisco State University. She has published frequently on topics in applied ethics (abortion, affirmative action, animal rights, environmental ethics) and is especially well known for her contributions to femnist philosophy. She is the author of three books, including *The Nature of Woman* (1980), *Gendercide* (1985), and *Moral Status* (1987).

The excerpt printed here is from her essay, "Future Generations," a chapter in *And Justice for All* (1982), edited by Tom Regan and Donald VandeVeer.

The next thing you might notice is the transition in sentence 4, "on the contrary," which clearly indicates that the author is disagreeing with a previous statement. Does this show that sentence 4 cannot be the opening sentence of the paragraph? No, because the author might be disagreeing with a statement in the preceding paragraph, which is not reprinted here. To try to resolve that issue, let's look at sentence 4 in another way.

Of the seven sentences that make up the paragraph, sentence 4 is the only one that seems to state the *thesis* around which the rest of the sentences in the paragraph cluster. Sentence 4 is the only sentence in which Warren states *her* position in no uncertain terms ("I would argue"). Furthermore, what she says in this sentence is at odds with what she says in all the other sentences in the paragraph — so it is unlikely to be the sentence that opens the paragraph. As we read over these sentences, one by one, we see that the clear thrust of the whole paragraph is to develop aspects of the argument *against* the idea that we, the living, have any moral obligations to the as yet unborn. In fact, the only sentence in the whole paragraph that does not develop this idea is sentence 4. In addition, sentence 4 contains the phrase "these facts," which must refer to "facts" *previously stated* — indeed, the very facts stated in the other sentences of the paragraph.

Here we have good reasons *against* putting sentence 4 at the beginning of the paragraph as well as against putting it somewhere in the middle of the paragraph. The contradictory statement in sentence 4 and its reference to earlier material are, in fact, good reasons for putting sentence 4 at the *end* — and thus viewing it both as Warren's objection to the ideas in the rest of the paragraph and as her introduction to the paragraphs that follow (not reprinted here) in which she presents her own argument. So, provisionally, let us put sentence 4 at the end. Our tentative sequence now looks like this: 7, . . . , 2, . . . , 4.

Next, is there any good candidate for the sentence that opens the paragraph? Except for sentence 4, all the other sentences share a theme — and that theme is expressed exactly once: in sentence 3. The "doubt" mentioned here about our obligations to future generations is developed in detail by all the other sentences (save 4). This confers unique prominence on sentence 3, so much so that it is likely to be the opening sentence we are looking for. So let's put it first, giving us this partial ordering: 3, . . . , 7, . . . , 2, . . . , 4.

That leaves us with three sentences still to put into sequence. Let's return to the issue of whether sentences 7 and 2 follow in strict sequence or whether some sentence intervenes. Notice that the statement in sentence 5 about the apparent oddity of claiming moral obligations to *"presently nonexistent people"* is closely linked to the statement in sentence 7 about "future people." No such link connects sentence 5 with any other sentence, so let's tentatively insert 5 immediately after 7, giving us this order: 3, . . . , 7, 5, 2, . . . , 4.

We are now left with only two sentences, 1 and 6, but there are still several possible places to put them. Closer scrutiny reveals that sentences 1 and 6 are unique in that each mentions *contingency*. This suggests that they go together as a pair, without any other sentence between them. But in which sequence: 6, 1 or 1, 6? Notice that sentence 6 amplifies the doubt that is mentioned at the end of sentence 2. Perhaps, then, 6 immediately follows 2. If it does, then our sequence looks like this: 3, 7, 5, 2, 6, . . . , 4.

Only sentence 1 remains to be inserted. This sentence pretty well summarizes the argument against moral obligations to future generations as developed by sentences 3, 7, 5, 2, and 6. In other words, once we've asserted sentence 1, there's no more to say (at least, in the sentences of this paragraph) to develop the argument of the paragraph — all that remains is to accept or reject the conclusion: that we have no moral obligation to future generations. Warren, as we have already noticed, rejects that conclusion. For these reasons, we can rather confidently propose the following final sequence: 3, 7, 5, 2, 6, 1, 4.

The Reconstructed Paragraph

Those who doubt that we have *any* moral obligations with respect to future generations may doubt this because they are troubled by a number of peculiar features about the relationship between ourselves and not-yet-existent people. First, there is the fact that future people (by definition) do not exist *now*. It may seem odd to claim that we have moral obligations to *presently nonexistent people*. Second, the very existence (in the future) of future generations is in doubt. Not only do we not know whether or not there will be human beings one hundred or one thousand years from now, or how many of them there will be, but the existence or nonexistence of future persons, as well as *which particular individuals* will exist in the future, is to some extent contingent upon our own actions. Either the *contingency* of future generations or our *ignorance* about them might be thought to defeat any claim that we have specific moral obligations regarding them. I would argue, on the contrary, that, as important as these facts are, they do not show that we lack moral obligations with respect to future generations.

Some Afterthoughts   Philosophers are not alone in being tempted to ignore crafting their paragraphs in a reader-friendly manner. What matters, a serious writer may well think, is not whether the paragraph is nicely structured; what alone matters is whether what is written is *true* and whether the argument of a given paragraph is *sound*. Yes. And since the truth of a sentence asserted in a paragraph does not depend on *where* in the paragraph it is placed, and since the soundness of an argument does not depend on the *sequence* in which the premises and conclusion are asserted, why bother much about that sequence? Why, indeed?

The answer ought to be clear: The purpose of an argumentative paragraph is not only to *inform* but also to *show* the reader by effective use of words, sentences, and paragraphs that the writer is correct. It is not (like a passage in a diary) merely a device for the writer to get thoughts onto paper in whatever order they tumble out. Readers cannot be effectively informed and persuaded if they are left groping for the connections between sentences. Writing and reading prose are essentially *linear* activities; writers cannot state everything in an argument at once (recall the epigraph from Rousseau at the head of chapter 3), so they must choose the order in which they place every sentence within its context — and sequence can make a difference in clarity, if not in cogency. Readers, for their part, can take in only one sentence at a time, and they will be better able to follow the reasoning in a piece of writing and be persuaded by it if the writer has used transitions and other such cues to indicate sequence and the relative importance of ideas. Where the connections between ideas are not clear, communication between writer and reader is likely to be frustrated.

Some of the same kind of reasoning that went into reconstructing the paragraph by Warren can usefully be applied to each of your own paragraphs, as you critically analyze what you have written.

EXERCISE 12: The External Logic of Paragraphs — Reinserting Paragraph Indents

Introduction   Just as a good paragraph will have its internal logic — that is, a logical sequence in its content, sentence by sentence — a page or two of paragraphs will have their sequential logic from paragraph to paragraph. We can call this the *external logic of paragraphs,* the logic *between* paragraphs, in contrast to the logic *within* a paragraph.

Here's an exercise to develop a sense of the logic between paragraphs. The instructor hands out a sheet or two of philosophical prose from which all the paragraph markings (the indents) have been deleted. The student's task is to reinsert the paragraph indents where they belong (or at least where the author put them), based on whatever cues can be identified.

You can try your hand at an exercise of this sort by paragraphing the following text, taken from "Rejecting All Lies," the opening section of the book, *Lying* (1978), by American philosopher Sissela Bok (b. 1934). The original had seventeen paragraphs — or twenty if you create a new paragraph (as she did) for each of the three quoted passages. For ease of reference, every fifth line has been numbered in the margin and the footnotes have been deleted.

SISSELA BOK
from *Lying*

The simplest answer to the problems of lying, at least in principle, is
to rule out all lies. Many theologians have chosen such a position;
foremost among them is St. Augustine. He cut a clear swath through
all the earlier opinions holding that some lies might be justified. He
claimed that God forbids all lies and that liars therefore endanger   5
their immortal souls. He defined lying as having one thing in one's
heart and uttering another with the intention to deceive, thereby
subverting the God-given purposes of human speech. His definition
left no room at all for justifiable falsehood. And he confessed that
this troubled him: He worried about lies to ailing persons, for in-   10
stance, and lies to protect those threatened by assault or defilement.
He allowed, therefore, that there are great differences among lies
and that some are much more abhorrent than others. He set up an
eightfold distinction, beginning with lies uttered in the teaching of
religion, the worst ones of all, and ending with lies which harm no   15
one and yet save someone from physical defilement. These last are
still sins and cannot be justified or advised to anyone, yet they can
much more easily be pardoned. And he concluded that:

> It cannot be denied that they have attained a very high standard
> of goodness who never lie except to save a man from injury; but   20
> in the case of men who have reached this standard, it is not the
> deceit, but their good intention, that is justly praised, and some-
> times even rewarded. It is quite enough that the deception should
> be pardoned, without its being made an object of laudation.

The impact of Augustine's thinking on this subject was immense.   25
Up to the time that he wrote, many different opinions had held
sway. Even for Christians, the Bible had seemed to give examples of
dissimulation and lying which made it difficult to object categorically to all lies. But Augustine explained these in such a way that he
could continue to maintain that God forbade all lies, while distin-   30
guishing among lies according to the intention behind them and the
harmfulness of their effects. These distinctions reappear in the
penitentials of the early Middle Ages and are fully treated and worked
out in the systematic works of the high Middle Ages, culminating in

Sissela Bok was born in Sweden, schooled in Switzerland and France, and earned
her Ph.D. from Harvard in 1970. She has served on the faculty at several universities
in the Boston area, including Harvard, M.I.T., and Brandeis. Currently she is a Distinguished Fellow at Harvard's Center for Population and Development Studies. For
more than two decades she has been widely recognized for her work on many
issues in bioethics. Her books on moral topics of interest to the general public —
including *Lying* (1978), *Secrets* (1982), *Mayhem* (1998), and *Euthanasia and Physician-Assisted Suicide* (1998, with Gerald Dworkin and R. G. Frey) — have earned
her many honors and awards. Reprinted here is a brief excerpt from *Lying*.

the treatment given to lying in the *Summa Theologica* by Thomas 35
Aquinas. Throughout, Augustine's prohibition of all lies as sinful
held sway. But such a doctrine turned out to be very difficult to live
by. Many ways were tried to soften the prohibition, to work around
it, and to allow at least a few lies. Three different paths were taken:
to allow for pardoning of some lies; to claim that some deceptive 40
statements are not falsehoods, merely misinterpreted by the listener;
and finally to claim that certain falsehoods do not *count* as lies. The
first built upon Augustine's eightfold hierarchy, going from the most
grievous lies to those most easily pardoned. Aquinas set a pattern
which is still followed by Catholic theologians. He distinguished 45
three kinds of lies: the officious, or helpful, lies; the jocose lies, told
in jest; and the mischievous, or malicious, lies, told to harm someone. Only the latter constitute moral sins for Aquinas. He agreed
with Augustine that all lies are sins, but regarded the officious and
jocose lies as less serious. The pardoning function came to grow 50
more and more important and ultimately created great discord within
the Church. Should one be able to tell lies and then have them
wiped from one's conscience? Ought it to be possible to do so repeatedly, perhaps even to plan the lies with the pardon in mind?
And by what means should the pardon be sought? To arrive at reli- 55
able answers to such questions was a tormenting task when views
differed so sharply and when error might result in punishment after
death. The two other paths around Augustine's strict prohibition
occasioned similar disputes. They assumed, in effect, that certain
intentionally deceptive statements are not lies in the first place. They 60
might then be used in good conscience. One such was the "mental
reservation" or "mental restraint." It took its lead from Augustine's
definition of lying as having one thing in one's heart and uttering
another, but it *left out* the speaker's intention to deceive as part of
the definition. It thereby allowed the following argument: If you say 65
something misleading to another and merely add a qualification to it
in your mind so as to make it true, you cannot be responsible for the
"misinterpretation" made by the listener. Some argued that such
mental reservation could be used only for a just cause and when
there was a chance for the deceived to make the correct inference. 70
Others went very far in expanding its usage — to the point where a
clever person could always find the convenient mental reservation
for any falsehood he wanted to convey. Needless to say, this doctrine aroused intense controversy, both within and outside Catholic
circles. This is how Pascal begins his polemic against it in his *Pro-* 75
vincial Letters:

> "One of the most embarrassing of these cases is how to avoid
> telling lies, especially when one wants to induce a belief in a
> false thing. This purpose is admirably served by our doctrine of
> equivocation, according to which, as Sanchez has it, "it is permit- 80
> ted to use ambiguous terms, leading people to understand them
> in another sense from that in which we understand them our-
> selves'."
> "I know that, father," said I.

"We have published it so often," continued he, "that at length   85
everyone has learned about it. But do you know what is to be
done when one finds no equivocal words?"

"No, father."

"I though as much," said he; "this is something new: It is the
doctrine of mental reservations. 'A man may swear', as Sanchez   90
says in the same place, 'that he never did such a thing (though he
actually did it), meaning within himself that he did not do it on a
certain day, or before he was born, or understanding any other
such circumstance, while the words which he employs have no
such sense as would discover his meaning; and this is very con-   95
venient in many encounters, and always very justified when
necessary for health, honor, or the good.'"

"Indeed, father! Is that not a lie, and perjury to boot?"

The mental reservation turned out to have a long history, especially in court proceedings. Since oaths in court were originally sworn   100
in the name of God with the fear that He might strike down those
who took His name in order to support falsehoods, some argued
that a silent reservation, audible to God but not to the court, might
avoid this fate. Thus, an adulterous woman might swear that she
had not wronged her husband, adding silently that at least she had   105
not done so that week, or at a certain house, thereby escaping her
husband's wrath and a certain death, while not believing herself
perjured in the eyes of God. Resorting to mental reservations and
other internal disclaimers to outward acts has been a matter of life
and death in those many periods when religious persecution has   110
raged. In the sixteenth century, for example, the so-called
Nicodemites, who had converted to Lutheranism or Calvinism, tried
to escape persecution by concealing their religious views and by
participating in the Mass. They sought to justify this behavior on
religious grounds, but Calvin condemned them in the harshest terms,   115
advising them to emigrate from Catholic areas rather than to take
part in "papist ceremonies." Nor is the mental reservation altogether
a thing of the past. We still swear to omit it in many official oaths of
citizenship and public office. And some still recommend it. A well-
known Catholic textbook advises doctors and nurses to deceive pa-   120
tients by this method when they see fit to do so. If a feverish patient,
for example, asks what his temperature is, the doctor is advised to
answer: "Your temperature is normal today," while making the mental reservation that it is normal for someone in the patient's precise
physical condition. The final way to avoid Augustine's across-the-   125
board prohibition of all lies seeks to argue that not all intentionally
false statements ought to count as lies from a moral point of view.
This view found powerful expression in Grotius. He argued that a
falsehood is a lie in the strict sense of the word only if it conflicts
with a right of the person to whom it is addressed. A robber, for   130
instance, has no right to the information he tries to extort; to speak
false to him is therefore not to lie in the strict sense of the word. The
right in question is that of liberty of judgment, which is implied in
all speech; but it can be lost if the listener has evil intentions; or not
yet acquired, as in the case of children; or else freely given up, as   135

when two persons agree to deceive one another. Grotius was a lawyer, and views such as his brought many to believe that if lies were
not actually unlawful, they were morally acceptable, bringing no
blame to the liar. Such an argument oversimplifies his thinking, but
it is a fact that Grotius helped to bring back into the discourse on   140
lying the notion, common in antiquity but so nearly snuffed out by
St. Augustine, that falsehood is at times justifiable. Among those
who discussed such doctrines with their students in ethics was Kant.
Between 1775 and 1781, long before he had published his own works
of moral philosophy, he gave yearly lectures on ethics at the Univer-   145
sity of Königsberg and used the required textbook, which discussed
the familiar distinctions from Aquinas and Grotius. To judge from
notes taken by students, edited in this century, Kant expounded on
this material in a lively way, using cases as illustrations. It is all the
more striking, then, that when Kant finally published his own words   150
on moral philosophy, his treatment of lying should expressly have
taken a distance from all such subtleties. His views set forth the
strongest arguments we have against all lying. Kant takes issue, first,
with the idea that any generous motive, any threat to life, could
excuse a lie. He argues that: 155

> Truthfulness in statements which cannot be avoided is the formal
> duty of an individual to everyone, however great may be the
> disadvantage accruing to himself or to another.

This is the absolutist position, prohibiting all lies, even those
told for the best of purposes or to avoid the most horrible of fates.   160
For someone holding such a position, to be called a liar was a mortal insult — perhaps cause even for legal action or a duel; to be
proved a liar could lead to self-exile out of shame. Kant's view, if
correct, would eliminate any effort to distinguish among lies, since
he rejects them all. He takes the duty of truthfulness to be an "un-   165
conditional duty which holds in all circumstances"; a lie, even if it
does not wrong any particular individual, always harms mankind
generally, "for it vitiates the source of law." It harms the liar himself,
moreover, by destroying his human dignity and making him more
worthless even than a mere thing. Kant also rejects the way around   170
Augustine's prohibition that consists in defining certain falsehoods
as not being lies. He defines a lie as "merely an intentional untruthful declaration to another person" and dismisses the idea that we
owe the duty of speaking the truth only to those who have a right to
the truth. On the contrary, truthfulness is a duty which no circum-   175
stances can abrogate. Whatever else may be said about Kant's position, it seems to have the virtue of clarity and simplicity. Others may
argue about when to lie, but he makes a clean sweep.

Discussion   Obviously, the first paragraph beings with line 1, at the
first word, "The." Other paragraphs easy to identify are the three that
begin with a line of quotation, and three more than begin immediately
after the end of each quotation. Starting out this way yields paragraphs

after line 19 and beginning at line 25, after line 76 and beginning with line 99, after line 155 and beginning with line 159. Seven paragraphs, thirteen to go! Now it gets a little tougher.

Beginning with line 3, Bok tells us about St. Augustine's rigid views against lying. Could there be a paragraph break somewhere between lines 3 and 18? If there isn't, the paragraph becomes fairly long, as one after another of St. Augustine's views are listed. Perhaps a paragraph break could be made at line 12 (guided by the "therefore") or at line 14 (guided by mention of his "eightfold distinction"). Let's make a break at line 14.

Bok brings her discussion of St. Augustine's views to an end by shifting her attention to the views of St. Thomas Aquinas. Her phrase "Three different paths" in line 39 suggests that we should expect each of the three "paths" to have at least one paragraph to itself. This would yield a paragraph break at lines 42, 58, and 125.

If we look closely at line 55, we might want to insert a paragraph break at this line for two reasons. (1) We can end a paragraph with the three questions in lines 52–56, and let the following declarative sentence begin a paragraph that answers those questions. (2) The four sentences beginning in line 58 introduce the second and third of the three "paths" mentioned earlier in line 39. So far, twelve paragraphs, with eight to go.

In line 75, the shift of attention to Pascal's views might well be the occasion for making a new paragraph, so let us insert one there.

Lines 107–111 is the last of Bok's text devoted to the Scholastic thinkers, followed by the first to refer to more recent thinkers (Calvin in line 115, for example). So we might well begin a paragraph at line 111. Line 117 introduces us to several sentences discussing the current status of "mental reservations." These sentences interrupt the historical flow of Bok's discussion, and so suggest that we might introduce a paragraph beginning with line 125. Line 125, beginning "The final way . . .", surely indicates that a new paragraph begins there. Now we have sixteen paragraphs.

The first mention of Kant in line 142 suggests a new paragraph. What follows are some fourteen sentences (plus one quotation) devoted to Kant's views. Can this long stretch be broken up into two or more paragraphs? Yes, it can. Look at line 152; here Bok lays the basis for explaining Kant's "strongest arguments . . . against all lying." That suggests a new paragraph at line 153. Her mention that "Kant also . . ." in line 170 suggests that this might introduce a new paragraph, so let us do so. We now have but two more paragraph breaks to locate.

What to do? There are two possibilities. One is that we have overlooked some cues (subtle ones, no doubt) that Bok has provided to introduce the missing two. The other is that she has inserted two more paragraphs than her text really needs. The true story is a bit more complex.

First, Bok inserted paragraphs beginning at line 163 and 170. Both appear in her discussion of Kant and will strike many readers as inessential. In fact, the paragraph break at line 163 turns one medium-length paragraph into two rather short ones for no apparent reason. Much the same is true of her paragraph beginning with line 170.

But that is not all. Bok had no paragraph beginning with line 12 or with line 14. Instead, she had one beginning with line 6. A paragraph break is no doubt needed somewhere. Putting it at line 6 rather arbitrarily breaks up the sequence of sentences beginning "He," "He," "He," and "His" and leaves us with a somewhat abrupt opening paragraph. Second, Bok did not have a paragraph beginning with line 75, despite the fact that the mention of Pascal marks a new topic. One suspects that she did not want a paragraph break at line 75 because she has one in the next line, beginning the long quotation. But other writers might prefer to tie Pascal more closely to what follows (the quote) than to what preceded (the discussion of "mental reservation").

The Reconstructed Text

The simplest answer to the problems of lying, at least in principle, is to rule out all lies. Many theologians have chosen such a position; foremost among them is St. Augustine. He cut a clear swath through all the earlier opinions holding that some lies might be justified. He claimed that God forbids all lies and that liars therefore endanger their immortal souls.

He defined lying as having one thing in one's heart and uttering another with the intention to deceive, thereby subverting the God-given purposes of human speech. His definition left no room at all for justifiable falsehood. And he confessed that this troubled him: He worried about lies to ailing persons, for instance, and lies to protect those threatened by assault or defilement. He allowed, therefore, that there are great differences among lies and that some are much more abhorrent than others. He set up an eightfold distinction, beginning with lies uttered in the teaching of religion, the worst ones of all, and ending with lies which harm no one and yet save someone from physical defilement. These last are still sins and cannot be justified or advised to anyone, yet they can much more easily be pardoned. And he concluded that:

> It cannot be denied that they have attained a very high standard of goodness who never lie except to save a man from injury; but in the case of men who have reached this standard, it is not the deceit, but their good intention, that is justly praised, and sometimes even rewarded. It is quite enough that the deception should be pardoned, without its being made an object of laudation.

The impact of Augustine's thinking on this subject was immense. Up to the time that he wrote, many different opinions had held sway. Even for Christians, the Bible had seemed to give examples of dissimulation and lying which made it difficult to object categorically to all lies. But Augustine explained these in such a way that he could continue to maintain that God forbade all lies, while distinguishing among lies according to the intention behind them and the harmfulness of their effects. These distinctions reappear in the penitentials of the early Middle Ages and are fully treated and worked out in the systematic works of the high Middle Ages, culminating in the treatment given to lying in the *Summa Theologica* by Thomas Aquinas.

Throughout, Augustine's prohibition of all lies as sinful held sway. But such a doctrine turned out to be very difficult to live by. Many ways were tried to soften the prohibition, to work around it, and to allow at least a few lies. Three different paths were taken: to allow for pardoning of some lies; to claim that some deceptive statements are not falsehoods, merely misinterpreted by the listener; and finally to claim that certain falsehoods do not *count* as lies.

The first built upon Augustine's eightfold hierarchy, going from the most grievous lies to those most easily pardoned. Aquinas set a pattern which is still followed by Catholic theologians. He distinguished three kinds of lies: the officious, or helpful, lies; the jocose lies, told in jest; and the mischievous, or malicious, lies, told to harm someone. Only the latter constitute mortal sins for Aquinas. He agreed with Augustine that all lies are sins, but regarded the officious and jocose lies as less serious. The pardoning function came to grow more and more important and ultimately created great discord within the Church. Should one be able to tell lies and then have them wiped from one's conscience? Ought it to be possible to do so repeatedly, perhaps even to plan the lies with the pardon in mind? And by what means should the pardon be sought?

To arrive at reliable answers to such questions was a tormenting task when views differed so sharply and when error might result in punishment after death. The two other paths around Augustine's strict prohibition occasioned similar disputes. They assumed, in effect, that certain intentionally deceptive statements are not lies in the first place. They might then be used in good conscience.

One such as the "mental reservation" or "mental restraint." It took its lead from Augustine's definition of lying as having one thing in one's heart and uttering another, but it *left out* the speaker's intention to deceive as part of the definition. It thereby allowed the following argument: If you say something misleading to another and merely add a qualification to it in your mind so as to make it true, you cannot be responsible for the "misinterpretation" made by the listener. Some argued that such mental reservation could be used only for a just cause and when there was a chance for the deceived to make the correct inference. Others went very far in expanding its usage — to the point where a clever person could always find the convenient mental reservation for any falsehood he wanted to convey. Needless to say, this doctrine aroused intense controversy, both within and outside Catholic circles. This is how Pascal begins his polemic against it in his *Provincial Letters:*

> "One of the most embarrassing of these cases is how to avoid telling lies, especially when one wants to induce a belief in a false thing. This purpose is admirably served by our doctrine of equivocation, according to which, as Sanchez has it, 'it is permitted to use ambiguous terms, leading people to understand them

in another scene from that in which we understand them our-selves'."

"I know that, father," said I.

"We have published it so often," continued he, "that at length everyone has learned about it. But do you know what is to be done when one finds no equivocal words?"

"No, father."

"I thought as much," said he; "this is something new: It is the doctrine of mental reservations. 'A man may swear', as Sanchez says in the same place, 'that he never did such a thing (though he actually did it), meaning within himself that he did not do it on a certain day, or before he was born, or understanding any other such circumstance, while the words which he employs have no such sense as would discover his meaning; and this is very convenient in many encounters, and always very justified when necessary for health, honor, or the good.'"

"Indeed, father! is that not a lie, and perjury to boot?"

The mental reservation turned out to have a long history, espe-cially in court proceedings. Since oaths in court were originally sworn in the name of God with the fear that He might strike down those who took His name in order to support falsehoods, some argued that a silent reservation, audible to God but not to the court, might avoid this fate. Thus, an adulterous woman might swear that she had not wronged her husband, adding silently that at least she had not done so that week, or at a certain house, thereby escaping her husband's wrath and a certain death, while not believing herself perjured in the eyes of God.

Resorting to mental reservations and other internal disclaimers to outward acts has been a matter of life and death in those many periods when religious persecution has raged. In the sixteenth cen-tury, for example, the so-called Nicodemites, who had converted to Lutheranism or Calvinism, tried to escape persecution by concealing their religious views and by participating in the Mass. They sought to justify this behavior on religious grounds, but Calvin condemned them in the harshest terms, advising them to emigrate from Catholic areas rather than to take part in "papist ceremonies."

Nor is the mental reservation altogether a thing of the past. We still swear to omit it in many official oaths of citizenship and public office. And some still recommend it. A well-known Catholic text-book advises doctors and nurses to deceive patients by this method when they see fit to do so. If a feverish patient, for example, asks what his temperature is, the doctor is advised to answer: "Your tem-perature is normal today," while making the mental reservation that it is normal for someone in the patient's precise physical condition.

The final way to avoid Augustine's across-the-board prohibition of all lies seeks to argue that not all intentionally false statements ought to count as lies from a moral point of view. This view found powerful expression in Grotius. He argued that a falsehood is a lie in the strict sense of the word only if it conflicts with a right of the person to whom it is addressed. A robber, for instance, has no right to the information he tries to extort; to speak falsely to him is therefore not to lie in the strict sense of the word. The right in question is that of liberty of judgment, which is implied in all speech; but it can be lost if the listener has evil intentions; or not yet acquired, as in the case of children; or else freely given up, as when two persons agree to deceive one another. Grotius was a lawyer, and views such as his brought many to believe that if lies were not actually unlawful, they were morally acceptable, bringing no blame to the liar. Such an argument oversimplifies his thinking, but it is a fact that Grotius helped to bring back into the discourse on lying the notion, common in antiquity but so nearly snuffed out by St. Augustine, that falsehood is at times justifiable.

Among those who discussed such doctrines with their students in ethics was Kant. Between 1775 and 1781, long before he had published his own works of moral philosophy, he gave yearly lectures on ethics at the University of Königsberg and used the required textbook, which discussed the familiar distinctions from Aquinas and Grotius. To judge from notes taken by students, edited in this century, Kant expounded on this material in a lively way, using cases as illustrations.

It is all the more striking, then, that when Kant finally published his own works on moral philosophy, his treatment of lying should expressly have taken a distance from all such subtleties. His views set forth the strongest arguments we have against all lying.

Kant takes issue, first, with the idea that any generous motive, any threat to life, could excuse a lie. He argues that:

> Truthfulness in statements which cannot be avoided is the formal duty of an individual to everyone, however great may be the disadvantage accruing to himself or to another.

This is the absolutist position, prohibiting all lies, even those told for the best of purposes or to avoid the most horrible of fates. For someone holding such a position, to be called a liar was a mortal insult — perhaps cause even for legal action or a duel; to be proved a liar could lead to self-exile out of shame.

Kant's view, if correct, would eliminate any effort to distinguish among lies, since he rejects them all. He takes the duty of truthfulness to be an "unconditional duty which holds in all circumstances"; a lie, even if it does not wrong any particular individual, always harms mankind generally, "for it vitiates the source of law." It harms the liar himself, moreover, by destroying his human dignity and making him more worthless even than a mere thing.

Kant also rejects the way around Augustine's prohibition that consists in defining certain falsehoods as not being lies. He defines a lie as "merely an intentional untruthful declaration to another person" and dismisses the idea that we owe the duty of speaking the truth only to those who have a right to the truth. On the contrary, truthfulness is a duty which no circumstances can abrogate. Whatever else may be said about Kant's position, it seems to have the virtue of clarity and simplicity. Others may argue about when to lie, but he makes a clean sweep.

The Closing Paragraph

Just as a strong opening paragraph gets your paper off to a good start, a closing paragraph ought to provide a satisfying finish and a sense of completeness. There is an important difference between a paragraph that genuinely concludes your paper and a paragraph that happens to be the last one.

Closing paragraphs are often ineffective because the writer has only a vague idea of their purpose. Or the writer thinks that the closing paragraph should merely *summarize* the whole paper. The problem with a concluding paragraph that summarizes is that it is often unnecessary, especially if the paper is short. Why devote a whole paragraph (which can easily amount to ten percent or more of the paper) to summarizing a three- or four-page paper? If readers can't keep the main points of such a short paper in mind, then there's something fundamentally wrong with the way the paper was organized in the first place. Also, if the paper is really arguing only one or two points, a summary of its conclusions is probably superfluous. In general, close your paper with a summary paragraph only when the paper is fairly long and the argument fairly complex. (For instructive examples of good closing paragraphs, look at the student essays by Steven Calcote, p. 67; David Hoberman, p. 74; and Stacey Schmidt, p. 87.)

So what should a closing paragraph do? There are at least a couple of possibilities. You can end your paper by showing that what you have been arguing *leads into another problem* — one that you do not have space or occasion to deal with, however. (This was the strategy Ellen Wheeler used in her essay on p. 100.) A closing paragraph of this sort indicates that you can see beyond the assigned topic and point to new vistas that invite future investigation.

Another kind of closing paragraph is one in which you *draw several threads of your paper together* and state forcefully and concisely what you have shown — and perhaps what you have not settled or even explored. Such a paragraph is similar to a summary, but it does not merely reassert points made clearly in the paper. Rather, it answers a question implicit in readers' minds: What are the chief points the writer has made and how are they connected to each other?

A final note: In a short (three- or four-page) paper it is often best simply to end your paper without any special closing paragraph. Instead, close by finishing your discussion of whatever is the last point or issue in the paper.

Choosing a Title

Essays customarily have titles, and this is also true of student essays submitted in philosophy courses. How should you choose a title for your essay? What makes one title better than another? And why do titles matter?

The answers to all of these questions lie in the *purpose* of a title. To get at that purpose, ask yourself: What do I as writer want to tell my readers about my paper right at the start — and tell them in a way that arouses their interest? At the minimum, you ought to indicate something about the *topic* of your paper. A title that fails to indicate the topic, however interesting or witty it might otherwise be, fails to be reader-friendly; instead, it just confuses or misleads.

Suppose, for example, you are writing a paper on Plato's dialogue *Meno,* a text frequently used in introductory philosophy courses. In particular, your essay focuses on the famous scene in which Socrates, as he explores the rudiments of the Pythagorean theorem with a slave boy, argues for two distinctions. One is between teaching and learning; Socrates claims that he is not teaching the slave boy, but that the slave boy is nonetheless learning geometry. The other is between knowledge and true belief; Socrates claims that the slave boy has true beliefs about geometry, but not knowledge. A first pass at a title for such an essay might look like this:

Plato's Theory of Knowledge in Meno

Though somewhat informative, this title is not specific enough; Plato has a fair amount to say about the nature of knowledge in *Meno,* apart from Socrates's discussion with the slave boy. As a second pass, you might revise your title:

Socrates and the Slave Boy in Meno

That narrows the subject, but now there is no reference at all to the epistemological issues central to the exchange between Socrates and the slave boy. As a third try, you might write:

Learning vs. Teaching in Plato's Meno

Now you've got a title that is descriptively accurate and appropriately narrow, although all reference to the slave boy has been dropped. Still, this title is acceptable.

Note: You can overstress informativeness and descriptive accuracy in a title, thereby sacrificing something at least as important: arousing readers' interest. As a title, "Learning vs. Teaching in Plato's *Meno*" lacks any zip or wit, and so you might strive for something more intriguing. What you want in your title is information *and* interest.

Suppose that after studying the dialogue, you are convinced that, contrary to Socrates's claim, he really did teach the slave boy some basic geometry, in particular how to get the right answer to the question "What is the size of a square double in area to a given square?" You've decided you're going to argue that Socrates's disavowal of teaching the slave boy is just wrong. So you might put the title in the form of a question that points to such an argument:

Does Socrates Really Know What Teaching Is?

But perhaps that title is a bit too cute, as well as too sweeping. Another title that also would suggest your line of argument is this one:

Does the Slave Boy Really Learn without Being Taught?

Or you might want to take an even bolder line, with this title:

Why Socrates Was Wrong in Thinking
He Did Not "Teach" Meno's Slave Boy

As with the opening paragraph, your title may be one of the very *last* things you write, since only after your paper is actually drafted do you know for certain what you think about the topic and the conclusions you have reached. And as this discussion shows, an essay often has many possible titles, some obviously much better than others. Since there is no guarantee that the first one that occurs to you will be the best you can think of, it's worth playing around with several possible titles before you finally fix on one. Remember that no philosophy paper ever got an A just because it had a superb title; but many a teacher was alerted to expect a good paper by nothing more than a glance at a really interesting title.

REVISING

With phase one of the writing process — drafting your essay — behind you, you are now ready for the next phase: revising your draft. Now the real work of *writing* begins! In improving your draft, you have two different tasks to carry out. First and foremost, there is *revising* that you have written. This is done by bringing in new thoughts on the content, new organization to reflect more accurately the structure of your thoughts, better (shorter or longer, fewer or more) quotations a further reflection indicates, new arguments based on evidence that you overlooked or hadn't yet thought of when initially drafting the paper.

But revisions of this sort will not by themselves have any beneficial effect on your writing. That is because revising is independent of *editing,* which involves conscious attention to the language (not the content) of the essay in an effort to make sure that it meets the standards of good prose. Revising and editing, in that order, are needed to turn your writing into prose in which you can take pride.

Writing Is Rewriting

Writing, as any experienced writer will tell you, really is largely a matter of *re*writing — and then rewriting again, fine-tuning the content and language until your paper makes the points you want it to make.

Start the revision process by typing or printing out a hard copy of your whole paper. (A handwritten draft is okay, but do not plan to submit your final paper in handwriting.) It is difficult to adequately revise an essay of more than a page or so without being able to see all of it laid out on a desk (or a bed or the floor). How else are you to see simultaneously the opening and closing paragraphs? The overall structure and sequence? The errors that escape your eye on the computer screen but glare forth once they are in black and white on paper? Don't be surprised if it turns out that you need to print out *several* drafts of your paper, one for each set of revisions you make. A nice clean hard copy can be of immense help to you in revising your essay.

What is it that you will set out to do in revising your essay? The tasks fall into roughly two categories. Some have to do with the *content* of the essay:

- Have you fully answered the question(s) in the assignment or fully developed all aspects of the paper topic?
- Are the quotations you have used apt, concise, and to the point?
- Have you supported your assertions and inferences adequately and as well as you can?
- Have you defined key terms as needed?

Considerations of these sorts were mentioned in the previous chapter in connection with drafting a philosophical essay. Making substantive changes like these is not so easy, however, after you have labored hard to get words onto paper. Most of us are understandably reluctant to unweave what we have just woven. Nevertheless, adopting a critical (*evaluative,* not *hostile*) attitude to your own prose is essential if your work is to be improved for public consumption, even if the public consists only of your instructor.

Other revision tasks have to do with your *writing* itself. A wide variety of considerations fall into this category. You need to do the following:

- Construct an outline of your paper to verify that you have given proper prominence to important ideas and have correctly subordinated less important ideas (examples, asides). Even if you drafted your paper from an outline, constructing an outline of the finished paper can be helpful. Remember, it is not enough that your paper has a structure; that structure must be evident to the reader.
- Tighten up your language; prune away needless words.
- Enliven your language by avoiding the passive voice. (For example, "Plato was taught by Socrates," a sentence in the passive voice, is less direct than "Socrates taught Plato," in which the subject, "Socrates," acts instead of being acted upon.)
- Use the first-person singular pronoun "I" where appropriate; don't be afraid to take active responsibility for your own views, and don't use the third person to refer to yourself ("This writer believes . . .").

- Check your grammar, watching out especially for the kinds of errors you know you are prone to make. Common errors include tense shifts, dangling modifiers, and subjects and verbs that do not agree. (See pp. 137–40.)
- Tie your prose together by effective use of transitional phrases between sentences and paragraphs. (See pp. 57–58.)
- Verify your spelling, making use of a spell checker if you have one on your computer. But don't rely entirely on a spell checker, because it can't distinguish between words such as "principal" and "principle," "affect" and "effect," or "infer" and "imply." (These and other key terms that are often misused and misspelled are discussed in more detail on pp. 133–36.)

All these reminders may be obvious, but that is not to say they are unimportant. Other questions to ask of your paper include the following:

- Is your *title* interesting and apt? (See pp. 125–27.)
- Does the *opening paragraph* get your paper off to a good start? (See pp. 107–09.)
- Have you introduced quotations from other sources with effective *lead-ins?* (See pp. 162–63.)
- Does the paper have the overall structure you want, as an *outline* of the paper may help you decide? (See p. 128.)
- Have you adequately *cited and documented all your sources,* to avoid confusing your readers and risking *plagiarism?* (See pp. 165–68.)

The foregoing are a mixture of formal and stylistic concerns, all of which must be addressed in the course of finishing your draft. In this chapter we'll review several of these concerns in greater detail.

Reviewing Your Paper for Word Choice (Diction)

The best way to learn how to use words effectively and appropriately is through practice. The more you read and write philosophy, the more comfortable you will become using the language of the discipline. Though it's not possible to cover all the subtleties of philosophical language here, the next three sections will help you avoid problems with word choice that crop up frequently in student papers.

Avoiding Sexist Language

In a recent book discussing John Stuart Mill's famous work *On Liberty,* we find this passage:

There can be little doubt that Mill believed that, given an appropriate range of relevant experience, men would in fact prefer activities involving the exercise of their best powers of discrimination and judgment over activities that do not. Mill is not committed to the view that men always display this preference —

he is not bound to hold the absurd view that, as between beer-drinking and wine-bibbing, men who know both always favor the latter on the ground of its greater demands of discrimination on the palate.

The three occurrences of the word "men" in this paragraph will raise eyebrows today among many readers — and not only those who aspire to be "politically correct." Each is *sexist* because it unnecessarily and inappropriately specifies the gender of a group of people. There is no reason in the context of this passage why "men" should be preferred either to "women" or to gender-neutral terms like "we," "men and women," "humans," or "people"; nothing distinctive about men, in contrast to women, is at issue. Today, it is increasingly rare for writers to use "men" to refer to both men and women, so much so that an author who persists in the older usage is likely to mislead readers into thinking that only males are being referred to.

One might try to defend the use of "men" in the quoted passage on two grounds. First, the author is writing about Mill's essay, and in that essay Mill himself never hesitates to use what today we would regard as sexist language. (This, by the way, is rather ironic, since Mill more than any other philosopher of the previous century took it upon himself to identify and attack the disadvantages men thrust on women, as his little book *The Subjection of Women* demonstrates. It did not occur to him, apparently — any more than it did to other writers of the day — that sexist language itself could be a source of oppression and subjection of women.) If male-centered language was a feature of Mill's own writing, so the argument goes, then it cannot be inappropriate in a discussion of his views. Second, certain readers may associate "beer-drinking and wine-bibbing" more with men than with women. To the extent that there are reasons to hold such a bias, one might argue, the use of the term "men" in this example is not clearly sexist.

These arguments are not very convincing. As to the first, no jarring or otherwise inappropriate note would be introduced into the discussion of Mill's text by using gender-neutral language. (And if Mill were alive today, it is highly unlikely that he would persist in the use of what he would surely agree was sexist language.) As to the second argument, one might concede the point — and still wonder why the author chose an example appropriate to a male stereotype rather than one appropriate to women or one equally appropriate to both men and women.

Very well, then, how might one avoid sexist language in this passage? There are many ways; for example, in the first case, instead of writing "relevant experience, *men* would in fact prefer," one could just as well write "relevant experience, *people* would in fact prefer." In the second case, instead of writing "the view that *men* always display this preference," one could write "the view that *we* always display this preference." In the third case, instead of writing "as between beer-drinking and wine-bibbing, *men* who know both," one could write "as between beer-drinking and wine-bibbing, *people* who know both." Further, one could offer a different example instead of "beer-drinking and wine-bibbing," something like "as between rock music and Schubert sonatas" or "as between television sitcoms and Shakespeare's plays."

To sum up, avoid gender-specific words or examples where they are not needed (far more frequently than many writers realize, they *are* unnecessary). Use gender-neutral expressions where possible (recall the preceding examples). Third, if you want to use gender-specific language or examples, strike a balance between those that are male-focused and those that are female-focused.

As this discussion indicates, you can often avoid sexist language with only a moment's reflection, and you can do it without obviously artificial and distracting results (which is what happens when, for instance, a writer uses male-specific terms or examples in even-numbered paragraphs and switches to female-specific language in odd-numbered paragraphs).

One of the most economical ways to avoid needlessly gender-specific language is to *shift from the singular to the plural*. Instead of writing, for example, "A careful reader would realize that he . . . ," write instead "Careful readers would realize that they. . . ."

In their eagerness to avoid sexist language, students often end up violating one of the most elementary rules of good grammar: Pronouns must agree in number with their antecedents, the words to which they refer. Consider the following sentence:

```
Anyone who thinks knowledge is justified true belief will
change their minds after reading Gettier's essay.
```

The indefinite pronoun "anyone," used as the subject, is singular, not plural; thus, the possessive pronoun that refers back to "anyone" must also be singular. But the pronoun "their" is plural. How did this error come about? Perhaps because the writer was trying to avoid sexist wording, like the following:

```
Anyone who thinks knowledge is justified true belief will
change his mind . . .
```

How can you avoid these phrasings, but not at the cost of a grammatical error? One way is to change the subject itself from the singular to the plural:

```
Those who think knowledge is justified true belief will
change their minds. . . .
```

The solution to the problem of sexist language is not to make a fetish of gender-neutral language. As for such now-familiar phrases as "he or she" and "she or he" (and their abbreviated versions, "he/she" and "s/he"), used by many writers in the name of fairness to both sexes, they are tiresome to read and often show a want of sensitivity and imagination. The solution lies in greater sensitivity to ways in which habits of language can conceal attitudes one would not consciously want to defend and in greater imagination in exploiting the resources of our vocabulary and grammar.

Using Latin Terms Correctly

Scholarly writing in books and professional journals often contains Latin terms and abbreviations. You should be familiar with these terms; however, avoid overusing them in your own writing. In most cases, the English equivalents of Latin expressions are preferable because they are less formal and easier for readers to understand.

Following is an overview of Latin terms that you are most likely to encounter while reading and writing philosophy.

cf. Short for "confer," meaning "compare." Use this abbreviation when you want readers to compare what you have just written or quoted with information from another source. For example, ". . . as in Hume's *Treatise* (but cf. Hume's first *Enquiry,* part VIII)." Be careful not to make the common error of thinking that "cf." means "see" or "consult." Use "cf." only when you want to make a comparison.

e.g., i.e. "E.g." abbreviates the Latin words "exempli gratia," which mean "for the sake of example." Thus, if you wish to cite Hume, say, as an example of an empiricist philosopher, you might write:

```
Several empiricists--for example, Berkeley, Hume, Mill-- . . .
```

But you could instead write this:

```
Several empiricists--e.g., Berkeley, Hume, Mill-- . . .
```

The abbreviation "i.e." stands for the Latin words "id est," meaning "that is." Suppose, to make a concept absolutely clear to your readers, you describe it or expand on it like this:

```
Russell's theory--his theory of descriptions-- . . .
```

But you might say the same thing this way:

```
Russell's theory--i.e., his theory of descriptions-- . . .
```

As you see from these examples, "e.g." and "i.e." have completely different roles: "e.g." introduces an example and "i.e." introduces an explanation or equivalent idea.

et al. Short for "et alii," meaning "and others." Use this abbreviation to save writing out a full list of names, such as the multiple authors of a book or the members of some class. For example, "The logical positivists (Carnap, Reichenbach, et al.) frequently argued. . . ." Note that a period follows "al." because it is an abbreviation, but no period follows "et" because it is a full Latin word ("and").

etc.   Short for "et cetera," meaning "and so forth." Use it when you don't want to write out a full list of items. For example, "This view is consistent with other theories, hypotheses, etc." Avoid "etc., etc." One etc. is always enough.

op. cit., loc. cit., ibid.   These abbreviations are all used in bibliographic footnotes to refer to information in an earlier note. "Op. cit." is short for "opere citato" and means "in the work cited" — that is, the book or article already documented in full (author, title, etc.) in a previous note. "Loc. cit." is short for "loco citato" and means "in the place cited," that is, the very page mentioned in an earlier note. "Ibid." is short for "ibidem," meaning "in the same place," and refers to a source documented in an *immediately* preceding note. Writers often use "ibid." to avoid having to repeat an author's name, the title of a work, and other publication information in a subsequent reference to the same source. (Be aware that "op. cit.," "loc. cit.," and "ibid." are being used less and less frequently in footnotes. Increasingly, authors are using an abbreviated form of a source — for example, a shortened title or the author's last name — in subsequent references.)

sic   This is not an abbreviation, so it requires no period. It means "so" and draws readers' attention to the exact words used by a speaker or writer you are quoting. "Sic" usually appears in brackets after an error in the speaker's or writer's words and indicates that you are reproducing the error intentionally. Often it points out a striking oddity worthy of notice. For example, ". . . as Johnson pointed out, because of 'the well-known statue [sic] of limitations.'"

viz.   Short for "videlicet," meaning "namely." It is used to introduce information that identifies or more fully describes something. For example, ". . . Russell's 'Lectures on Logical Atomism,' viz., the lectures so titled that he published in 1918."

Commonly Confused Words

Philosophers have frequent occasion to use some words that are often misspelled and even more often misused because they are confused with another word similar in pronunciation, spelling, or meaning. The following list, though far from complete, offers some helpful distinctions among such words. (For additional vocabulary and definitions of interest, see the glossary, pp. 187–94.)

affect, effect   Philosophers write endlessly about *causes* and their *effects*, but rarely about *affects* and their causes. Most often, "affect" is used as a verb and "effect" is used as a noun. ("Though Absolute Idealism greatly affected British philosophy in the late nineteenth century, few of those effects are visible today.") When "affect" is used as a noun, it typically refers to feelings and their expression ("She took the news without visible affect") and is roughly a synonym for "emotion" or "feeling." When used as a verb ("Did the disturbance outside affect your concentration?"), "affect" always indicates some form of causal influence. "Effect" can also be used as a verb ("Further revisions in your paper will not effect much improvement in your grade"); because it is then roughly a synonym for the verb "cause." It's no wonder there is confusion between "affect" and "effect."

allusion, illusion   An allusion is something to which one refers (or alludes). An illusion is a deceptive appearance of things, such as the mirage of water on a hot stretch of desert or on a highway in Nevada. Notice that "illusion" is not based on a verb, but "allusion" is. ("Her allusion was to a neglected passage in Plato's *Republic*." "He alluded to the case of sticks appearing bent in water as an optical illusion.")

ambiguous, vague   Something is *ambiguous* when there is more than one way to interpret it in context. Consider this example from America's premier philosopher, W. V. O. Quine (1908–2000): "Their mothers bore them." Are their mothers tiresome and boring, or did their mothers give birth to them? By contrast, an expression is *vague* if it is difficult to interpret in any specific way. Just how much of a man's hair needs to be gone before he can properly be described as *bald*? A *small* elephant is still much larger than a *large* mouse.

deduce, deduct   These two verbs are sometimes confused, probably because their noun form, "deduction," is the same. One *deduces* a conclusion from certain premises — and the resulting deduction is either valid or not. Hence, "deduces" is roughly a synonym for "infers." However, one *deducts* the cost of business travel from one's income tax; the resulting deduction may or may not be allowed. Thus, "deducts" is roughly synonymous with "subtracts." Philosophers constantly are concerned with deductions of the first sort, but rarely (except around April 15) with those of the second sort.

denote, connote, mean   Words and phrases — especially common nouns—have meaning in two different ways. First, they *refer to* or *denote* something; thus the term "horse" denotes or refers to all the members of the biological species *equus,* the animals (past, present, future) in the real world. Strictly, the denotation of a common noun, such as "horse," is the class of all horses; terms such as "unicorn" denote the null class, since there are no unicorns. Second, all of these words *con-*

note or have as their *sense* certain features typical, characteristic, or essential to the members of the class. Thus, the connotation or sense of the word "horse" includes being a mammal with four feet and hooves, suitable for riding, etc.

We need the distinction between sense and reference because we need to be able to explain how two terms can refer to the same thing (as "water" and "H_2O" do), and yet not mean exactly the same thing (we knew what water was long before we knew that it was H_2O). We also need to be able to explain how terms that have no application (as is true of "unicorn" and "hobgoblin," since there are no such things) nevertheless are not meaningless and do not mean the same thing.

John Stuart Mill popularized the verbs "connote" and "denote," along with their associated nouns, in his *System of Logic* (1843). Most philosophers today shun these two words and use instead the pair of nouns "sense" (for connotation) and "reference" (for denotation). These terms owe their popularity to the influential German mathematical logician Gottlob Frege (1848–1925). He designated the two kinds of meaning as *Sinn* and *Bedeutung,* and the English terms "sense" and "reference" are, respectively, the standard translations of his German.

dilemma, paradox   A *dilemma* is a predicament in which all the alternatives are unattractive. For example, the novel *Sophie's Choice* is built on the dilemma Sophie faces when a Nazi officer tells her to choose between her two children; she may save one, but the other will be exterminated — a tragic choice if ever there was one. A *paradox* is a statement or conclusion that is counterintuitive but that nevertheless seems to follow by impeccable logic. Paradoxes are as old as Zeno of Elea (fifth century B.C.), who argued that motion is impossible: Before an arrow can hit its target, it must go half the distance; but before it can go half the distance, it must go a quarter, and so on. In essence, it must pass through an infinite series of distances. But nothing can pass through an infinite series of distances. By this logic, it seems impossible for an arrow to hit its target. But arrows can hit their targets. You figure it out!

feel, think   In common speech and writing we often use the verb *feel* when our feelings are not at issue. (For example, "I feel that Nietzsche's views on morality are far more interesting than Kierkegaard's.") Perhaps the idea is to suggest some uncertainty or tentativeness in what one *thinks*. In any case, you are well advised to say "I think" when in fact it is what you think or believe that is at issue. Save the verb "feel" for the occasions when it is someone's feelings you wish to report ("Sometimes we feel guilty when in fact we are not guilty").

immanent, eminent, imminent   God is said to be *immanent* (as opposed to *transcendent*) just to the extent that God is thought to enter into history and directly into our lives, say through answering our prayers. A philosopher is *eminent* just to the extent that he or she is well known to other philosophers and holds views that are highly regarded and widely discussed, in contrast to other philosophers of lesser eminence or no eminence whatever. The due date for an essay in your philosophy course is *imminent* if it is only a few days (or hours) away.

infer, imply   This pair of verbs is chronically misused. Persons *infer* when, like Sherlock Holmes, they draw a conclusion from certain premises. Thus, an *inference* is the conclusion someone draws from premises, circumstances, or events. Persons *imply* when they hint or suggest something without explicitly saying it. ("Wittgenstein's views in his *Philosophical Investigations* imply a rejection of most of his earlier views of the *Tractatus*.") Thus, one who asserts both "All crows are black" and "That bird is a crow" implies the unstated proposition "That bird is black." An *implication* is something that follows from something else. Words or other signs by themselves often imply things; they never infer anything. Only people (and perhaps some animals) infer things. Thus, a brand-new wristwatch in good working order lying on a remote sandy beach implies that someone quite recently lost or discarded this watch on or near the spot; and if you found such a watch, you might infer just that.

necessary and sufficient conditions   A condition is *necessary* just in case in its absence something cannot happen. For example, adequate moisture in the air is a necessary condition of snow or rain. Necessary conditions can be expressed with the connective "only if." ("It will snow only if there is enough moisture in the air.") A condition is *sufficient* for a result if whenever the condition occurs, then so does the result. ("Given the amount of moisture in the air, the sudden drop in temperature to below zero Celsius was sufficient for it to snow.") Or, to take another example, a sufficient condition of being excused from meeting the deadline of a paper assignment is a note from your doctor. Sufficient conditions can be expressed with the connective "if." ("If you bring a doctor's excuse, that will be sufficient.") A given condition may be sufficient but not necessary, necessary but not sufficient, neither, or both.

principle, principal   "Principle," a noun that means a fundamental *rule,* figures frequently in philosophy ("the principle of excluded middle" in logic, "the principle of charity" in hermeneutics, and "the principle of utility" in ethics and political theory). "Principle" is often used in the plural, as in "principles of inference" or "principles underlying our moral code." "Principal," although it can be a noun (as when, in finance, one contrasts principal and interest), is usually an adjective and is roughly synonymous with "chief," "paramount," or "major." ("My principal point in this paper is that. . . .") "Principal" is rarely used in the plural.

Reviewing Your Paper
for Grammar and Punctuation

Though you should focus primarily on the content and organization of your philosophical essay, don't overlook the finer points of good writing. Errors in grammar and punctuation can detract — sometimes seriously — from an otherwise strong paper. Such errors can make you appear careless and thus undermine the authority of your writing. It's important, then, to check for problems with grammar and punctuation after you have made major revisions in content.

This section is intended to alert you to major errors to look out for in your papers. Of course, it's not within the scope of this book to thoroughly cover the conventions of good writing. For such detailed advice, you should consult a writer's handbook.

Grammar

The following questions cover some of the most common grammatical errors. You might want to use the questions as a checklist to help identify and correct problems in your writing.

Are your sentences parallel in structure? To make sentences logical and clear, items in a series or grouped ideas should be expressed in a consistent, or parallel, form. The following sentence is not in parallel form:

```
In this paper I intend to discuss the morality of eutha-
nasia, show why doctors ought not to assist in euthana-
sia, and that euthanasia is not a moral right.
```

To be grammatically consistent with the rest of the sentence, the last clause ("that euthanasia . . .") should begin with a verb. The following revision makes the sentence elements parallel:

```
In this paper I intend to discuss the morality of eutha-
nasia, show why doctors ought not to assist in euthana-
sia, and argue that euthanasia is not a moral right.
```

Are modifiers placed properly? Modifiers, words or phrases that describe or limit other words, should be placed as close as possible to what they modify. Consider this sentence:

```
You only need to read chapter 1 to complete the exercise.
```

Because the modifier "only" is intended to limit what needs to be read—chapter 1—and nothing more, the sentence should be revised as follows:

```
You need to read only chapter 1 to complete the exercise.
```

Watch out, too, for dangling modifiers, which don't refer logically to what they are intended to modify:

> ```
> Serving in the Austrian Army during World War I while he
> wrote the Tractatus Logico-Philosophicus, it was one of
> Wittgenstein's most impressive works.
> ```

In this sentence, the dangling modifier "Serving in the Austrian Army during World War I . . ." does not refer logically to anything in the clause "it was one of Wittgenstein's most impressive works." The sentence could be reworked as follows:

> ```
> Serving in the Austrian Army during World War I while he
> wrote Tractatus Logico-Philosophicus, Wittgenstein pro-
> duced one of his most impressive works.
> ```

Do you avoid shifts in tense? Because shifts in the tense of your verbs can distract and disorient readers, strive for consistency. Notice the tenses of the underlined verbs in this example:

> ```
> Although Turing does not present a convincing positive
> argument--he replied to various objections and defended
> the imitation game as a fair test--he does provide a
> strong argument against the view that computing machines
> cannot play the imitation game.
> ```

The tense in this sentence shifts confusingly from the present ("does not present") to the past ("replied" and "defended") and then back to the present ("does provide"). Revised for consistency, the sentence would read:

> ```
> Although Turing does not present a convincing positive
> argument--he replies to various objections and defends
> the imitation game as a fair test--he does provide a
> strong argument against the view that computing machines
> cannot play the imitation game.
> ```

Because philosophical texts and ideas — even those that are hundreds of years old — endure and remain relevant, it is conventional to discuss them in the present tense, as in the preceding example.

Do you avoid shifts in point of view? Like tense shifts, shifts in point of view are distracting. Whether your point of view is the first person ("I" or "we"), second person ("you"), or third person ("he," "she," "it," "one," "they"), strive for consistency. Notice the underlined pronouns in the following example:

> ```
> Our philosophy course was challenging.  We discussed
> Kant's Critique of Pure Reason in the first two weeks.
> Then you had to write a fifteen-page paper on it.
> ```

The point of view shifts from the first person ("our" and "we") to the second person ("you"). Revised for consistency, the sentence would read:

> ```
> Our philosophy course was challenging.  We discussed
> Kant's Critique of Pure Reason in the first two weeks.
> Then we had to write a fifteen-page paper on it.
> ```

Do you avoid fragments and run-on sentences? Fragments are word groups that, though they are presented as complete sentences, are not complete. Run-on sentences, by contrast, are word groups that seem to "run on" because they have not been punctuated properly. It's easy to make both of these errors in a first draft, especially if you are working quickly. When revising your draft, look out for sentences like this:

```
Pythagoras's legacy had a great influence on classical
Greek and medieval European thought.  Especially in
mathematics, music theory, and astronomy.
```

"Especially in mathematics, music theory, and astronomy" is a phrase modifying "thought"; thus, it is a fragment, not a complete sentence. Attaching the fragment to the sentence that precedes it solves the problem:

```
Pythagoras's legacy had a great influence on classical
Greek and medieval European thought, especially in math-
ematics, music theory, and astronomy.
```

Now consider this example:

```
Pythagoras is best known for describing numerical rela-
tionships in right triangles, in fact, he saw numerical
relationships in all things.
```

The comma inserted between the two independent clauses doesn't give readers enough of a break; thus, the sentence is a run-on. Inserting a semicolon between the clauses solves the problem:

```
Pythagoras is best known for describing numerical rela-
tionships in right triangles; in fact, he saw numerical
relationships in all things.
```

The sentence could also be restructured as follows:

```
Though Pythagoras is best known for describing numerical
relationships in right triangles, he saw numerical rela-
tionships in all things.
```

Do your subjects and verbs agree? Subjects and verbs should agree in person (first, second, or third) and in number (singular or plural). When revising your papers, look out for errors like the following:

```
This group of theories were presented together in Davis's
final monograph.
```

Because the subject of the sentence is "group," a singular noun (not "theories"), the verb "were" should be replaced with "was."

Indefinite pronouns like "anybody," "each," "either," "everyone," "neither," and "none" are especially tricky. Though they often seem to be plural, such pronouns are singular; thus, errors like the following are common:

```
Each of the theories were supported by Davis's research.
```

To agree with the singular pronoun "each," the plural verb "were" should be replaced with the singular verb "was."

Do your pronouns and antecedents agree? A pronoun (a word that stands in for a noun) should agree with its antecedent (the word to which the pronoun refers), and vice versa.

```
A candidate must complete a semester of independent study
before they can enter the program.
```

The pronoun "they" is plural; thus it does not agree with its singular antecedent, "candidate." The following revision corrects the problem by making the antecedent plural:

```
Candidates must complete a semester of independent study
before they can enter the program.
```

Be careful when using indefinite pronouns, which, though singular, often seem to be plural.

```
No one will be eligible for the program until they have
completed a semester of independent study.
```

The pronoun "they" does not agree with its singular antecedent, the indefinite pronoun "No one." The sentence could be revised as follows:

```
No one will be eligible for the program until he or she
has completed a semester of independent study.
```

Since the "he or she" construction is awkward, one could rework the sentence this way:

```
To be eligible for the program, a candidate must have
completed a semester of independent study.
```

Punctuation

Following is an overview of some punctuation marks that are especially troublesome.

The apostrophe. When you want to refer to a book by Russell or to a doctrine advanced by Spinoza, you would of course write:

```
Russell's book      Spinoza's doctrine
```

That is, you would form the possessive of the proper name by adding an apostrophe followed by the letter "s." But suppose the proper name already ends with the letter "s," as do the names of St. Thomas Aquinas, René Descartes, and John Rawls, a contemporary American philosopher. In cases such as these, *follow the same rule:*

```
Aquinas's theory      Descartes's belief      Rawls's book
```

Don't make the blunder of confusing "its," the possessive form of "it," and "it's," the contraction of "it is." Like other possessive pronouns, such as "ours," "yours," and "theirs," "its" has no apostrophe.

Dash versus hyphen. The dash, formed by typing two hyphens (- -), works much like parentheses in that it allows you to insert a comment within a sentence. However, use dashes instead of parentheses when you want to interrupt a thought or draw attention to a parenthetical remark:

```
Freud's theories--whether or not you agree with them--
have been influential throughout this century.
```

Dashes are often favored over parentheses because they offer a lower and therefore less disruptive hurdle to the eye than do the vertical parentheses. (In your typewritten papers, do not put a space before or after the dash.)

By contrast, the hyphen is used, among other purposes, to divide a word at the end of a line. Such a hyphen tells readers that the letters to the left of the hyphen are a syllable or two of a whole word, the rest of which begins the very next line of type. Another use of the hyphen is to form compound modifiers, like "full-blown AIDS," "twenty-second entry," "half-baked ideas," and to form compound nouns, such as "city-state" and "philosopher-king." The hyphen is also used to replace the word "to," as in "pages 17-30." (Notice, however, that if you write "from" in front of "page," you must also write "to" and not use the hyphen. Thus, write "from page 17 to 30" or "pages 17-30," but *not* "from pages 17-30.") Finally, the hyphen is used to join some prefixes to their root noun, as in "anti-Semite," "pro-choice," and "self-conscious."

Parentheses versus square brackets. Parentheses mark off a digression or amplification, sometimes inside a sentence, sometimes after a sentence. Be careful not to overuse parentheses. A good rule of thumb is this: If the sentence you have written really needs the parenthetical material, perhaps you should replace the parentheses with a pair of commas, since parentheses are more of a barrier to the eye than are commas. Or perhaps the parenthetical information deserves a sentence of its own, on equal footing with the sentences before and after it.

Square brackets have a much narrower role than parentheses. Their primary use is to mark an insertion inside a quotation. They tell readers that the bracketed word or words are *not* in the original quotation (for further discussion, see "Integrating Quotations," p. 161). Brackets are also used for parenthetical insertions *inside* parentheses, as in the following example:

```
Descartes's argument for God in the "Third Meditation"
(according to most commentators, though not all [Bernard
Williams is an exception]) is far less important to his
project than is his argument in the "Fifth Meditation."
```

Revising Papers in Response to Others' Comments

Peer Review

Unless your instructor declares otherwise, you ought to seek out a roommate, a classmate, or some other student as a resource in helping you revise your essay. (Naturally, you'll offer to reciprocate the service.) Once you have written a first draft of your paper, the observations of a second reader can be most helpful. The flaws that writers fail to see in their own writing often are quickly spotted by a different pair of eyes. Thus, getting a *peer review* of your work-in-progress as it enters its final stages can be of real value.

Peer review can take several forms, two of which deserve mention. (Often these approaches are combined.) In one method, you give your reader a clean draft of your paper and ask that he or she mark up the draft with suggestions, corrections, questions, and other helpful comments. You can then refer to these comments as you develop the next draft.

Another style of peer review is to discuss your paper with your peer reader as soon as he or she has finished reading it. With this method, you can ask the reader to elaborate on whatever in your draft caught his or her attention, perhaps making it easier for you to see how to deal with problems the reader has noticed.

A discussion may take more of your reader's time than the first method and for that reason may not be so easy to arrange. But never mind: different strokes for different folks. Either system of peer review is better than not bothering to get another perspective on your draft. If peer review is unavailable, seek out your college writing center for help.

Whether or not peer review is available, one of the best ways to assess the quality of your own writing is to *read the draft aloud,* even if you have no audience. Far better than your eye, your ear will detect defects in tone, cadence, grammar, diction, and flow.

Some students (and instructors) worry about collaboration between students during the revision process. Of course, you do want to distinguish carefully between having someone point out what is confusing, incomplete, careless, or just plain wrong and having someone else solve these problems for you. If you seek a peer review from a student who is *not* in your philosophy course, and thus is unfamiliar with your paper topic, you minimize the likelihood that he or she will have too much influence on your writing. And if you choose your peer reader well, you maximize the chance that you will get some important insights for improving organization, clarity, and adequacy of explanation and argument, even though your peer reader has not done the relevant reading or heard classroom lectures and discussions related to your paper topic. Be sure, if you have any doubts about whether your instructor would object to peer review in either of the two forms just described, to explain your intentions and ask for permission.

Instructor Comments

Many instructors ask students to turn in first drafts of their essays so that the instructor can provide some guidance on how to develop the essays as well as bring errors and omissions to students' attention. After studying the marginal comments from the instructor, students then revise their papers accordingly and submit them for a grade. In exercise 13, we will see how one student, Peter Miller, revised his first draft in response to his instructor's comments.

EXERCISE 13: *Writing and Revising an Essay*

Introduction   The following text is chapter 13 of *Free Will and Responsibility* (1984) by Jennifer Trusted. In this chapter Trusted discusses some aspects of the perennial problem of freedom of the will. She focuses on the contrast between the two most popular theories, *libertarianism* and *determinism*. Determinism is the view that, because all our behavior is determined (caused) by physical events inside or outside our bodies, human freedom is an illusion. Libertarianism holds that, because not all our behavior is determined, human freedom is not an illusion; persons really can decide freely and responsibly what to do.

JENNIFER TRUSTED
The Concept of Freedom

Hitherto it has been assumed that we all (determinists and libertarians) know what freedom *is,* even if some of us doubt that it is possible to be free and to make a free choice. In respect of human behavior the concept of *free* actions has been contrasted with that of determined happenings, with the implication that any human act must either be free or be determined — that these are the only two possibilities and they are mutually exclusive.   1

We have discussed mitigating circumstances: ignorance, threats, and the like, but we have inclined to the Aristotelian view that,   2

Jennifer Trusted (b. 1924) earned her first degree at Cambridge in 1946 and her Ph.D. in philosophy at Exeter in 1973. She was teaching in England at the Open University and at Exeter when she published her first book, *Free Will and Responsibility* (1984), from which this excerpt is reprinted. In subsequent years she has published books in several areas of philosophy: *Moral Principles and Social Values* (1987), *Physics and Metaphysics* (1991), *Beliefs and Biology* (1996), *Introduction to the Philosophy of Knowledge* (1996), the *The Myth of Matter* (1999).

unless there is *physical* compulsion, an act is deemed to be free.[1] Mitigating circumstances might absolve or partly absolve from *responsibility,* but the choice made is still a free choice. For example, the bank clerk threatened with a gun may *choose* to hand over the money, but that is an action, not a happening, for *he could have chosen otherwise.* The threatening gun does not destroy freedom of choice, though in most circumstances it absolves the clerk from blame. In other circumstances, we may regard *moral* attitudes as compelling, but that is to recognize that moral *choice* is possible; the agent is free to make that moral choice. "When Luther thundered at the Diet of Worms 'Here I stand. I can no other. So help me God,' he was not denying, he was presupposing, that, in the most fundamental sense, he could!"[2]

When libertarians say that there is free choice, they are saying 3 that an action is free because the agent could have chosen to act differently and could in fact have acted differently. He or she could have chosen and acted differently despite all the physical conditions remaining the same.

However, this does not exclude libertarians from acknowledg- 4 ing that human actions depend on certain relevant physical conditions being satisfied. The distinction between them and determinists is that the latter account for human actions solely in terms of prior physical events (directly for physical determinists, indirectly for teleological determinists). What the libertarian thesis entails is that the same person could have taken a different decision and could have acted differently, if both external and internal *physical* conditions had remained the same. Therefore it is not inconsistent for libertarians to acknowledge that any given action can only take place if appropriate physical conditions are satisfied. When they say that a person "could have done otherwise" the "could" is meant unconditionally *within* the given physical context.

In an ordinary physical system (excluding subatomic events) we 5 believe this to be impossible. We hold that a given physical event is completely determined by the physical conditions and could not be otherwise if these physical conditions remained unaltered. This is why the libertarian claim strikes the determinist as fundamentally unreasonable, indeed nonsensical. But the essential feature of the libertarian case is that human actions are *not* like ordinary physical events.

However, it does not follow that human actions are *entirely* the 6 result of nonphysical causes (they patently are not) nor that intentions are independent of physical circumstances (again they patently are not). Therefore we must appreciate that human actions and even

---

1. In his "A Plea for Excuses," *Philosophical Papers,* ed. J. O. Urmson and G. J. Warnock (3rd ed., OUP, Oxford, 1979), J. L. Austin associates himself with Aristotle: ". . . 'free' is only used to rule out the suggestion of some or all of its recognized antitheses . . . 'freedom' is not a name for a characteristic of actions, but the name of a dimension in which actions are assessed . . . Aristotle has often been chidden for talking about excuses or pleas and overlooking the 'real problem': in my own case, it was when I began to see the injustice of this charge that I first became interested in excuses" (p. 180).

2. Antony Flew, *A Rational Animal* (Clarendon Press, Oxford, 1978), p. 63.

intentions may be at least *partly* determined and, having accepted this, we must alter our concept of freedom. Instead of being a concept like spherical or square which does or does not apply, it is to be regarded as a concept like difficult, or distant, or dim which may be applied in a given context and not in another because there are degrees of these qualities. A choice may be held to be relatively free, free within certain limits, partly free, or largely free. These gradations due to circumstances were appreciated by Aristotle but . . . he related them to responsibility rather than to freedom.

When we consider the relation of circumstances to degrees of   7
freedom, rather than to degrees of responsibility, we are concerned with freedom of choice, with freedom as to what we decide to do; that is, what we intend. Aristotle was also primarily concerned with intention, but we differ from him for he did not doubt that nearly all intentions were freely formed.[3] We do doubt this, and so we can argue that there can be absolution from responsibility even if there is no external physical compulsion. We think that there can be internal psychological compulsion.

What a libertarian has to show is that even if there are some   8
psychological factors which can affect intentions, so that some decisions are determined by internal factors, yet, at least in some instances, there can be an element of freedom. Determinists argue that the balance between internal and external factors can vary, and certain internal factors (such as phobias) may be more obviously compelling than others, but, at the last, there is no freedom. They say that if all the external and internal physical conditions remain unchanged, then whatever intention was formed, and whatever action was taken, could not have been otherwise. They will agree that the less compelling the psychological state *seems* to be, the more easily we can imagine that another intention and another action was possible, but this belief in an alternative is illusory.

Now we can all grant that, for any action, a great many physical   9
conditions must be satisfied; but libertarians are not disputing that physical conditions affect intentions and action. Their point is that, for the performance of an action, the intention is a necessary condition and that intention is not *entirely* physically determined. In other words they are asserting that intentions and decisions can be, at least partly, independent of all physical events. What we have to consider is whether this can be justified: if all physical conditions (external and internal) are fixed, can an individual *choose* whether and how to act? The libertarian says "Yes" and the determinist says "No."

Perhaps if we look at this question and its assumptions a little   10
more closely we may find a path out of the impasse. We need to consider the significance of "can" and "could" in different contexts. Even in one sentence there can be two different senses. For example: "I could have walked a mile in twenty minutes this morning but I could not have run a mile in one minute this morning."

---

3. He did think that persistent wrongdoing would corrupt the character so that freedom could be thus restricted. But ordinarily choice was free; Aristotle did not entertain our notion of psychological compulsion.

The first "could" implies that the act was not performed because 11 I *chose* not to take a walk; the second "could not" states that the act was not performed because it was physically impossible for me to do it. This shows that there are, at the ordinary commonsense level, significant differences in the way we make use of "can" and "could." But the differences are deeper than may appear on first consideration. Libertarians are prepared to agree with determinists that physical conditions[4] must be satisfied, and that, if they are not, then there can be no free choice. They are concerned with the former type of implication of "can" and "could." In such circumstances, they say, the choice is free and is the decisive cause of action (or nonaction).

We need to consider whether the connection between choice 12 and action, or decision and action, can be *causal*. Compare "If I choose then I can go through the door" with "If I am thin enough then I can squeeze through that gap." From the former you can infer that I can go through the door, whether or not I choose in fact to do so. From the latter you certainly cannot infer that I can squeeze through the gap whether or not I am thin enough.

Thus a choice, be it free or determined, is certainly not a condi- 13 tion of action in the way that physical conditions are conditions of action. Nevertheless, choice is some kind of condition — a different kind, but still a condition. J. L. Austin says: "One view is that wherever we have *can* or *could have* as our main verb, an *if*-clause must always be understood or supplied, if it is not actually present, in order to complete the sense of the sentence."[5] Austin wishes to draw our attention to the difference between "I could have if I had chosen" and "I could have if I had the capacity." He argues that, in the first case, any "if" that is added, is added in order to analyze the sentence; basically the sentence can be accepted as a simple, unconditional, categorical assertion. By contrast, in the second case, the "if" is required because the sentence is a true conditional. "To argue that *can* always requires an *if*-clause with it to complete the sense is totally different from arguing that *can*-sentences are always to be analyzed into sentences containing *if*-clauses."[6]

In our ordinary English usage, to say "I can" or "I could" implies 14 that all physical conditions are satisfied, but this is quite different from saying that the assertion is a conditional. If I say "I can ride a bicycle," I mean my statement to be taken categorically, not hypothetically: "We allow that, in saying that he could have, I do assert or imply that certain *conditions,* those of opportunity, *were satisfied:* but this is totally different from allowing that, in saying that he could have, I *assert something conditional.*"[7] We have to be careful with our "cans," as Austin says: "We are tempted to say that 'He can'

---

4. I have omitted consideration of psychological conditions, e.g. "I could not bring myself to watch a bullfight," because these can be related to past history and genetic makeup, thus to physical states of the brain, and therefore they can also be regarded as physically compelling. Austin's point is that, in ordinary usage, "can" and "could" imply that there are no restraining physical (including such psychological) conditions.

5. J. L. Austin, op. cit. (n. 1 above), p. 214.

6. Ibid. p. 217.

7. Ibid. p. 225.

sometimes means just that he has the ability, with *nothing said* about opportunity, sometimes *just* that he has the chance, with nothing said about ability, sometimes, however, that he really actually *fully can* here and now, having both ability and opportunity."[8]

Clearly choice is not a condition analogous to physical conditions but we must make a choice (take a decision) to carry out an action. Austin's opening question, "Are *cans* constitutionally iffy?" can be seen as posing our problem in another form. Near the end of his essay he writes: "In philosophy it is *can* in particular that we seem so often to uncover, just when we thought some problem settled, grinning residually up at us like the frog at the bottom of the beer mug."[9]

Libertarians want to lift that frog out of the beer mug and say that there are circumstances when with all physical conditions unaltered, choice could have been otherwise. Unfortunately [libertarians'] opinion can never be tested for, in any given circumstance, one choice is made and one action performed. There cannot be a repetition for it is impossible for the circumstances to be repeated. There is a necessary alteration in that the second choice must be influenced by the outcome of the first. Austin himself is undecided:[10]

> It has been alleged . . . that the things we ordinarily say about what we can do and could have done may actually be consistent with determinism. It is hard to evade all attempt to decide whether this allegation is true — hard even for those who, like myself, are inclined to think that determinism itself is still a name for nothing clear, that has been argued for only incoherently. At least I should like to claim that the arguments considered . . . fail to show that it *is* true, and indeed in failing go some way to show that it is *not*. Determinism, whatever it may be, may yet be the case, but at least it appears not consistent with what we ordinarily say and presumably think.[11]

We may see the problem as a problem where common sense takes account of psychological conditions by considering a set of concrete cases. Let us take a person X, and X's decision to answer or not to answer the doorbell. We assume that all relevant physical conditions are satisfied but there are other factors that must be taken into account. For example:

1. Someone with a gun demanded that X stayed very still.
2. X feared the arrival of a debt collector.
3. X was very tired.
4. X was listening to an interesting talk on the radio.
5. X was reading an interesting book.
6. X was "just sitting."

For Aristotle, X would make a free choice in all these circumstances, because not physically compelled. Today we would be in-

8. Ibid. p. 230.
9. Ibid. p. 231.
10. See also ch. 18.
11. J. L. Austin, op. cit., p. 231.

clined to argue that the different circumstances offered different degrees of freedom. The freedom in situation 1 barely counts as freedom, there is more in 2, probably yet more in 3, and so on. Our problem is whether, in any of these situations, with *all* the external and internal physical conditions remaining constant, X's choice could have been different.

We might be tempted to say that apart from situation 1 there was   19 scope for a free choice, but we should have to admit that one factor affecting the choice will be X's disposition. A determinist will maintain that the disposition (and hence X's decision) is determined by X's genetic constitution and past history. The illusion of freedom, the determinist would say, rests on the fact that a very small change in physical conditions (internal or external) could lead to the opposite decision; but change there must be for choice to be different. Prediction of X's decision (and action) may be difficult, indeed impossible, but this gives no ground for saying that X's choice is not determined by physical conditions alone. In an ultimate sense determinists allow no degrees of freedom for there is no real freedom. There can be degrees of predictability, but that is another matter.

Libertarians argue that different conditions, as for example in 1   20 to 6 above, give, in this case X, different degrees of freedom of choice. They contend that the determinist view of disposition as being the historically determined character (a passive result of genetic constitution and past history)[12] ignores the active personal decision taken in the situation. When we say that someone acts "out of character" we are referring to the determined historical character. But the fact that such a phrase as "out of character" makes sense indicates that there is another aspect of character. A decision taken at a given time is the result of conscious awareness of conditions *and* of conscious assessment of the probable result of the decision, that is its likely effect on the individual (internally and externally) and on others. It is this assessment which need not be totally dependent on physical conditions. A decision to take the "right" or "wrong" course of action will itself affect the historical character, and frequent "right" or "wrong" decisions can make permanent alterations in the historical character. As Aristotle said, "It is in our power to be decent or worthless." Libertarians need not deny that persistent decisions to do "wrong" may so debase the historical character that the conscious self is forcefully directed to the wrong decision. But, for libertarians, all conscious decisions are still made by the conscious self and that self, although it is influenced, and perhaps strongly influenced, by its historical character as well as by physical events, is not absolutely determined by them. The historical character may be as compelling as the man with the gun, but in neither case is the compulsion absolute. Nevertheless, it may be so effective that prediction of behavior is easy and, for practical purposes, is absolutely reliable.

---

12. Each person's historical character can be regarded as due to a physical brain program.

Yet though the influence of historical character may be so strong   21
that the decision is, for practical purposes, determined, this does
not undermine the libertarian thesis. Libertarians can admit that for
very good and very bad characters decisions are practically determined without losing their case. Their case rests on the assumption
that there is a conscious self which makes judgments that need not
be completely dependent on physical events. By contrast, determinists assert that judgments must be completely dependent on physical events.

To summarize: For determinists freedom is an illusion that arises   22
because there are many occasions when human actions are unpredictable. For libertarians there are degrees of freedom: The conscious self may be practically compelled or strongly influenced or
less strongly influenced by external and internal physical circumstances. But although certain decisions are, and potentially all decisions *could be,* determined by physical conditions, it does not follow that they *must* be. . . . If we insist, as determinists do, that all
decisions are physically determined, we are simply insisting on determinism as a metaphysical thesis; it becomes an act of faith. . . .

Sample Student First Draft with Instructor Comments

This was Miller's assignment:

Write an essay of 500 to 750 words on the following topic: In her
essay "The Concept of Freedom," from *Free Will and Responsibility,* Jennifer Trusted claims that freedom is not an all-or-nothing
concept like "square," but is a concept of degrees, like "difficult."
What is her argument for this view? What bearing does it have on
the dispute between determinists and libertarians?

Jennifer Trusted's Concept of Freedom
and Its Bearing on the Dispute between
Determinists and Libertarians

by

Peter L. Miller III

Informative title. Good.

Effective introduction   In her book entitled <u>Free Will and Responsibility</u>,   1

Jennifer Trusted claims that the traditionally accepted

view of freedom as an either/or (type of) concept is wrong.   *Wordy*

Instead she claims that freedom is a concept of degrees

Her?

or gradations. This (perception) of freedom necessitates a   *?*

reevaluation of the debate between determinists and

libertarians. (It) also suggests a (reclassification) of   *Explain* *?*

both views.   *Choppy. Tie together*

Short para. Attach it to next para?   (This) dispute has centered on (the debate of) whether   *Wordy*   2

there are any really free actions or whether they are all

determined happenings. (This) implies that any human

action must be one of the two.   *Vary your language.*

The (determinist) believes that all human actions are   3

Commas needed because "determined" = "caused."   determined, or caused, by prior physical events. (They)   *Pronoun does not agree with antecedent*

allow varying balances between internal and external

physical factors but deny that if the set of factors is

kept the same then more than one outcome is possible.   *Wordy*

Determinists also say that certain (internal factors--

i.e., psychological ones)--are strong and compelling while

weaker ones seem to open the door to other possible

Wrong word   intentions and actions. But these other possibilities

are (allusions) that arise because of the impossibility of

Put modifier by word it modifies.   measuring all of the minute actions that sum to cause

human action (accurately). In the end there is no freedom.

The libertarians, on the other hand, hold that even if

all of the internal and external physical factors re-

Avoid repetition.   mained (the same) (the same) person <u>could</u> have chosen differ-

Comma needed.

ently.   In other words, human actions are not entirely
determined by physical causes.

Trusted starts her argument here.   She states that | 4
for the libertarians to agree that any human action can
(only) take place if certain physical conditions are met is
not inconsistent with their viewpoint.   The ("could,") from *elliptical — expand this idea*

Somewhere, you need a full reference to this source → the libertarian's point of view, is understood to be
"meant unconditionally (within) the given physical context"
(Trusted, para. 4).   *Trusted's emphasis, or yours?*

A physical event is completely determined by physi- | 5
cal conditions.   A given event will not be different *Says who? You? Trusted?*
unless the conditions are altered.   Therefore, in an
Awkward. Can you be more specific? ordinary physical system (i.e., on a supra-atomic scale)
(the "could" from above) is impossible and thus seems
nonsensical to determinists.

Since, according to libertarians, human actions are | 6
not wholly determined by physical factors, they must not
be exclusively in an ordinary physical system.   Therefore, human actions are not ordinary physical events.
Nor are they entirely determined by nonphysical causes.
And intentions are not independent physical causes,
Quotation marks needed when you mention words as words. either.   Therefore, says Trusted, human actions and
intentions are _partly_ determined.   Furthermore, we must
alter the traditional concept of freedom: the terms
"totally free" and "totally determined" no longer apply.

Trusted now comes to her final conclusions.   Freedom | 7
This paragraph only restates Trusted's view. It doesn't explain it. is not a concept like "square"; that is, it is not an
either/or concept.   Rather, it is a concept like "diffi-
cult," a matter of degree or gradation.   Furthermore,
these gradations are due to the circumstances of a
situation.   *Wordy*

Specify what "this" refers to. (This) (serves to change) the goal of the libertarians | 8
in their debate against the determinists.   Now, instead
of having to prove that human actions are completely
freely chosen, they (only) need show that human actions in

Right word?

some small way are even slightly free. (Conversely,) the

task of the determinists is orders of (magnitude) harder:

Now they must prove that human actions are in no part, no

Avoid repetition.

matter how small, free.

Since freedom has the quality of (magnitude,) rather   9

than presence or absence, we can see that there will be

actions that are mostly determined. These will still

Is it scope or accuracy that their view lacks?

have a very small free component, but they will practi-

Awkward to speak of views as having subsets.

cally be determined happenings. In this way the deter-

minist (view) can be seen as a small (subset) of the liber-

tarian view. Thus, it seems that the determinists do not

have the (entire) picture of human actions. *Redundant*

To accept their view, that (determined) (happenings) are   10

Don't you mean human choices and actions?

Too many small paragraphs

caused entirely by physical conditions, even though those

conditions may often not be detectable, is "an act of

faith" (Trusted, para. 22) and unpr(oo)vable. *Typo.*

Thus, Jennifer Trusted's concept of freedom does   11

A good note on which to end

much to further the libertarian's cause. Indeed, it may

render the determinist view as incomplete.

Awkward

Discussion   The comments and corrections on Miller's essay — almost all of them addressed only to his writing, not to his development of the paper topic — are more than most instructors would have time to make. Reviewing the remarks, we see that Miller's paper has several major strengths and weaknesses.

Miller does a good job of describing the differences between determinist and libertarian views and sketching Trusted's argument. Also, his introduction and conclusion are effective. This first draft, however, suffers from two main faults: First, Miller presents his views in the form of too many short paragraphs. Second, in paragraph 7, he does not explain Trusted's view that freedom is a concept of degree. In this draft, he just restates her view.

Let's examine the original essay paragraph by paragraph and look at some key strengths and weaknesses.

Paragraph 1. Miller provides an effective opening. The revisions needed here are minor.

Paragraph 2. Here's the first of several tiny paragraphs in Miller's essay.

Paragraph 3. This paragraph suffers from various flaws, noted in the margins. Nevertheless it is helpful because it supplies readers with a partial definition of two key terms — "determinism" and "libertarianism" — fairly promptly and within a few lines of each other. Some sort of definition of these two terms is needed, as Miller appreciates, if readers are to follow his overall argument.

Paragraph 4. Notice here, and again in paragraph 8, the way the word "only" has been introduced at the wrong place in the sentence. On each occasion, Miller gives this word too much scope in the sentence; "only" should be placed immediately before the word or words it is meant to limit. As far as Miller's use of "could" in the third sentence of this paragraph, the term needs to be expanded into a phrase to help the reader see the connection to the previous paragraph.

Paragraph 5. Miller opens this paragraph with a sentence that has no attribution — a common error. Be sure you make it plain to your readers just *whose* belief or doctrine you are stating.

Paragraph 6. Note the instructor's comment at the end of this paragraph, drawing Miller's attention to the fact that quotation marks are needed around the terms "totally free" and "totally determined." Quotation marks are needed whenever words themselves are being talked about, rather than being used in the normal fashion to mention something else.

Paragraph 7. The instructor's comment that Miller has only restated — not explained (or justified) — Trusted's view that freedom is a concept of degree points to the most important philosophical weakness of this draft. Something in a more analytical vein needs to be added or the paper doesn't really develop the assigned topic adequately. (Look at the revised draft to see how Miller repaired this defect.)

Paragraph 8. The pronoun "This" that begins the paragraph is vague; Miller needs to add a noun or a phrase to specify what "This" refers to. Again, "only" needs to be placed next to the words it modifies.

Paragraph 9. The instructor's final comment on the paragraph, addressed to the adjective "entire," suggests that Miller needs to give a little further thought to just what the difficulty here is for the determinist if Trusted's account of freedom is correct.

Paragraph 10. The phrase "determined happenings are caused" is redundant. One cure is to drop the adjective; another is to recast the sentence entirely.

Paragraph 11. This tiny closing paragraph consists of two sentences of very different value. In his first sentence, Miller steps back nicely from his discussion and passes judgment on what it shows. But his second sentence is less successful; it's not really clear what he means. Whether it is best to end with a very short paragraph, such as this, or to join this paragraph to its predecessor is perhaps mainly a matter of taste. In a short paper such as this, a nice, brisk concluding sentence or two (as in Miller's first draft) can be quite effective. Yet the ending in the revised version may be even better.

Now read through the second draft of Miller's paper. Of course, there is still room for various improvements, in both style and content. A third draft might be better than the second draft in several ways. Be that as it may, the point here is to see the many improvements that can be made on a draft essay that is as good as Miller's first draft was.

Miller's Revised Essay

Jennifer Trusted's Concept of Freedom
and Its Bearing on the Dispute between
Determinists and Libertarians
by
Peter L. Miller III

In her book entitled <u>Free Will and Responsibility</u>,[1] Jennifer Trusted claims that the traditionally accepted view of freedom as an either/or concept is wrong. Instead, she claims that freedom is a concept of degrees or gradations. If she is right, then the debate between determinists and libertarians needs to be reevaluated, and both views need to be revised.

The dispute between determinists and libertarians has centered on whether there are any really <u>free</u> actions or whether they are all determined happenings. This implies that any human action must be one or the other. The determinist believes that all human actions are determined, or caused, by prior physical events. Determinists do allow varying balances between internal and external physical factors, but they deny that if the set of factors is kept the same then more than one outcome is possible. Determinists also say that certain internal (psychological) factors are strong and compelling, while weaker ones seem to open the door to other possible inten-

----

1. All quotations in this paper are from Jennifer Trusted, <u>Free Will and Responsibility</u> (Oxford: Oxford University Press, 1984).

tions and actions. But these other possibilities are
illusions that arise because of the impossibility of
accurately measuring all the minute actions that sum
to cause human action. In the end there is no freedom. The libertarian, on the other hand, holds that
even if all of the internal and external physical
factors remained the same, a given person could have
chosen differently. In other words, human actions
are not entirely determined by physical causes.

Trusted starts her argument here. She states
that for the libertarians to agree that any human
action can take place only if certain physical conditions are met is not inconsistent with their view.
The "could have chosen differently," from the
libertarian's point of view, is understood to be
"meant unconditionally within the given physical
context" (Trusted, para. 4, emphasis in the original).

But determinists hold that each physical event
is completely determined by physical conditions. A
given event will not be different unless the conditions are altered. Therefore, in an ordinary physical system (i.e., on a supra-atomic scale) the
"could," mentioned above, is impossible and thus
seems nonsensical to determinists.

Since, according to libertarians, human actions
are not wholly determined by physical factors, they
must not be exclusively in an ordinary physical system. Therefore, human actions are not ordinary
physical events. Nor are they entirely determined by
nonphysical causes. And intentions are not independent physical causes, either. Therefore, says
Trusted, human actions and intentions are partly
determined. Furthermore, we must alter the traditional concept of freedom: The terms "totally free"
and "totally determined" no longer apply.

Trusted now comes to her final conclusions.
Freedom is not a concept like "square"; that is, it
is not an either/or concept. Rather, it is a concept

like "difficult," a matter of degree or gradation. Furthermore, these gradations are due to the circumstances of a situation. Her six different kinds of responses a person might make to the doorbell ringing illustrate the different degrees of freedom in our choices and acts.

These conclusions change the goal of the libertarians in their debate against the determinists. Instead of having to prove that human actions are completely freely chosen, they need show only that human actions in some small way are even slightly free. Consequently, the task of the determinists is orders of magnitude harder: Now they must prove that human actions are in no part, no matter how small, free.

Since freedom has the quality of degree, rather than presence or absence, we can see that there will be actions that are mostly determined. These will still have a very small free component, but they will practically be determined happenings. In this way the determinist view can be seen as a special case of the libertarian view. Thus, it seems that the determinists do not have a correct picture of all human actions.

To accept their view, that human choices and actions are caused entirely by physical conditions even though those conditions may often not be detectable, is "an act of faith" (Trusted, para. 22) and unprovable. Thus, Jennifer Trusted's concept of freedom does much to further the libertarian's cause. Indeed, it may even show that the determinist's view is wrong.

Manuscript Preparation and Format

All that remains is to put your paper into final form. Whatever the length or topic, the paper ought to display certain standard features before it leaves your hands and goes into those of your instructor. In a philosophy paper there are rarely any special features (computations, graphics) that need to be incorporated, and — except where those are needed — the guidelines offered here are transferable to just about any paper you will need to write in college humanities and social science courses. (As you have no doubt already learned, different instructors have different ideas about the way they want student papers prepared for submission. Naturally, you shouldn't depart from explicit instructions on such matters.)

Paper   No matter how you draft your paper, type or print it for submission on unlined 8 1/2" × 11" white stock. Any other kind or size of paper poses problems. (Of course, lined paper is fine for in-class examinations, which are usually handwritten.)

Typing   Do *not* submit a handwritten paper unless your instructor explicitly gives you permission. Handwritten papers are extremely difficult and time-consuming to read, and their length is hard to judge. Don't risk prejudicing an instructor against your work before he or she has even begun to read it! When typing, be sure to *double-space* all text; footnotes or endnotes may be single-spaced — unless, of course, your instructor advises otherwise. (Most stylebooks recommend double-spacing long quotations — see "Long Quotations," p. 164.) Also, never type or write on both sides of a sheet; the benefits of saving paper are far outweighed by the disadvantages to the reader — especially a reader who, like your instructor, intends to comment on what you have written and may need the back side of the page to do so.

Title Page   Not all instructors require a title page. If your instructor doesn't require one, you should type your name, the name of your instructor, the title of the course, and the date on separate lines in the upper left corner of the first page of your paper. The title should be centered over the text.

If your instructor does require a title page, type the title first, centered, on a separate sheet of paper, followed by your name, the course title, the instructor, and the date, all centered. Page 159 shows a format that you might use.

Pagination   Be sure that your paper includes page numbers on all but the title page. This not only keeps the sequence of pages clear but also enables the instructor to refer to specific page numbers in comments.

Margins   Be sure to leave margins of at least one inch on all sides of your paper. This allows room for the instructor's comments and keeps pages from looking cramped with text. Aim to fill a page with typescript averaging no more than about 250 words.

Indentations   Conventional paragraphing requires that the opening line of each paragraph be indented five spaces from the left margin. Usually, long quotations are indented ten spaces and single-spaced.

Numbering Propositions   Your paper may focus on several propositions (assertions, theses, doctrines), which you compare or contrast at later points. Referring to the propositions is easier if you treat each as a separate paragraph and assign a number, in parentheses, to each one. This practice annoys some readers because it may require them to turn back a page or two to remember just what a particular proposition said. Nevertheless, it is economical and precise and enables you to easily relate two or more propositions — for example, "Notice how proposition (1) is implied by proposition (3)." Just be careful not to rely too much on numbering and cross-references; you don't want to try your readers' patience and powers of concentration. (To see how one student effectively referenced numbered propositions, turn to the paper by David Hoberman, p. 74.)

Footnotes or References   You must cite the sources of all quotations and other borrowed material. The method of *in-text citation* generally is adequate for this purpose. Lengthy asides not sufficiently important to be included in the text itself belong in a note, either at the foot of the appropriate page or at the end of the paper. (For more information about citing and documenting sources, see chapter 6.)

Bibliography   You must provide complete publication information for all books and articles cited in your paper. Usually this information is included at the end of the paper, in a bibliography or a list of works cited. (See pp. 172–75 for details about compiling a bibliography.) Other types of bibliographies are a list of works consulted and a list of works relevant to a given topic but not so far used to write a paper. (For an example of the latter type, see "A Student's Bibliography," p. 175.)

Stapling   Fix the sheets of your paper in proper sequence and staple them together unless your instructor tells you otherwise. Paper clips and straight pins have a way of falling off or attaching themselves to the paper that is stacked on top of or underneath them.

Binders   You may choose to put your paper in a plastic binder that is available at your college bookstore. But unless your instructor asks you to use such binders, you might as well save yourself the money. Even though bound papers look nice, they do not flip open and stay open easily, and instructors find it difficult to mark them.

A Final Checklist

Now that you are finished with your paper and have printed out (or typed) the final copy, it is time for one last review to assure yourself that you haven't overlooked any important elements. If you can answer "Yes" to each question in the following checklist, you will have done about all that is possible to make your paper the best piece of work that you can.

Sample Title Page

Was Abraham's Intended Sacrifice of Isaac Really Murder?
Some Reflections on Kierkegaard's
<u>Fear and Trembling</u>

Sally Jacobson

Philosophy 001A: Introduction
Professor Azzouni
April 22, 2002

Your purpose in reviewing your paper is twofold. First, there are some substantive matters that deserve one last look; although you cannot rewrite your paper now, you cannot afford to ignore these matters:

- Opening paragraph achieving its purposes?
- Central point, or thesis, clear?
- All aspects of the paper topic in the assignment explicitly identified and addressed?
- Quotations appropriately chosen?
- Quotation lead-ins sensible and sufficient?
- Sexist language avoided?
- Grammatical errors eliminated?
- Spelling errors eliminated?
- Transitions between paragraphs explicit and varied?
- Key terms defined during the course of argument?
- Assumptions and inferences clearly contrasted?
- Reasons for your opinions carefully and adequately stated?
- Conclusions to arguments clearly contrasted with their premises?
- Closing paragraph effective?

Next, you want to check out various details of manuscript preparation, especially these:

- Title (and subtitle, if any) concise, apt—and engaging?
- Title page, if required, contains all the appropriate information?
- Pages correctly numbered?
- Footnotes or endnotes, if any, numbered in proper sequence? (See chapter 6.)
- Quotations accurately transcribed from the original?
- Quotations and other borrowed material properly cited and documented?
- Ellipses, insertions, alterations, and emphases in quotations properly marked? (See chapter 6.)
- Pages carefully stapled together in correct sequence?

Note: Be sure to make a hard copy of your paper for your files, and do not erase your paper from your disc or hard drive.

6. Integrating Quotations and Citing Sources

By necessity, by proclivity, and by delight, we all quote.

— Ralph Waldo Emerson

INTEGRATING QUOTATIONS

In the course of writing essays or term papers, you will probably need to use quotations from assigned readings or from your instructor's lectures. In doing so, you must think about your *purpose* for quoting certain passages, lest these quotations do little more than show that you have read the relevant materials and extracted a few phrases here and there to retain something of their flavor.

Why Quote in the First Place?

The best reason for quoting an author's words is that the author has said something remarkable and has said it concisely, so that a paraphrase — putting another's ideas into your own words — will lose something from the original that is useful for you in one or more of your roles as a writer: expositor, interpreter, critic, or commentator.

By using quotations carefully and selectively, you show your readers that you have been attentive to the nuances, idiom, and vocabulary of your sources. Effective quotation is also indispensable in conveying the style of writing and reasoning in your sources, and this may prove helpful to you in your exposition and criticism of others' positions and points of view. (To see how one student used quotations effectively, take another look at Ellen Wheeler's paper on p. 100.) Quotation may even be essential, as when you want to criticize an author's position and thus want to state that position in the author's own words.

Pitfalls to Avoid in Quoting

As with all good things, quotation can be overdone. First, you need to keep an eye on the length of your quotations; don't let them get *too long* or they may overwhelm the points you wish to make with them. Be sure to trim away all of the author's language that is superfluous for your purposes. (See p. 163 for advice on using ellipses to show omissions.)

Second, quoting too frequently from your sources can make your paper look like a cut-and-paste job, with passages from sources held together by scattered sentences of your own. Such a tactic might indeed convey how the authors whom you quote reason — and convey it better than paraphrasing and less-frequent quotation would. But too little of such a paper is really your work; you cannot expect your instructor to think very highly of a paper that consists largely of quotations from sources, however expertly chosen and cleverly stitched together the quotations may be.

Third, one or more of your quotations may *not be apt,* either because your prose doesn't provide adequate context for the quotation or because you have not located the best passage in the reading to illustrate the point you want the quotation to make. You will avoid such problems if you make sure that the quotation you choose is

- correctly quoted in your paper,
- apt and really supportive of the point you want to make, and
- effectively woven into the context of your prose.

Assuming that you are satisfied that a certain quotation is appropriate for your paper, your next task is to make sure that it is properly introduced. This is accomplished by writing a suitable lead-in.

Lead-ins

Lead-ins are words or phrases that set up a quotation and tie it logically to the rest of the paper. To illustrate, suppose you are writing a paper evaluating some of the dozen objections to utilitarianism that John Stuart Mill discusses in chapter 3 of his *Utilitarianism* (1860). The following quotation states the last (and one of the most important) of these objections, and you intend to discuss it at length:

> Again, defenders of utility often find themselves called upon to reply to such objections as this — that there is not time, previous to action, for calculating and weighing the effects of any line of conduct on the general happiness.

To set up this quotation effectively, you would need to supply some context for it and adjust the quotation itself:

```
The last and most important of the objections to utili-
tarianism that Mill discusses is that "there is not time,
previous to action, for calculating and weighing the
effects of any line of conduct on the general happiness."
```

This sentence contains only those words of Mill's that are central to your purpose and it reads smoothly. Notice, too, that the lead-in words "and most important" help readers see why you are using this quotation.

Frequently, the best way to integrate a quotation into your paper is to alter it slightly, in any of four ways: *inserting* a word or phrase not in the original; *deleting* a word or phrase from the original; *altering* a word or some letters in a word to make the quotation fit into your context; or *emphasizing* a word or phrase being quoted.

Insertions

To make a quotation fit smoothly into your text, you may have to insert a word or phrase within brackets, as in the following example:

> `As Hobbes points out, where there is no effective govern-`
> `ment "the life of man [would be] solitary, poor, nasty,`
> `brutish and short."`

If the writer hadn't inserted the verb "would be," the quoted sentence would have been ungrammatical because it has no verb.

Deletions

Sometimes the passage you want to quote can be usefully abbreviated to eliminate irrelevant material or to make the quotation fit better within the grammar and context of your writing. Whenever you delete words from a quotation — whether at the beginning, middle, or end — always indicate the deletion by inserting an *ellipsis,* three dots with a space before and after each one. Suppose that in quoting from Kant's *Critique of Pure Reason,* you wanted to omit some words from the interior of a quotation. You might write:

> `Kant opens the `<u>`Critique`</u>` by asserting: "We are in posses-`
> `sion of . . . `<u>`A Priori Knowledge`</u>` and even the Common`
> `Understanding is never without Them."`

The three dots take the place of Kant's words "Certain Modes of."

Suppose that instead of dropping words from the middle of the quotation, you wanted to omit some words from the end. You might write:

> `Kant opens the `<u>`Critique`</u>` by asserting: "We are in Posses-`
> `sion of Certain Modes of `<u>`A Priori`</u>` Knowledge. . . ."`

In this case, the period immediately after "Knowledge" is the period that ends the sentence that includes the quote; the next three periods are the ellipsis indicating that some words have been omitted from the end of the quote itself.

Alterations

In English, the initial letter of the first word of a sentence is always capitalized. (You should spell out any number that you cannot avoid putting at the beginning of a sentence.) Students often violate this rule because they want to begin a sentence with a quotation, but the first word they want to quote is not capitalized in the original. To avoid this problem, capitalize the first word in the quotation and enclose the capital letter in *brackets* to show readers that the letter was not capitalized in the original. For example, Benedict Spinoza (1632-1677) begins Proposition 21 of his *Ethics* (1677) as follows:

```
All things which follow from the absolute nature of any
attribute of God must for ever exist. . . .
```

Suppose you want to begin a sentence with Spinoza's words "the absolute nature." You would write the sentence like this:

```
"[T]he absolute nature of any attribute of God," Spinoza
declares, "must for ever exist. . . ."
```

Conversely, you can use brackets to lowercase a letter that is capitalized at the beginning of a sentence in the original:

```
Spinoza declares that "[a]ll things which follow from the
absolute nature of any attribute of God must for ever
exist."
```

Emphasis

Occasionally, there will be a word or two in a quotation that is so important for your purposes that you want to draw readers' attention to it. The standard way to emphasize such words is to *underline* (or italicize) them and then add a parenthetical note indicating that you have added the underline as an emphasis. Here's an example:

```
As Nietzsche rightly said, "Punishment is overdetermined
by utilities of all kinds" (emphasis added).
```

A somewhat different problem arises when you want to quote a passage that contains a word or phrase that the author has emphasized. To let your readers know that the emphasis is not yours, add a disclaimer right after the quotation, in this manner:

```
As Jennifer Trusted noted, "the intention is a necessary
condition and that intention is not entirely physically
determined" (emphasis in original).
```

Long Quotations

If you want to quote at length from a source, say a whole paragraph or half a dozen long sentences, the usual practice is to set the quotation off as an extract, thus displaying the text. To do this, *indent* the whole passage ten spaces, and double-space between lines. Because the indented passage is clearly an extract, you don't have to enclose it in quotation marks. Remember to introduce the quotation with a lead-in; usually, the lead-in is followed by a colon. For example:

```
In his Thoughts Out of Season, Nietzsche acknowledged the

influence of Schopenhauer in some detail.  In his own

words:
```

> In order to describe properly what an event my
> first look into Schopenhauer's writings was for
> me, I must dwell for a minute on an idea that
> recurred more constantly in my youth, and
> touched me more nearly, than any other.

AVOIDING PLAGIARISM

What is plagiarism? Why is it objectionable, indeed, unlawful and morally wrong? How can it be avoided?

Writers plagiarize when they use another's words or ideas without suitable acknowledgment. Plagiarism amounts to *theft* — theft of language and thought. Plagiarism also involves *deception,* whether intentional or not. A writer who uses the words or thoughts of another without proper acknowledgment deceives readers as to the true source of the ideas and language.

Thus, plagiarism is doubly wrong: It wrongs the person from whom the words or thoughts were taken and to whom no credit was given; and it wrongs the reader by fraudulently misrepresenting the words or thoughts as though they are the writer's own.

To fix these ideas more clearly, let's take a closer look at an example of plagiarism. Here's a passage from Alan M. Turing's essay "Computing Machinery and Intelligence" (1950):

> The idea behind digital computers may be explained by saying
> that these machines are intended to carry out any operations
> which could be done by a human computer. The human computer
> is supposed to be following fixed rules; he has no authority to
> deviate from them in any detail. We may suppose that these rules
> are supplied in a book, which is altered whenever he is put on to
> a new job. He has also an unlimited supply of paper on which he
> does his calculations. He may also do his multiplications and
> additions on a "desk machine," but this is not important.

Now suppose, having read Turing's paragraph, you were to write in your paper the following:

> The idea of a digital computer is that of a machine that
> does anything a human computer can do. The human follows
> definite rules, which he finds in a book. He has all the
> paper he needs for his calculations and may also have a
> desk calculator to check his arithmetic.

Such a paragraph is a *paraphrase* of Tuning's passage. It also *plagiarizes* the original. First, it does not acknowledge the Turing paragraph as its source. In addition, the only difference between the two paragraphs is that, in the second, a few words or phrases have been changed, but all the *ideas* of the second paragraph are clearly contained in the original.

One can even imagine a version of the paragraph in which hardly any of the words are from the original — yet the paragraph counts as plagiarized because the *ideas* are all Turing's:

```
The notion of a digital computer is the notion of a
machine that can do whatever rational tasks you or I can
do. Definite rules govern the human thinker, we shall
assume; and these rules are explicitly written out in
some rule book.  The rules are adjusted for each task our
human computer is to perform.  There is plenty of paper
available on which to write down any calculations, and we
might even imagine that the human has a handy desk calcu-
lator available on which to do the necessary arithmetic.
```

Again, this paragraph tracks the original thought by thought and adds nothing whatever to it. The verbal changes are purely cosmetic — as though they were designed to conceal the fact that the ideas have been appropriated from another source. Clearly, what is missing is some suitable acknowledgment to Turing's essay as the source of the ideas. You could add such an acknowledgment by introducing the whole paragraph with words such as these:

```
As Turing explains it, the notion of a digital com-
puter . . .
```

Of course, it is perfectly all right to convey Turing's ideas through an acceptable *paraphrase,* perhaps with an apt *quotation* or two:

```
In his paper "Computing Machinery and Intelligence," Alan
M. Turing explains the idea of a digital computer by
reference to a human computer.  "The human computer is
supposed to be following fixed rules," he says, and
"these rules are supplied in a book," suitably adjusted
for each new task. Turing allows the human to have plenty
of paper and the assistance of what he calls a "desk
machine"--what we'd call a hand or desk calculator.
```

The reader who comes across this passage in your paper will have no doubt whatever as to your source and your indebtedness.

One way to avoid plagiarism is never consciously to use the words or ideas of another writer. But this cure can be as bad as the disease. It is often not merely convenient but essential to one's own purposes as a writer to use the words or phrases of another. For example, as mentioned before, you may want to quote exactly what someone else has written so that you can proceed to criticize it. By all means, do it. If we never used the words or ideas of another person, the world of scholarship would be impossible. Objections properly arise only when you borrow the words or ideas of another without suitable acknowledgment.

What counts as suitable acknowledgment? You should *mention the author's name,* at the minimum, and use quotation marks around any words you have taken directly from a source. Usually you should provide complete publication information for the source somewhere in your paper.

Scholars and writers will divide, however, over certain cases. For example, in the student paper on page 87, Stacey Schmidt quotes many phrases from G. M. A. Grube's translation of Plato's *Republic,* without mentioning this particular translation as the source of the quotations. Is that plagiarism? No, because the quotation marks make it clear that Plato's text in English translation is being quoted. However, papers submitted in class should probably specify the translation. Or consider Ellen Wheeler's essay on Descartes and Turing (p. 100), where no publication information is provided for the sources of the many quotations. Is that plagiarism? No, although it might be argued that the documentation is inadequate. Wheeler could easily have repaired that defect by adding a footnote at the bottom of the first page of her essay, separated from the text above by a line; for example:

```
    All quotations are from Descartes, Discourse on
Method, translated by Haldane and Ross, or from Turing,
"Computing Machinery and Intelligence," Mind (1950).
```

Such a note suffices to avoid any appearance of plagiarism, even if it is not enough to enable readers to check quotations and other borrowed material for accuracy against the originals, for which a page or line reference for every quotation is required.

Problems can arise, of course, when a writer unwittingly appropriates a word or phrase from another. For example, one sometimes hears the phrase "a moral equivalent to war." The phrase refers to the need to provide opportunities — especially for young men — to show courage, dedication, loyalty, and even self-sacrifice, qualities celebrated of men in battle ever since Homer's *Iliad,* but minus the carnage of warfare. Not everyone realizes that "a moral equivalent to war" is a phrase the American philosopher William James (1842–1910) made famous in an essay of that title published in 1910. Thus, a student writing an essay on, say, the morality of pacifism, might write something like this near the end:

```
The antipacifist is right, at least to this extent, that
we need a moral equivalent to war.
```

Is this plagiarism from James? Can plagiarism be unintentional, and is it excusable if done in ignorance? The answer to these questions is "Yes." Of course you can use a phrase that is in common circulation even if you don't know its origin. But if you do know the source, cite it. The student who knows that James invented this phrase should certainly have written something like this:

```
The antipacifist is right, at least to this extent:  We
do need--as William James said early in the previous
century--a moral equivalent to war.
```

Despite admonitions against plagiarism, students still commit it; a news item in *The Boston Globe* of December 15, 1993, reported a study of MIT students showing that about one-fifth of those sampled admitted to having used the work of another (a fellow student or some other source) without proper acknowledgment. The news report did not indicate the extent to which MIT philosophy students were typical or atypical in their plagiarism. Nor did the report indicate whether plagiarism has increased with the growing practice of collaborative learning, in which students work together on a common writing or research project but are expected to turn in individual papers.

Since most students enroll in philosophy courses out of genuine interest in the subject, not because they are required to do so for graduation, there may be less incentive for them to cheat (and plagiarism is a form of cheating). Is it excessively optimistic to hope that once you understand both what is morally objectionable about plagiarism and how easily it can be avoided, you will conscientiously seek to avoid it — and not only in your philosophy courses?

CITING AND DOCUMENTING SOURCES

Let's begin by confessing that it's a nuisance to have to inform your readers of the sources on which you have drawn for your essay. The effort to do so — with footnotes, bibliography, and all the checking for accuracy that implies — just feels like pure drudgery. And pedantry. Who really wants or needs this information, anyway? Nevertheless, there are persuasive arguments against dismissing the responsibility to inform readers of your sources.

Consider, for example, a case in which you want to incorporate a sentence from an assigned reading into your paper. You put the sentence in quotation marks but leave it at that, without any footnote or other reference to your source. Now put yourself in the position of your reader. The reader can see, thanks to your quotation marks, that the words are not your own. But whose are they? Where do they come from? The reader cannot answer these questions because you have provided no way to check the quotation against the original. Why should your reader care? Perhaps in order to verify whether you have quoted your source accurately (maybe the quotation looks fishy) or possibly to evaluate whether you have quoted out of context or in some other way misled the reader (and perhaps yourself). More positively, the quotation may be so interesting that the reader would like to read more from its source. A scrupulous reader will be alert to all these points; so will a scrupulous writer.

There is also a fourth reason for proper citation and documentation of sources — avoiding *plagiarism* (see p. 165).

To properly acknowledge sources, you should *cite* them briefly in the text and then provide complete publication information (*documen-*

tation) for them somewhere in your paper. You can cite sources by numbers that correspond to numbered footnotes or endnotes containing publication information. Or you can provide a brief, parenthetical citation of the source in the text of your paper and include more detailed publication information elsewhere, perhaps in a bibliography or a list of works cited at the end of your paper. (Find out which method your instructor prefers.)

Whatever method of citation you use, remember this simple rule: When citing a book's title, either *underline* the title or put it in *italic* font. For other texts — essays and chapters in books especially — put the title in *quotes*. Never use both underlining and quotes or italic and quotes.

Numbered Footnotes or Endnotes

With this method, you number sources in the text in sequence, starting with 1. These numbers are keyed to notes at the foot of the page or at the end of the paper. (In published books and articles, you will sometimes see that the footnotes are numbered afresh, starting with 1, for each page of text that has any notes. You are better advised to number your notes in one sequence from the beginning to the end of your paper. That way, no two notes ever have the same number and so their sequence is less likely to be confused as you prepare your paper for submission.) Insert the numerals into your text wherever it is most appropriate (usually at the end of a sentence), and be sure to put the numerals in superscript type, like this:

    `. . . as Bertrand Russell explains.`[1]

If you choose to document such a reference in a *footnote,* place the note at the bottom of the page on which the reference appears. Be sure always to separate the last line of your text from your first footnote like this:

```
-------------------------------------------
     1. Bertrand Russell, The Problems of Philosophy
(Oxford: Oxford University Press), 38.
```

If you have footnoting software on your word processor, it may automatically insert such a line.

If you choose to document your references in endnotes, include the notes, numbered in sequence, at the end of your paper under the heading "Notes."

Which system is best: footnotes or endnotes? Footnotes have the advantage of providing information immediately, at the foot of the page, so readers don't have to thumb to the back of the paper to see what you're referring to. However, if your notes are nothing but references to your sources (in contrast to *discussion notes,* in which you amplify some point in your text and thus carry on part of your argument in your notes), then many readers will be glad to have such routine information out of the way at the back of the paper. Also, endnotes are a boon to the writer (somewhat less so now, with the availability of footnoting software) because they can be easily added or subtracted, revised and deleted, without affecting the spacing on the pages on which they appear. Most instructors will accept either method, as long as you are consistent.

In-text Citation

In recent years it has become increasingly common (both in published writing and in student papers) to give up footnotes and endnotes, along with all those numerals scattered across the pages of the essay, in favor of an abbreviated in-text reference to a source. Such a reference is enclosed in parentheses. Suppose you were quoting from Bertrand Russell's *Problems of Philosophy* and wanted to refer to page 93. Here's how an in-text citation to that page would look:

> "Knowledge by acquaintance takes two forms" (Russell, 93).

Or you might write it this way:

> "Knowledge by acquaintance takes two forms," according to Russell (93).

That is, you can choose whether to put the author's name inside the parentheses along with the page number or outside the parentheses as part of the sentence itself, with only the page number in parentheses. Such a brief form of citation will suffice, provided your instructor is amenable and that two conditions are satisfied: First, no other book or article by Russell is also cited in your paper; second, somewhere in your paper you record the basic bibliographical information about this source — author, title, publisher, and date. Here is how such a bibliographic note might look, placed at the bottom of the first page on which a reference to Russell appears:

> ---
> All page references in this paper are to Bertrand Russell, <u>The Problems of Philosophy</u> (Oxford: Oxford University Press, 1912).

If you prefer, this information can be given in the text itself, where you first quote from Russell, or at the end of your paper. (Notice, by the way, that book titles are always underlined, the conventional way when typing to indicate italics. If you use a computer that allows you to type in italics, do so for book titles. Never both underline and italicize. Essay and article titles are set inside quotation marks; never underline or italicize them.)

Multiple Sources

In a paper in which you cite more than one source, you must use a slightly more complex system than that just described.

Several Works by the Same Author   When you want to refer to several different writings by Bertrand Russell, you must modify the in-text citation method in one of two ways.

One method is to include a key word or phrase from the particular title of Russell's that you are citing, thereby providing a unique reference for each of your sources. Thus, instead of writing "(Russell, 93)" — suitable when only one work by Russell is being cited in your paper — you would write "(Russell, *Problems,* 93)," using an obvious abbreviation of the title. Of course, you need to be sure the abbreviation you choose for each source is clear and unique. If one of the sources by Russell is an article or essay rather than a book, you'd put the abbreviated version of the title in quotation marks, like this: (Russell, "Logical Atomism," 42).

Another method uses year of publication instead of short titles to provide unique references to sources by the same author. To refer to Russell's *Problems of Philosophy,* page 93, as apart from his other writings, you would cite "(Russell 1912: 93)," since 1912 was the year *Problems of Philosophy* was first published and you are not citing anything else published by Russell in 1912. If you were, you would use letters with the years (1912a, 1912b) to distinguish between titles published in the same year. In your bibliography, these works would be listed in alphabetical sequence with the entry for 1912a (referring to Russell's essay "The Essence of Religion," published in 1912 in the *Hibbert Journal*) preceding the entry for 1912b (referring to his book *Problems of Philosophy*).

Several Works by Different Authors   Consider now a case in which you want to refer not only to works by Russell but also to books or articles by his colleagues G. E. Moore (1873–1958) and Ludwig Wittgenstein (1889–1951). If you cite but one item from each author, you can use the briefer form of in-text citation explained on page 170. Thus, your in-text citations would look like these:

```
(Russell, 93)      (Moore, 112)      (Wittgenstein, 38)
```

But suppose you want to cite more than one item from each of these authors. In this case, you must use the more complex scheme explained above, so that each citation includes a unique reference to each source. Thus, you would include in-text citations like these:

```
(Russell, Problems, 93) (Russell, "Theory," 114)
(Moore, Principia, 112) (Moore, Ethics, 78)
(Wittgenstein, Tractatus, 38) (Wittgenstein, Investiga-
tions, 44).
```

Remember: When you refer to more than one book or article as a source for your paper — whether by one or several different authors — you must include a bibliography or list of works cited at the end of your paper, in which you give full publication information for each source: author's name; full title of the book, article, etc.; and place and date of publication. (See "Preparing Your Bibliography," p. 172.)

Special Cases Some writers pose special problems in citation; Wittgenstein is a good example. If you were to include an in-text reference to his *Tractatus Logico-Philosophicus* in the form "(Wittgenstein, *Tractatus,* 4.442)," you would be relying on the reader knowing that "4.442" refers to a particular numbered *proposition,* the page on which it appears being unnecessary. But if you were to refer to this book in the form "(Wittgenstein, *Tractatus,* 4)," it would not be clear whether you are referring to the *proposition* numbered 4 or to the *page* numbered 4. A parallel problem arises in references to Wittgenstein's other writings. For example, if you were to refer to his *Philosophical Investigations* as "(Wittgenstein, *Investigations,* 144)," you would leave the reader confused: Does the "144" refer to the *page* so numbered? Or does it refer to the *paragraph* so numbered? (This paragraph appears on page 57 of the first edition of this work published in 1953.) To get around this problem, it would be best to precede numbers cited with "p." for "page," "para." for "paragraph," or "s." for "section."

References to Plato, Aristotle, Kant, and many other philosophers pose similar problems arising from the proper manner in which to refer to pages (or even the lines) from their texts. These matters are too recondite to discuss here; however, you need to stay alert to possible exceptions to and complications in the general rules discussed in this section. In any case, remember this rule: *If in doubt about how to cite and document your sources, ask your instructor for advice.*

Preparing Your Bibliography

In every essay in which you refer to other sources, you must include bibliographic information about those sources. When you cite but *one* work, you can include such details in a footnote or endnote, in the manner described in the previous section (see p. 169). But when you cite more than one item, you will need to prepare a list that provides complete bibliographic information for all the books and articles used in your paper. This list, appended to your essay, usually appears under the title "Bibliography" or "Works Cited."

The information in each bibliographic entry falls into three parts: the name of the author or editor, the title of the work, and publication information (place, publisher, and year). Each of these three parts to your citation should end with a period.

The entries for the sources in your bibliography or list of works cited should be arranged in alphabetical order by the surname of the authors or editors, with the first author's name in each entry given last name first. (If the work has two or more authors, only the first author's name is entered last name first.) Thus, if you are citing works by Moore, Russell, Ayer, and Wittgenstein, their names would appear in the list as follows:

```
Ayer, A. J.
Moore, G. E.
```

```
Russell, Bertrand.
Wittgenstein, Ludwig.
```

Titles of books, encyclopedias, and periodicals should be under-lined (or italicized if you have a computer that can produce italics), whereas the titles of essays and articles should be enclosed in quotation marks.

For more information on citation and documentation, you can con-sult any of several stylebooks. The grandparent of them all is *The Chi-cago Manual of Style* (14th ed., 1993), first published by the University of Chicago Press in 1906. *The MLA Handbook* (5th ed., 1999), published by the Modern Language Association, is another style guide typically used in the humanities. But you probably won't have any use for the detailed scholarly advice such guides offer. For your purposes, you will not go far wrong if you use the following examples to guide the con-struction of your bibliography. These examples cover the main types of sources you are likely to include in a paper for a philosophy course. (For the sake of consistency, these examples are based on *Chicago* style. If your instructor prefers that you use some other style, you should do so.)

A Book by One Author

```
Richard, Mark. Propositional Attitudes: An Essay on
       Thoughts and How We Ascribe Them. Cambridge: Cam-
       bridge University Press, 1990.
```

A Book by More Than One Author

```
Hofstadter, Douglas R., and Daniel C. Dennett. The Mind's
       I: Fantasies and Reflections on Self and Soul. New
       York: Basic Books, 1981.
```

A Journal Essay or Article by One Author

```
Azzouni, Jody. "A Simple Axiomatizable Theory of Truth."
       Notre Dame Journal of Formal Logic 32 (Summer 1991):
       458-93.
```

An Essay in an Edited Volume

```
Cartwright, Helen Morris. "Parts and Places." In On Being
       and Saying: Essays for Richard Cartwright, edited by
       Judith Jarvis Thomson, 175-214. Cambridge: MIT
       Press, 1987.
```

Two or More Works by the Same Author

Daniels, Norman. <u>Am I My Parents' Keeper? An Essay on
    Justice between the Young and the Old</u>. New York:
    Oxford University Press, 1988.

---. <u>Just Health Care</u>. Cambridge: Cambridge University
    Press, 1985.

Notice the three hyphens beginning the entry for the second of two books by Daniels. This is the standard way to avoid typing the author's name more than once. Notice also that the books are listed in alphabetical order by the first main word of their titles. (Articles, such as *a, and,* and *the,* don't count; but prepositions — as in John Stuart Mill's book *On Liberty* — do.)

An Article from an Encyclopedia or Other Reference

Dennett, Daniel C., and John C. Haugeland. "Intentional-
    ity." In <u>The Oxford Companion to the Mind</u>, edited by
    Richard L. Gregory, 383-86. Oxford: Oxford Univer-
    sity Press, 1987.

An Edited Collection or Anthology

Daniels, Norman, ed. <u>Reading Rawls: Critical Studies of a
    Theory of Justice</u>. Oxford: Basic Blackwell, 1975.

A Book Review

White, Stephen L. <u>Review of Freedom and Belief</u> by Galen
    Strawson. <u>Philosophical Review</u> 100 (January 1991):
    119-22.

A Translation of a Classic Work

Aristotle. <u>On Rhetoric</u>. Edited and translated by George
    A. Kennedy. New York: Oxford University Press, 1991.

The current edition of *The Chicago Manual* does not offer advice on how to document Internet sources, but the following model is a good one to use for *Chicago*-style documentation:

Author's name. "Document title or subject line." <u>Title of
    complete work or Web site</u> (if applicable). Date of
    Internet publication or communication. <URL> or
    other retrieval information (date of access). Text
    division (if applicable, rather than a page number).

Web Site

```
The American Philosohical Association. apaOnline. 27
     August 2001. <http://www.udel.edu/apa/> (28 August
     2001).
```

Article in an Online Journal

```
Hibbets, Maria. "The Ethics of Esteem." The Journal of
     Buddhist Ethics 7 (2000). <http://jbe.gold.ac.uk/7/
     hibbets001.html> (28 August 2001).
```

E-mail Message

```
Beck, Candice. "Research on the Death Penalty." 14 August
     2001. Personal e-mail (25 October 2001).
```

A Sample Bibliography

Suppose your instructor wanted you to expand your knowledge on the general subject raised by the writing exercise in chapter 4 on the excerpts from Descartes and Turing (pp. 91 and 93). The directions for such an exercise might look like this:

> Go to the library and identify eight books, articles, and book reviews (at least one of each) published since 1950 on the general topic of the nature of human consciousness. List what you find in a carefully prepared bibliography, and turn it in at the next class meeting.

A bibliography compiled in response to this assignment might look like this:

A Student's Bibliography

```
     A Bibliography on the Nature of Human Consciousness
                              by
                        Eugene Leach

Churchland, Paul S. Neurophilosophy: Toward a Unified
     Science of the Mind/Brain. Cambridge: MIT Press,
     1986.
Dennett, Daniel C. Consciousness Explained. Boston:
     Little, Brown, 1991.
```

---. Review of The Self and Its Brain: An Argument
    for Interactionism by Karl R. Popper and John C.
    Eccles. Journal of Philosophy 76 (1979): 91-97.

Flanagan, Owen. The Science of the Mind. 2nd ed.
    Cambridge: MIT Press, 1991.

Harnad, Stephen. "Consciousness: An Afterthought."
    Cognition and Brain Theory 5 (1982): 29-47.

Kitcher, Patricia. "Phenomenal Qualities." American
    Philosophical Quarterly 16 (1979): 123-29.

Putnam, Hilary. "Brains and Behavior." In Analytical
    Philosophy, 2nd series, edited by R. J. Butler,
    1-19. Oxford: Basil Blackwell, 1965.

Rorty, Richard. "Contemporary Philosophy of Mind."
    Synthese 59 (1970): 323-48.

Turing, Alan M. "Computing Machinery and Intelli-
    gence." Mind 59 (1950): 433-60.

Vendler, Zeno. The Matter of Minds. Oxford: Clarendon
    Press, 1984.

7. Using Library and Online Resources

There is nothing imaginable so strange or so little credible that it has not been maintained by one philosopher or another.

— René Descartes

Printed materials of many sorts are available in your college library to assist in developing your understanding of the majority of philosophical questions that might be of interest to you. Whether you consult these materials out of curiosity or as part of an assignment, the volumes on your library's reference shelves will help you improve your grasp of philosophy. The sooner you acquaint yourself with them — ideally during your first philosophy course — the better. Four different sorts of resources are discussed here.

For quick consultation and advice, your best bet is a one-volume *philosophical dictionary,* in which explanations of the essential words and phrases of philosophy (as well as some brief biographical information about famous philosophers) are available.

For a more thorough discussion of major topics (an essay of several columns or even pages), you must turn to a *multivolume encyclopedia of philosophy.*

Dictionaries and encyclopedias alike present information in a predigested, encapsulated form; you cannot easily see a philosopher *thinking* about a philosophical problem in such materials. For that, you need to turn to other kinds of resources.

One kind is a *series of books* written to present the reader with a state-of-the-art examination of a subject, such as ethics. Some of these series (there are several) approach their subjects in a fairly elementary manner; others are more advanced. All are useful to the student looking for more information and discussion than can be found in a dictionary or encyclopedia.

A far better and more exciting — but also more daunting — source is the *professional journals,* in which philosophers write articles, essays, discussion notes, and book reviews for each other. You will find at first reading that most of this material is beyond your grasp; very well, at least you can begin to get a sense of how professionals discuss philosophical issues. And you may be pleasantly surprised to discover that in many cases the material in these journals *is* accessible to you; in such instances you will have the gratification of being able to listen in on the current dialogue in the field.

In the next sections you will find further details about each of these kinds of resources. You are bound to learn something from trying to put one or another of them to use.

PHILOSOPHICAL DICTIONARIES

Like other fields, philosophy has its own distinctive vocabulary — the technical terms of the trade — and philosophers often give specialized meaning to words in ordinary language. To help sharpen your usage of philosophical terminology, you can of course get some help from the standard dictionary that ought to be handy on your desk. But for more complete and precise information about philosophical terminology, you should consult one of the several good philosophical dictionaries now available. Library staff can help you find them. The best-known and probably most widely available such volume is *The Dictionary of Philosophy,* edited by Dagobert Runes (New York: Philosophical Library, 1942). In three hundred pages of double-column text, it contains more than four thousand entries. Its chief merit is the many excellent entries, written by the eminent American logician Alonzo Church (1903–1995), explaining and defining logical terms. It is, however, significantly out of date and omits much that is now current in the vocabulary of Western philosophy. (One unusual feature of the book is its emphasis on the terminology of Asian and Indian philosophy.)

Simon Blackburn, a British philosopher, has written *The Oxford Dictionary of Philosophy* (Oxford: Oxford University Press, 1995), a book that should be on library reference shelves everywhere. With nearly three thousand entries from "Aristotle" to "Zen," all written by Blackburn, the volume offers extensive coverage not only of the most recent technical terminology but also of important concepts in Chinese, Indian, Islamic, and Jewish philosophy.

Comparable in size, scope, and recency of publication is *The Cambridge Dictionary of Philosophy,* edited by the American philosopher Robert Audi (Cambridge: Cambridge University Press, 1995). Nearly a thousand pages contain over four thousand entries on topics from the medieval philosopher Pierre Abelard to the ancient Middle Eastern religion Zoroastrianism. Unlike Blackburn's solo authorship of the dictionary for Oxford, Audi enlisted nearly four hundred colleagues to write the entries for this Cambridge dictionary.

Four other volumes, all in paperback (but unlikely to be found in any except the largest paperback bookstores), are quite valuable. Any student majoring in philosophy ought to have one of these books handy. The oldest is *A Dictionary of Philosophy,* Second Edition., edited by Antony Flew (New York: St. Martin's Press, 1984), and first published in 1979. Flew enlisted the help of more than thirty of his British colleagues to produce a 380-page, double-column volume; entries vary in length from one-sentence definitions to substantial essays. Noteworthy are the brief biographical sketches of all classic and many contemporary philosophers and the many definitions of concepts in formal logic. Some effort has been made to include terms and persons of importance in non-Western philosophy.

The most recent of the dictionaries is *The HarperCollins Dictionary of Philosophy,* Second Edition, by Peter A. Angeles (New York: HarperCollins, 1992). Angeles provides more than three thousand entries. His biographical sketches are noticeably briefer than those in the Flew dictionary, and his topic entries are written in a brisker style that gives at least the appearance of greater precision in definition and explanation.

The smallest and least comprehensive of these books is *The Philosopher's Dictionary,* Second Edition, by Robert M. Martin (Orchard Park, N.Y.: Broadview Press, 1991). In 250 pages Martin manages to define or discuss more than two thousand items — but only because his entries are extremely short; none is more than a middling paragraph long. Students who consult this dictionary will nevertheless thank the author for his unpretentious style.

Finally, there is *A Dictionary of Philosophy,* Second Edition, by A. R. Lacey (London: Routledge, 1990). Lacey's entries are single-column and vary in length from a sentence to more than a page; his book has fewer total entries than any of the other dictionaries mentioned. He covers dozens of basic concepts, and for every important topic or figure there is a short bibliography — something none of the other dictionaries provides.

ENCYCLOPEDIAS, BOOK SERIES, AND SPECIALIZED REFERENCES

You will probably do a better job on some of your writing assignments in a philosophy course if you seek help along the way from books that are not assigned reading but that probably are available in your college library. These materials fall into three broad classes: standard encyclopedias and related references in philosophy; various series of books spread across the whole field of philosophy; and more specialized volumes on some of the topics introduced but not thoroughly discussed in this book.

Encyclopedias and Related References

The reference section of your college library is certain to have one or more of these resources. For information about leading philosophers, their doctrines, key technical terms, and perennial problems of philosophy, these concise and comprehensive sources are invaluable. In addition to the one-volume philosophical dictionaries (discussed in the previous section), there are various *encyclopedias of philosophy*. By far the most popular such resource is the six-volume *Encyclopedia of Philosophy,* edited by the American philosopher Paul Edwards (New York: Macmillan, 1967). It is currently undergoing a complete revision. All major topics, persons, and issues in Western philosophy are discussed in this encyclopedia, many at considerable length.

The largest and most recent is the *Routledge Encyclopedia of Philosophy* in ten volumes compiled under the general editorship of Edward Craig. Published in 1998, it boasts more than two dozen subject editors, British, Canadian, and American. Its nearly two thousand entries, spanning Eastern and Western philosophy, make it not only the largest but also the most thorough of all such encyclopedias. In 1999, Professor Craig published a much-reduced version of his *Encyclopedia* in a one-volume edition, *The Concise Routledge Encyclopedia of Philosophy.* Another volume is the *Companion Encyclopedia of Asian Philosophy* (London: Routledge, 1996), a one thousand page volume covering all the major Asian philosophical, ethical, and religious traditions.

No less useful for beginners, in part just because of its relatively compact one-volume size, is *The Oxford Companion to Philosophy* (Oxford: Oxford University Press, 1995), edited by the British philosopher Ted Honderich. More than a dictionary but less than an encyclopedia, this thousand-page volume has more than two thousand entries written by some two hundred scholars. In scope and detail it rivals some multivolume encyclopedias.

Routledge in London also publishes a one-volume *Concise Encyclopedia of Western Philosophy and Philosophers,* Third Edition (1990), edited by the British philosophers J. O. Urmson and Jonathan Ree. Another new British publication is the *Blackwell Companion to Philosophy,* edited by Nick Bunnin and P. Tsui-James (Oxford: Blackwell, 1995). It has some three dozen articles by as many authors, each on a major field or figure in Western philosophy. The book is designed less as an encyclopedia and more as an introductory survey of the entire field of Western philosophy.

More specialized resources are also available. The three-volume *Encyclopedia of Ethics,* Second Edition, edited by Lawrence C. and Charlotte B. Becker (New York: Garland, 2001), is of great value to students writing papers on any of a wide variety of topics in ethical theory, applied ethics, and related matters. Similarly, *The Oxford Companion to the Mind,* edited by Richard L. Gregory (Oxford: Oxford University Press, 1987), is a comprehensive one-volume guide for students writing on topics in philosophical psychology, cognitive science, philosophy of mind, and related fields. Since 1992, Routledge has published a whole series of one-volume "companions," each on a special area of philosophy. Currently, there are volumes available for ethics (edited by Peter Singer), aesthetics (edited by David Cooper), metaphysics (edited by Jaegwon Kim and Ernest Sosa), contemporary political philosophy (edited by Robert E. Goodin and Philip Pettit), epistemology (edited by Jonathan Dancy and Ernest Sosa), and philosophy of mind (edited by Samuel Guttenplan). As of 2001, twenty-two volumes in this series have been published.

Several other encyclopedias on the border between philosophy and other disciplines also deserve at least a mention. The four-volume *Encyclopedia of Bioethics,* edited by Walter T. Reich (New York: Free Press, 1978), was published in a revised edition of five volumes in 1995. *The Encyclopedia of Nonviolent Action,* edited by Christopher Kruegler and others, was published in New York by Garland in 1996. Also published in 1996 is *The Encyclopedia on War and Ethics,* edited by the American philosopher Donald A. Wells and published by Greenwood.

The History of Philosophy

Beginners often approach philosophy by studying its history. Of course the best way to do that is to read texts that reprint the main writings of the major philosophers of the past. But students often want not only to read but to read *about* a given philosopher. Unfortunately, there is no standard one-volume history of Western philosophy suitable for this purpose. The most recent book aimed at meeting this need is *The Oxford History of Western Philosophy,* edited by Sir Antony Kenny (Oxford: Oxford University Press, 1994). This book ought to be a welcome addition to every college library. A more ambitious and comprehensive series being published in England is the *Routledge History of Philosophy,* edited by G. H. R. Parkinson and S. G. Shanker, in ten large volumes; each runs to about four hundred pages and is edited by a different scholar.

Other new series provide a more selective focus on the history of philosophy. Blackwell, in Oxford, England, has undertaken a novel series of "dictionary" volumes, each one devoted to a major classic philosopher and written by an expert in the field. Every book is a compendium of materials (including a biography) about a selected philosopher; so far, volumes on Descartes, Hegel, Heidegger, Hobbes, Kant, Locke, Rousseau, and Wittgenstein have been published.

A somewhat similar series — *Cambridge Companions to Philosophy* — is under publication by Cambridge University Press in England. Volumes are now available on Plato, Aristotle, Aquinas, Descartes, Locke, Leibniz, Hume, Kant, Hegel, Marx, Freud, Heidegger, Sartre, and Foucault, and more than a dozen others are projected. Each book contains essays by a dozen or so specialists. One of these "dictionaries" or "companions" would be of considerable value for any student writing a paper on, say, Descartes or Hegel. A third such series, edited by Tim Crane and Jonathan Wolff, both of University College, London, has been undertaken by Routledge. Each of these *Routledge Philosophy Guide Books* focuses on a classic text by a great philosopher (for example, Locke's

Essay Concerning Human Understanding) and offers a comprehensive introduction to the work. The first volumes in this series appeared in 1995.

Another series of substantial and scholarly volumes is *The Arguments of the Philosophers,* published in London by Routledge under the general editorship of Ted Honderich. Each volume, written by a distinguished European, British, or American scholar, is devoted to the entire work of a major philosopher, like Socrates or Wittgenstein. Some two dozen volumes have been published so far. The authors have been given considerable freedom; thus, their treatments of philosophers vary in style, length, emphasis, and detail. Nevertheless, the student who wants to know what Hume or Descartes thinks about a certain topic cannot do much better than to consult the relevant volume in this series.

Fields of Philosophy

Students hungry for more information about a given area of or set of problems in philosophy than any of the encyclopedias can provide might well look into the appropriate volume in the series *The Foundations of Philosophy* (Englewood Cliffs: Prentice Hall). This series consists of fifteen books (originally published in both paperback and hardcover) written by a distinguished group of (mostly) American philosophers. Originally written in the 1960s, these volumes have been revised and kept up to date in most cases; several of them are now in their third or fourth edition. Each volume runs about two hundred pages, and every major field of philosophy — ethics, logic, philosophy of science, epistemology, and so on — has its own volume, written in a style intended to be accessible to beginners. Most good libraries have some or all of the volumes in this series.

A very different series of books focused on particular problems of philosophy has been published by Oxford University Press under the general title *Oxford Readings in Philosophy.* More than thirty of these paperback volumes have been published (some are now out of print). Libraries hesitated to buy them because they were available only in paperback. But they are widely used, especially in more advanced courses. Each volume consists of a dozen or so articles selected from philosophical journals, with an introduction and bibliography by the editor (most of them British philosophers). No concessions were made to the needs of beginners; the materials reprinted in these books are (or were, at the time of their original publication) state-of-the-art thinking by some of the most important and influential philosophers.

More Specialized Resources

Among the many topics mentioned but not discussed at length in this book, several receive thorough treatment in other volumes. From among dozens of such volumes, two in particular deserve mention.

Virtually all introductory books to informal logic discuss fallacies, informal and formal. One book devoted entirely to this subject is

S. Morris Engel's *With Good Reason: An Introduction to Informal Fallacies,* Fourth Edition. (New York: St. Martin's, 1990).

There are dozens of textbooks on informal logic, critical thinking, and methods of argument, all of which cover in greater detail the issues discussed in chapter 3. One of the better such books, by Robert J. Fogelin and Walter Sinnott-Armstrong, is *Understanding Arguments: An Introduction to Informal Logic,* Sixth Edition (San Diego: Harcourt, 2001), first published in 1978 (with Fogelin as the sole author).

JOURNALS

The Readers' Guide to Periodical Literature, a well-known index to magazine articles, is of little or no use to students writing philosophy papers, because it rarely includes anything of philosophical interest. Philosophers just do not publish in *The National Review, Reader's Digest,* or *Field and Stream* — and the journals in which they do publish are not indexed in *The Readers' Guide.*

Philosophers typically publish short works like essays, articles, and book reviews in scholarly journals, just as scholars in other disciplines do. These journals are largely unread by and unknown to the general public. They are usually published four times a year (a few appear more frequently) and bound in softcover.

Today, dozens of philosophical journals are published regularly in English; unfortunately, because of their number, steadily rising cost, and the demands they make on library shelf space, only the largest university research libraries can subscribe to more than a few. But most college libraries are likely to subscribe to some of these journals, with back issues bound and available (but not circulating) on their shelves. The articles, discussions, and book reviews in these journals can be of great use to students. Although intended for an audience of professional academic philosophers — your teachers — the contents of journals are not always so technical or difficult as to be wholly inaccessible to beginning students. Many of the essays that students read in textbooks for introductory "problems in philosophy" courses were originally published in scholarly journals.

Philosophical journals can be divided into two groups: those that publish material in every subfield of philosophy and those that specialize in one subfield. In the first category are the two oldest and most widely read journals published in the United States: *The Journal of Philosophy* (1904–), published monthly and edited by members of the philosophy faculty at Columbia University, and *The Philosophical Review* (1892–), published quarterly and edited by members of the Cornell University philosophy department. The best-known rival to these two in scope and prestige is the quarterly journal *Mind,* published in England since 1892. Two other journals of broad scope are *Philosophical Studies* (1950–), edited in this country, and its older companion, *Analysis* (1933–), published in Great Britain. These journals publish more frequently and in issues of only a few dozen pages. They offer very short essays of three or four pages on the narrowest of topics.

In the category of specialized journals in a subfield of philosophy, the oldest and probably the best-known and most widely read is *Ethics,* founded in 1891 and published by the University of Chicago Press. Its subtitle, *An International Journal of Social, Political, and Legal Philosophy,* indicates its scope. More recently, *Philosophy and Public Affairs* (1971–), published by Princeton University Press, has become a widely recognized forum for discussions in social, political, and legal philosophy.

Virtually every area of philosophy — history; formal logic; phenomenology; applied ethics; aesthetics; philosophy of religion, education, law, and science, to name but a few — has at least one journal catering to the interests and needs of scholars and students.

How can you find your way through this vast literature and zero in on the handful of essays or reviews on your particular interest? *The Philosopher's Index* (1967–) — available in print in quarterly volumes, through CD-ROM, and now on the Internet — can help. Hardcover volumes of the *Index* will give you information about some 15,000 journal articles and 5,000 books published since 1940. The CD-ROM version — the key to a treasure trove of philosophical literature — makes available information about more than 175,000 articles and books. If your college library does not subscribe to the printed version, ask your reference librarian for help in determining whether the computer facilities in your library provide access to this resource. If you want to access the *Index* on the Internet, learn how by an e-mail inquiry to fells@bgnet.bgsu.edu.

But the best way to learn what philosophical journals have to offer is to browse through the current issues on the periodical shelves in your library, looking for material of interest and letting things catch your eye and attention that you were *not* looking for. Because journal articles are generally short — typically no longer than a chapter in a book — you can skim them on the spot, perhaps making a note of authors, titles, journal numbers, and pages for future reference. Just as war is too important to be left to the generals, your philosophical education is too important to be left to the classroom and to particular writing assignments. Let your curiosity lead you down unfamiliar paths; don't be afraid to explore the vast terrain that lies all about you in the journals (including the back issues bound and shelved in the library stacks), because that is where today's philosophers are working on today's philosophical problems. Take some initiative to deepen and widen your philosophical education.

INFORMATION ON THE WEB

In addition to the printed books and journals discussed above, it is increasingly possible to get helpful information from the Internet. Although a valuable resource, the Internet should be approached with caution. The seemingly infinite number of Web sites available to users boggles the mind and can lead to more research problems than an un-initiated student can handle. Some of what is available will not help you write a better paper, either because the information is too specialized to be of much use (except to advanced undergraduates and graduate students) or because the information source is not designed with student paper writing in mind. Also, each Web site you use in the course of researching a topic must be scrutinized carefully, and its merit, or lack of merit as the case may be, determined, in order to evaluate the relevance and reliability of the information being provided. Below are some guidelines to keep in mind as you surf the Net.

Evaluating and Using Web Sources

- Refine your search topics as much as possible to eliminate superfluous material.
- Rely primarily on primary sources rather than secondary sources in your research, but remember that secondary sources can supply important background information on many topics.
- Determine the credentials and affiliation of authors, as well as the motivation behind their work.
- Evlauate the arguments, assumptions, and biases of the authors and ask yourself if their work will negatively affect or complement your work.
- Ascertain whether the conclusions of the authors are supported by reliable references.
- Investigate the merits of other cited Web sites.
- Deduce the date that each Web site was made available and how frequently it is updated or revised.

Online Resources

The following Web sites may prove useful to you in your online research.

A Dictionary of Philosophical Terms and Names, located at <http://www.philosophypages.com/dy/>, lets you have all the advantages of a multivolume dictionary without leaving your computer. A somewhat similar resource is the *Internet Encyclopedia of Philosophy* at <http://www.utm.edu/research/iep>. Enter a term in the *Encyclopedia*'s search box and it will retrieve relevant articles and encyclopedic entries. Another helpful gateway Web site is *Philosophy in Cyberspace* at <http://www-personal.monash.edu.au/~dey/phil>. It is less comprehensive but more selective than some of the other sites mentioned here. Maintained by a graduate student in philosophy, this site is well organized and frequently updated. One of the best gateways to just about any topic in the field of philosophy is *EpistemeLinks.com,* located at <http://www.epistemelinks.com/>. It offers links far and wide, is updated regularly, and is second to none in its scope.

Several other useful sites are maintained by academics in the field. *Ethics Update,* maintained by Lawrence M. Hinman of the University of San Diego, focuses on popular and professional information on ethics for students and instructors. It can be found at <http://ethics.acusd.edu/index.html>. *The Guide to Philosophy on the Internet,* located at <http://earlham.edu/peters/philinks.htm>, and *Hippias: Limited Area Search of Philosophy on the Internet* at <http://hippias/evansville.edu> are both edited by Peter Suber, a professor of philosophy of Earlham College. *Hippias* is a selective Web search engine that focuses only on philosophy resources. Finally, *apaOnline,* the Web site of the American Philosophical Association can be found at <http://www.udel.edu/apa>.

In addition to the Web sites mentioned above, each of which offers access to a wide range of information, there are three more-specialized resources you might find interesting. One is *Gallery of Philosophers,* featuring pictures of Western philosophers since the ancient Greeks. It is located at <http://watarts.uwaterloo.ca/PHIL/cpshelle/Gallery/gallery.html>. Another source of interest is *Historical Women of Philosophy,* which introduces the reader to many important thinkers who slipped through the cracks of mainstream recorded history because of their gender. Its coverage begins with the pre-Socratics and ends in the seventeenth century. See for yourself at <http://www.geocities.com/Athens/Forum/9974/>. Lastly, there is *The Philosophical Lexicon,* created by philosophers Daniel Dennett and Joe Lambert. It amusingly converts the proper surnames of well-known philosophers, living and dead, into other parts of speech. Difficult to appreciate the humor unless you already know something about the philosopher in question. As an example, here's what the *Lexicon* does for the late Paul Grice, of Oxford and U.C. Berkeley, highly regarded and deservedly so: "*grice,* n. Conceptual intricacy. 'His examination of Hume is distinguished by erudition and grice.' Hence, *griceful,* adj. and *griceless,* adj. 'An obvious and griceless polemic.'" Hmm. Not to everyone's taste, perhaps, but for the cognoscenti it will cause a giggle or two. Look it up at <http://www.blackwellpublishers.co.uk/lexicon/>.

A Glossary of Philosophical Terms

Philosophy, like other academic fields, has its own technical vocabulary. Some of it is of interest only to specialists and professionals; you will not miss much if you fail to master all of this jargon, because much of it has limited transfer value from one philosopher, or philosophical text or problem, to another. But there are other terms that form a large part of the working vocabulary of every philosopher, and you need to be familiar with these terms so that you can understand and use them as needed. (Some of these words and phrases — often confused with each other or otherwise misused — have common currency outside of philosophy; the most conspicuous examples have been listed and explained on pp. 133–36.) Several good one-volume dictionaries, encyclopedias, and handbooks are available to guide your word choice and satisfy your curiosity for greater detail and a fuller account of the terminology of philosophy (see pp. 177–86). Here it will suffice to identify and define several dozen such terms. (Where you see "q.v." [Latin for "which see"] after a word or phrase in this list, it means that word or phrase appears as an entry in its own right.)

Ad hoc   Latin for "to this," said of assumptions, hypotheses, or claims that are invented on the spot to save an argument.

A fortiori   Latin for "from the stronger," a phrase used to indicate "all the more." Thus, if all persons are mortal, a fortiori — all the more obviously — you are mortal.

Agnosticism   In religious matters, the doctrine that we do not have enough evidence to decide whether God exists or does not exist. In general, a suspension of belief because of inadequate evidence one way or the other. See also **skepticism.**

Altruism   The belief that we ought to look out for the welfare of other living creatures, notably other humans. Opposed to **egoism** (q.v.).

Analogy   A similarity between two things, often determined by a comparison based on said resemblance; *disanalogy* is the dissimilarity between two things. In philosophy of religion, the argument from **analogy** (that God's nature as designer and creator of the universe is to be determined by analogy with a craftsman and the product of his art) was searchingly criticized by Hume (see p. 11).

Analytic   A proposition is said to be **analytic** when its truth can be determined by analysis, that is, without reference to experience or other evidence. Thus, "A circle is a closed plane figure, all points on the circumference of which are equidistant from the center" is an analytic proposition. It is highly controversial whether any propositions of philosophical interest are **analytic.** The opposite of **synthetic** (q.v.) and roughly equivalent to **tautology** (q.v.).

Antithesis   The opposite or negation of a **thesis** (q.v.). Thus, "God lives" might be viewed as the **antithesis** or contradictory of the **thesis,** "God does not live" (or more informally, "God is dead" or "There is no God").

A posteriori   A belief or proposition is **a posteriori** (literally, "from what comes after") to the extent that its truth can be determined only by reliance on experience and observation. The opposite of **a priori** (q.v.).

A priori   A belief or proposition is **a priori** (Latin for "from what comes before") if its truth is determined intuitively and thus not by reference to experience and observation. The opposite of **a posteriori** (q.v.).

Argument   One or more reasons for a belief, intended to support or give a reason for that belief. For a fuller discussion, see pages 55–57.

Atheism   The belief that there is no God (much less any gods).

Behaviorism   A branch of experimental psychology founded early in the twentieth century, according to which the proper subject of study in scientific psychology is not mental phenomena (accessible, if at all, only by introspection), but actual behavior (publicly observable movements of the animals or humans under study).

Biconditional   The propositional connective, "if and only if."

Categorical imperative   Proposed by Immanuel Kant the **categorical imperative** says: Act in such a manner that the principle on which you act could be universalized (i.e., accepted by anyone else in that situation).

Cogito ergo sum   Descartes's famous Latin epigram, "I think therefore I am."

Conscience   The ethical norms (prohibitions, requirements, principles) that each of us possess within and to which we turn as we struggle to decide what we ought to do, or not do, in a given case. Thus, a conscientious person is one who relies on his or her **conscience** in deciding how to act in difficult cases, in contrast to acting **against con-**

science, that is, acting according to popular desire, official commands, or other sources of authority outside oneself.

Consequentialism A variety of ethical theories that agree in taking the actual or probable consequences (results, outcomes) of our actions as the criterion for deciding whether the action is right or wrong. The most popular form of **consequentialism** is **utilitarianism** (q.v.).

Consistency Two or more beliefs or propositions are **consistent** if and only if all can be true together at the same time.

Contingent A proposition or event is **contingent** to the extent that its truth or occurrence depends on some other proposition or event, and the latter is not a necessary truth. Thus, a person's knowledge that a certain proposition is true is **contingent** on the person understanding the proposition in the first place.

Contradiction A belief or proposition **contradicts** another belief or proposition to the extent that if either is true the other must be false.

Counterexample Any example — genuine or imaginary — that contradicts a given theory or hypothesis. Thus, in *The Subjection of Women,* John Stuart Mill cites Queen Elizabeth I, Queen Victoria, and Joan of Arc as **counterexamples** to the generalization that women lack the necessary intelligence and fiber to lead and rule.

Definition An explanation of what a term or phrase means. **Definitions** come in various forms, such as ostensive, contextual, formal, and synonymous. For details see pages 59–62.

Deism The belief (popular among philosophers during the Enlightenment) that God is like a cosmic watchmaker; He wound up the universe through the natural laws He created but has not thereafter interfered with human life. Thus, there have been no miracles, and prayers are futile. Not to be confused with **theism** (q.v.).

Deontology From the Greek, "dei," meaning "I must"; the view that the morality of our conduct is to be determined by our intentions and the principles on which we act, not the results or consequences of our actions. A deontological approach to ethics gives pride of place to justice, the principles of right conduct, our duties and obligations; their priority, it is claimed, makes these concepts indefinable by reference to good or bad consequences.

Determinism The belief that all human actions are caused by events over which persons have no real control, just as events in the physiocochemical world are caused by other events over which no one has any control.

Dialectic For Plato, **dialectic** meant mainly dialogue, the back-and-forth of serious conversation and debate aimed at finding the truth about something. For Kant, **dialectic** meant the unavoidable back-and-forth of human reasoning when we grapple with things beyond any possible experience and are led to embrace what seem to be necessary but opposite conclusions. Hegel found **dialectic** in history; Marx found it in political economy.

Dualism   The doctrine of metaphysics that holds that ultimate reality consists of two fundamentally different kinds of things, usually mind and matter.

Egoism, ethical and psychological   **Ethical egoism** is the normative doctrine that each of us ought to pursue our own advantage regardless of its effects on others (except where those effects impinge on our interests). **Psychological egoism** is the empirical claim that we are hard-wired by our genes so that we cannot in fact act otherwise than by trying to advantage ourselves even at the expense of others.

Emotivism   A theory in metaethics to the effect that all ethical utterances are expressions of personal feeling; derisively called the Boo!-Hurrah! theory. If "wrong" in the judgment "Murder is wrong" is nothing but the venting of personal dislike for murder, then "wrong" is semantically equivalent to expletives such as "Boo!" or "Ugh!" The same holds true for "Honesty is a virtue" and "Hurrah!"

Empiricism   The doctrine associated with such British thinkers are Berkeley, Locke, and Hume. It basically holds that all propositions — other than definitions, including logical and mathematical truths — are such that their truth or falsity must be determined by some sort of experience or observation. Opposed to **rationalism** (q.v.).

Equivalent   Two beliefs or propositions are **equivalent** just in case whatever makes one of the beliefs or propositions true (or false) does the same for the other.

Fallacy   Loosely, any error in reasoning. For a discussion of fallacies, see pages 195–98.

Hedonism   The belief that the only thing good in itself (and hence not good only because it leads to good things) is pleasure and the absence of pain.

Hypothesis   A belief or proposition whose truth is uncertain, usually owing to inadequate evidence or inconsistency with prevailing theory, but which nonetheless may be true and is worth further consideration.

Idealism   Diverse metaphysical doctrines associated with Plato, Berkeley, and Hegel, according to which ideas (variously defined) are the ultimate reality.

Induction   Inference from a sample to a generalization. Contrasts with **deduction**. For further details, see pp. 57, 134.

Intuition   A mental process to be contrasted with sensation, observation, excogitation, memory, imagination, calculation, and deliberation. Said to be the source of certain basic a priori truths in logic (the whole is greater than any of its parts), ethics (let your conscience be your guide), and in other areas of philosophy. When one cannot offer an argument for a proposition, yet is certain of its truth, it is not uncommon to claim to know that proposition **intuitively.**

Logical positivism   An influential movement in Anglo-American philosophy during the middle third of the twentieth century, according to which all meaningful propositions could be sorted into the **analytic** (q.v.) and the **synthetic** (q.v.), with the result that metaphysical propositions, belonging in neither category, were strictly meaningless. Mathematical propositions, being necessarily true, were analytic.

Materialism   The metaphysical doctrine that ultimate reality is material stuff. A version of **atomistic materialism** was defended by Democritus, Plato's rival; Marxism is **historical** and **dialectical materialism.**

Metaethics   The study of the concepts and principles of normative ethics and the meaning of ethical terms. For a fuller discussion, see page 4.

Modality   The mode or manner in which something is asserted. There are many different kinds of modalities, the most familiar being temporal (past, present, future), deontic (required, permitted, forbidden), and alethic (necessary, possible, actual).

Natural law   Laws concerning the nature of things and not owing their existence to any human authorities. Includes both scientific laws of nature (the laws studied in physics, chemistry, etc.) and normative laws regulating human conduct (the norms of ethics, jurisprudence, etc.).

Nominalism   Any doctrine in logic or metaphysics that claims there are no general abstract entities (the property of being red, the number 17) but only concrete particulars (the red of that red rose, the numeral "17").

Non sequitur   Latin for "it doesn't follow." A conclusion in an argument is a **non sequitur** when it does not follow logically, that is, cannot be deduced from the argument's premises.

Predicate   The attributive term of a declarative sentence or proposition. Thus, "wise" is the **predicate** term in the sentence "Too few philosophers are wise." Aristotelian logic required identifying the predicate in a subject-predicate declarative sentence in order to construct **syllogisms** (q.v.) and test for their validity.

Prima facie   Latin for "on first appearance." A person's right might be said to be **prima facie** if it is a right on its face, or at first sight. But it might not be a true right (it is a right *only* **prima facie**) because it can be overridden by other moral considerations.

Proposition   The kind of assertion that can be either true or false. What a declarative sentence expresses. **Syllogisms** (q.v.) are constructed out of categorical propositions, each of which in turn is built out of four concepts: A quantifier (All/None/Some) + subject term + verb (is/are) + predicate term. For example, All men are mortal.

Rationalism   The philosophy common to Descartes, Spinoza, and Leibniz (the so-called Continental rationalists) and their followers, which holds that some truths about the world can be known by "the light of nature," "common sense," or "intuition," that is, without prior observation or other experience. Such truths are supposed to be **a priori** (q.v.) but not **analytic** (q.v.), hence not trivially true.

Rationalize/Rationalization   To **rationalize** a proposition is to give it a rational defense or explanation. A **rationalization,** however, is a reason for belief or action that conceals the real reason. ("His support for lower taxes is not, as he claims, based on the unfairness of higher taxes; it is just an unconscious **rationalization** of his selfishness.")

Realism   Opposed to **idealism** (q.v.), sentimentalism, romanticism. In metaphysics, **realism** is the belief that things — physical objects, natural laws, our own bodies, perhaps abstract entities such as numbers — in fact exist outside and independent of our minds.

Relativism, cultural and ethical   According to **cultural relativism** ethical norms vary from culture to culture and depend for their legitimacy on how effective they are in holding a culture together. Anthropologists have shown that cultural relativism is true. **Ethical relativism,** a normative doctrine, holds that there are no objective principles of right and wrong conduct by which one can evaluate the norms of any given culture.

Scholasticism   The style of philosophizing popular in the late Middle Ages in Europe. Practiced in the medieval universities of France, Italy, and England by Dominicans, Franciscans, and other scholar-monks. Such a student was called a *scholasticus* (Latin).

Skepticism   A skeptic is one who doubts claims of knowledge on the grounds that either the available evidence is inadequate to support the claim or it is impossible in principle for the claim to be reasonably asserted or denied. Akin to **agnosticism** (q.v.).

Social contract   The theory that we owe obedience to the law and to those who enact and implement it; we have tacitly agreed to suspend our natural right to rule ourselves in favor of authorizing procedures by which means a government can be created to form a political society. Classically defended in various forms by Hobbes, Locke, Rousseau, and Kant.

Subject   The grammatical topic of a sentence or proposition. Thus, "philosophers" is the **subject** of the sentence "Most philosophers are professors."

Sub specie eternitatis   Latin for "under the aspect of eternity," a phrase made famous by Benedict Spinoza. It reminds us that things often look different if we take a long (indeed, an eternal) view: In the short view, our bias and our ignorance distort good judgment.

Syllogism, categorical and hypothetical Syllogistic reasoning was pioneered by Aristotle as the principle form of deductive logic. A **categorical syllogism** consists of three categorical propositions, two as premises and one as the conclusion: For example, all men are mortal, all Greeks are men, therefore all Greeks are mortal. There are 256 possible forms of such syllogisms, not all of which are valid. A **hypothetical syllogism** consists of two premises and a conclusion; the major premise is a hypothetical (or if-then) proposition and the minor premise is a categorical proposition. For example, if the thermometer reads 212°F or higher, the water must be boiling; the thermometer in this bowl of water reads 212°F; therefore the water must be boiling.

Synthetic The opposite of **analytic** (q.v.). Thus, a sentence or proposition is **synthetic** if its truth value cannot be determined solely by analysis, that is, by reference to nothing but the meaning of its constituent terms.

Tautology A sentence or proposition is a **tautology** if and only if it can be seen to be true by nothing more than the meaning of the terms or the syntax of the words used to state it. For example, "all wise philosophers are wise" is a **tautology** of the form "all X Y is X". Here, the meaning of the constituent terms is irrelevant. What matters is the form. ("Business is business" looks like a **tautology** because it has the form "X is X"; but the form in this case is misleading.) "All philosophers are lovers of wisdom" is an implicit **tautology** because "philosophy" means "love of wisdom." All **tautologies** are **analytic** (q.v.).

Teleology Originally, an Aristotelian doctrine related to his theory of the four kinds of cause. On that theory, in addition to the formal, efficient, and material causes of things, there are also *final causes,* goals or aims (in Greek, "telos") toward which things (not just living things) strive. **Teleological** explanations account for events or the properties of things by reference to their telic (or goal-directed) properties, that is, the way some feature of the thing contributes to its achievement of some purpose, goal, or final end.

Theism In monotheism, (as in traditional Judaism, Christianity, and Islam), the doctrine according to which there is but one God whose nature is both immanent and **transcendent** (q.v.). Polytheism (many gods) and pantheism (God is in all things) are other forms of **theism.** Contrast **Deism** (q.v.).

Thesis The **thesis** of an argument is whatever the argument is designed to affirm or deny (see p. 24). In Hegelian dialectic (q.v.), the **thesis** affirms a proposition, the antithesis denies that proposition, and the synthesis transcends this contradiction and gives rise to a new **thesis.**

Thought experiment In contrast to a real experiment, in chemistry or physics or biology, a **thought experiment** is conducted entirely in the imagination in an effort to test the consequences of some hypothesis or idea. Thus, Turing's "imitation game" (see pp. 93–94), designed to help us decide whether machines can "think," is a **thought experiment,** an arm-chair exercise.

Transcendent/transcendental   A belief or proposition is **transcendent** if it refers to matters beyond any possible experience. A belief or proposition is **transcendental** if it is universally and necessarily true. Both ideas come to prominence in Kant's epistemology and metaphysics.

Utilitarianism   The ethical theory associated with the views of Jeremy Bentham (1748–1832), James Mill (1773–1836), and his son John Stuart Mill. **Utilitarianism** is the principle that we always ought to choose the act, or type of act, that will maximize the balance of good over evil for all affected.

Fallacies

Critical readers need to be alert to errors in reasoning — **fallacies, as they are called** — that can be detected in the writings of others, just as critical thinkers will endeavor to avoid making such errors in the first place. Fallacious reasoning has been studied and discussed since Aristotle, and philosophers have identified many kinds of errors in reasoning that appear and reappear with some frequency. It may prove useful, therefore, to have at hand a list of standard fallacies. The following list of twenty fallacies is by no means exhaustive, but it does identify many of the most frequent and familiar types of such errors.

Ad hominem   The attempt to discredit an idea or proposition by pointing to some flaw or fault in the behavior or character of the person who is the source of the idea or proposition. "Bertrand Russell's philosophical ideas must be wrong because he was so often cruel and indifferent to the needs of those close to him."

Affirming the consequent   If you assert a hypothetical proposition (such as "If it rains then the streets will be wet") and you also assert the consequent of that hypothetical ("The streets are wet"), and think that these two assertions prove the conclusion ("It must have rained"), you commit the fallacy of affirming the consequent. The streets can get wet in ways other than by rain; perhaps they are awash from flooding, or maybe the street cleaners flushed the street.

Ambiguity   Switching from one sense of a key term to another in the course of an argument. John Stuart Mill once wrote: "The only proof capable of being given that an object is visible, is that people actually see it. . . . In like manner, . . . the sole evidence it is possible to produce that anything is desirable, is that people actually desire it." Mill failed to notice the ambiguity in the suffix -*able*/-*ible*. In reference to visible things, it means "*can* be seen." But in reference to desirable things, it means either "*can* be desired" or — more likely — "*ought* to be desired."

Appeal to authority   The attempt to support an idea or proposition not by relevant evidence but by pointing to the authorities who believe it. "If Nobel prize–winning chemist Linus Pauling thinks that megadoses of vitamin C will cure the common cold, he must be right." Well, he was wrong, or so more recent research has established. His authority as a theoretical chemist did not make him an authority on nutrition.

Appeal to force   The attempt to support a belief or proposition by threatening one who refuses to believe. "If logic and reason can't convince you, maybe this persuader [a loaded gun] will do the trick." Yes, the threat of force may get you to do as the gunman wants, but it is not evidence that his argument is correct.

Appeal to ignorance   The attempt to support a belief by appealing to what we don't know. "For all we know, the death penalty is a better deterrent than imprisonment." "Yes, but for all we know, innocent people are occasionally executed." Neither side in this argument gives any *reason* for agreement; ignorance on these matters is not a valid reason to support *either side*.

Appeal to pity   The attempt to persuade someone to accept your beliefs or grant your desires by begging them to pity you. "Your Honor, I know I am guilty of killing my parents, but have mercy on me — after all, I'm an orphan." Good for a laugh but not for an excuse or justification.

Appeal to tradition   The attempt to support a belief by pointing out that it has a long history behind it. "What was good enough for our forebears ought to be good enough for us." Really? Couldn't times have changed in relevant ways, thus giving us a good reason for putting tradition aside?

Denying the antecedent   If you assert a hypothetical proposition (such as "If Jones rides a fast horse, then he can get to the station on time") and deny the antecent ("Jones does not ride a fast horse") and believe that these two assertions prove the negation of the consequent ("Jones cannot get to the station in time"), you commit the fallacy of denying the antecedent. There are other ways Jones could get to the station on time, such as by hiring a taxi.

Division   Attributing to an individual a property of the class of which the individual is a member. "All the richest people in town live upon the hill; since Jones lives up on the hill he must be one of the richest people in town."

False analogy   The United States got involved in Vietnam in the 1960s in part because government officials relied on a false analogy, specifically a domino analogy: "If Vietnam goes Communist, so will Laos and Cambodia, followed by Thailand and Burma, until the whole of Southeast Asia will be Communist." But these governments did not fall over each other like a row of dominos.

False dichotomy (or black and white fallacy)   Identifying two alternatives and insisting that they are exhaustive and exclusive, when they are not. During the Cold War, any action that looked like appeasement of the Soviet Union provoked this debate: "I'd rather be dead than Red." "Well, I'd rather be Red than dead." As history shows, there were other alternatives; millions of people around the globe rejected Communism and lived to tell the tale.

Gambler's (or Monte Carlo) fallacy   "Since I've flipped heads five times in a row, there is a high probability that on the next toss I'll get a tails." No, the probability of tails on the next toss is exactly what it was on the first and all other previous tosses, 1 out of 2, or 0.5.

Many questions   The classic example is the question "Have you stopped beating your wife?" How should a bachelor reply? The question presupposes a prior question "Are you married?" to which the bachelor's answer would be "No," thus, obviating the original question. For the married man, too, the questioner presupposes a prior question "Did you ever beat your wife?" to which the true answer might be either "Yes" or "No." Only in the former case could the question "Have you stopped beating your wife?" be correctly answered "Yes" or "No."

Oversimplification   "Grade inflation in college classes today is rampant because teachers are afraid their students will otherwise give them poor evaluations, which could lead to little or no salary raise, nonreappointment, and even denial of tenure." This explanation is an oversimplification, even if it is part of the overall explanation. For example, students need high grades if they aspire to professional training in medicine, law, or business. Many instructors dislike awarding grades (as distinct from evaluating student work). During the Vietnam War, when grade inflation began, faculty were reluctant to give their male students lower grades, lest they be made more vulnerable to the draft.

Poisoning the well   In his *New Introductory Lectures* (1933), Sigmund Freud wrote that "no one has a right to join in a discussion of psychoanalysis who has not had particular experiences that can only be obtained by being analyzed oneself." Really? This pronouncement destroys at a stroke every criticism ever made by someone outside the psychoanalytic movement, no matter how intelligent, fair-minded, and thorough the criticism might be.

Post hoc, ergo propter hoc   Latin for "after this, therefore because of this," this is a version of confusing correlation with causation. If your hair starts to fall out after you've changed your diet, it doesn't necessarily follow that your new diet caused your hair loss.

Red herring   Distracting someone's line of thought by inserting an attractive digression from the topic. "You think the problem of AIDS in Africa is serious — well, let me tell you about the problem of overpopulation there."

Slippery slope   Objecting to taking a first step in a certain direction on the grounds that later steps will be irresistible and ruinous. "If we legalize the right of doctors to assist their patients who want to die, it's just a question of time before doctors will be killing their patients without bothering to get their consent." Neither logical necessity nor actual experience (today, in the Netherlands) tells us that physician-assisted suicide is the first step down a slippery slope to disaster.

Straw man   A maneuver in which one imputes to the opponent a thesis that is an exaggeration or misrepresentation of the opponent's real position, and thus easily knocked down (hence, metaphorically, a position made of straw). "If you advocate take-home exams, you might as well advocate letting students cheat on their exams. But that's a silly and outrageous idea!"

Acknowledgments *(continued)*

Edmund Gettier, "Is Justified True Belief Knowledge?" *Analysis,* vol. 23 (1963), pp. 121–23. Reprinted by permission of the author.

Garrett Hardin, from "Living on a Lifeboat," *BioScience,* vol. 24, October 1974, pp. 561–68. Copyright 1974 by American Institute of Biological Sciences. Reproduced with permission of American Institute of Biological Sciences via Copyright Clearance Center.

Penelope Maddy, from "Indispensability and Practice," *The Journal of Philosophy,* vol. 89 (June 1992), p. 275. Reprinted by permission of *The Journal of Philosophy,* Columbia University.

Ernest Nagel, from "Philosophical Concepts of Atheism." In J. E. Fairchild, ed., *Basic Beliefs.* New York: Sheridan House, Inc., 1959, 1987.

Friedrich Nietzsche, from *On The Genealogy of Morals & Ecce Homo* by Friedrich Nietzsche, edited by Walter Kauffman, translated by Walter Kauffman & R. J. Hollingdale, copyright © 1967 by Random House, Inc. Reprinted by permission of Random House, Inc.

Robert Nozick, from *The Nature of Rationality,* by Robert Nozick, p. 3. Copyright © 1993 by Princeton University Press. Reprinted by permission of Princeton University Press.

Plato, from *Republic,* trans. G. M. A. Grube, Hackett Publishing Company, Inc. 1974. Reprinted by permission of Hackett Publishing Company, Inc. All rights reserved.

Bertrand Russell, from "Three Essentials for a Stable World," *Fact and Fiction* by Bertrand Russell. Routledge, 1994. Reprinted by permission of Routledge.

Judith Jarvis Thomson, from "A Defense of Abortion," *Philosophy and Public Affairs,* vol. 1 (1971), pp. 48–49. Copyright © 1971 by Princeton University Press, Reprinted by permission of Princeton University Press.

Jennifer Trusted, "The Concept of Freedom," from *Free Will and Responsibility* by Jennifer Trusted (Oxford University Press). Copyright © Jennifer Trusted 1984. Reprinted by permission.

Alan M. Turing, "Computing Machinery and Intelligence," *Mind,* vol. 59 (1950), pp. 433–460. Reprinted by permission of Oxford University Press.

Mary Anne Warren, from "Future Generations" in Tom Regan and Donald VanDeVeer, eds., *And Justice for All.* Rowman & Littlefield, 1982, p. 147. Reprinted by permission of the author.

Index